Rings of Dissent

SPORT AND SOCIETY

Series Editors
Aram Goudsouzian
Jaime Schultz
Founding Editors
Benjamin G. Rader
Randy Roberts

For a list of books in the series, please see our website at www.press.uillinois.edu.

Rings of Dissent

Boxing and Performances of Rebellion

Edited by
RUDY MONDRAGÓN,
GAYE THERESA JOHNSON,
and DAVID J. LEONARD

Foreword by
DAVE ZIRIN

Afterword by
MARK ANTHONY NEAL

UNIVERSITY OF ILLINOIS PRESS
Urbana, Chicago, and Springfield

Manufactured in the United States of America
1 2 3 4 5 C P 5 4 3 2 1
♾ This book is printed on acid-free paper.

Cataloging data available from the Library of Congress

LCCN 2025016617
ISBN 978-0-252-04686-5 (cloth : alk.)
ISBN 978-0-252-08898-8 (paper : alk.)
ISBN 978-0-252-04842-5 (ebook)

Contents

Foreword

DAVE ZIRIN

In the entire cultural constellation of these United States, boxing is perhaps the most evocative lens for understanding our collective history. The sport's brutality and bigotry as well as its crassness and corruption exist alongside a beauty and athletic derring-do that rises to the level of ballet or at least its own kind of pugilistic poetry. This is US history in a nutshell: a battle between the most odious kinds of oppression and the efforts of people in utterly inspiring fashion to rise up and shrug aside the boot on their necks. The morality play of what takes place in the ring, how the crowd cheers, and the reaction as the punches land tells an electric story about the era when the fight takes place. As this volume makes clear, the manner in which people train, the relationships with their fellow boxers and trainers, and their very walk to the ring tell that story as well.

For the historian, boxing, known as "the sweet science," offers an almost embarrassment of riches of material. If one wants to teach about the white supremacy and violence that defined the first part of the twentieth century, a professor could not do much better than to tell the story of "The Galveston Giant," Jack Johnson, with his world-traveling efforts to become the first Black heavyweight champion and the ugly political and prosecutorial backlash that ensued. If one wanted to speak about the Great Depression in the 1930s, the story of "The Cinderella Man," James Braddock, speaks to the resilience of the poor and their search for escape. Braddock's tale translates that story as well as any lecture on Hoovervilles and bread lines. As war clouds gathered over Europe and radical multiracial labor movements began to impact the United States, the ensuing rise of "The Brown Bomber," Joe Louis, and his two fights against Hitler's favorite boxer, Max Schmeling—and the writings of Richard Wright about Harlem's reaction to the fight—are a terrific window into this people's history that's all too hidden. Certainly, any look at how the 1950s became the 1960s and the civil rights movement became a push for Black Power, would study the affection for President Kennedy's favorite boxer, Floyd Patterson—a devout integrationist—and then the subsequent rise of Cassius Clay, who, of course, shocked the world when he announced that he had joined the Nation of Islam and would be known as Muhammad Ali. The late 1960s is in so many respects the story of Ali, including his resistance to the Vietnam War draft and the influence he had on a rising generation that was willing to say no to war. In the 1980s, boxing again had its national moment when Mike Tyson became the center of the tabloid frenzy that defined so much of the decade.

Time and again, this sport has given us the richest possible window into this country, and yet it has seemed in recent years that the window has closed. The opposite of love is not hate but indifference, and boxing has experienced a wave of indifference in the broader pop cultural firmament. The sport's status has diminished on the national landscape because of a variety of factors. There is the corruption of the warring boxing federations, which breeds an utter public mistrust of the rankings. There are the parasitical promoters praying at the altar of pay-per-views, which limits the reach of their audience. There are new—and very hypocritical—cultural norms where sports fans claim to be repulsed by the violence and attendant head injuries in boxing yet still consume football in mammoth gulps, not to mention the niche following of mixed martial arts. But we still need boxing not only to understand our past but also to comprehend the present.

This is what makes *Rings of Dissent* such an invaluable contribution to our understanding of sports and our society. It reopens that window with a series of essays that place the present of boxing exactly where it should be: as a lens to understand our world. This book has the immediacy of the great boxing writing of the past by figures such as James Baldwin, Gay Talese, and Joyce Carol Oates while keeping its feet planted in the present. It is both academically rigorous and immediately accessible, with something in it for boxing fans and detractors alike. But the book also takes a look at the hidden histories of fighters like Ralph Dupas by Dr. Louis Moore and his remarkable story of wanting to be perceived as white in the middle of the Jim Crow South.

The parts of the book that place it most resolutely in the present are those that deal with the fighters themselves, particularly Latinx boxers. Learning about their struggle against Trump's anti-immigrant invective and the use of not only their words but their very ring entrances to have a political dialogue with fans is an eye-opener and a window to our present that is as important as anything that has been provided by the past. The tale of the legendary Gleason's Gym and the way trainers and boxers have come together to form a "moral economy" of mutual help and understanding amid this most violent of endeavors with one another smash preconceptions about what it is we have been consuming.

This is not just a book about boxing and its place in our culture. In a sense this book is hip-hop, and not only because it includes a fascinating interview about boxing with rap lyricist Jasiri X. The book has a rhythm and a flow that sometimes feels like watching a great MC and other times like you are watching a master of footwork cut off and dance around the ring.

One of my favorite boxing quotes comes from fighter Buster Mathis, who when asked by his son if he should play football or box, said, "Son, play football because nobody plays boxing." This book isn't playing, but everyone should get in the rhetorical ring and dance with what its authors bring to the arena.

INTRODUCTION

Rollin' with the Punches

Boxing, Struggle, and Dissent

GAYE THERESA JOHNSON, DAVID J. LEONARD,
and RUDY MONDRAGÓN

Deontay "The Bronze Bomber" Wilder emerged from a tunnel and entered the ring walkway. With over eight hundred thousand pay-per-view buys in North America alone, this was the most-viewed heavyweight title fight since Mike Tyson and Lennox Lewis in 2002. Wilder seized the moment. Adorned in a forty-thousand-dollar custom-made suit by statement-art designers Cosmo Lombino and Donato Crowley, he commenced a nearly five-minute ring entrance to defend his World Boxing Council World Heavyweight title against fellow undefeated challenger Tyson "The Gypsy King" Fury. As is customary for champions, Wilder entered the ring second. A row of screens along his left side projected single iconic images of Black luminaries, creating a digital entourage composed of Frederick Douglass, Nipsey Hussle, Harriet Tubman, Kobe Bryant, Maya Angelou, Malcolm X, Jackie Robinson, Martin Luther King Jr., and Muhammad Ali. D Smoke, a rising star from Inglewood, California, preceded Wilder, performing "Black Habits I," which extols "Black magic, Black excellence, Black habits, this Black medicine, everything Black."[1] The crowd roared as the 6′7″ Wilder emerged into view, adorned with a black and rhinestone head mask and crown, chest plate, skull shoulder pads, and a mask with red glowing lights around his eyes. In an interview with TMZ, Wilder explained that the suit was designed to remind viewers of "a lot of men and women that paved the way for us. This is Black History Month and I'm going to be paying tribute to that" (McFarlane 2020). Wilder and his team used this visual montage to bring a Black past into a present, spotlighting the precarity of Black life. The suit itself was so spectacular that it generated its own news coverage apart from the fight's outcome. Nyree McFarlane (2020) later wrote, "The fight didn't go his way, but the loss shouldn't take the shine off Deontay Wilder's elaborate, intricately designed ring walk outfit." The combination of powerful statements made by Wilder and his team in the minutes before the fight were precise, enduring, and curated for a worldwide audience. Wilder followed a tradition among Black, Indigenous, and Latinx professional fighters who have used expressive culture, visibility, financial resources, proximity to the media and press, and celebrity platform to make powerful statements about community, politics, and identity.[2]

Boxing is about more than a fight in a ring. It is bigger than its titles, a single competition, or a legendary fight night. The most celebrated stories in the history of boxing are about fighters—both winners and losers—who are the most underestimated, most determined, and the least likely to succeed. And some of the least recognized stories are about the communities these boxers come from and the often unnamed people and circumstances that shape both promise and possibility in the ring. These stories recall the accumulation of hours of practice in under-resourced gyms, the pooling of community resources, and the conversion of humble contexts into powerful statements about home, nation, race, and identity.

Rings of Dissent is about the brilliance, contradiction, liberation, and capitulation that exist in previously overlooked sites of resistance among boxers and their communities. We argue that subversive and often contradictory performance practices are everywhere in boxing. We draw attention to the cultural politics and performances of marginalized boxers to reveal the structures of power and practices of agency that are always at work around Black, Brown, and queer bodies. We believe that understanding boxing's centrality in the social practices and cultural politics of communities of color creates an opportunity to study power, race, immigration, gender, and capital in a new way.

We also hope that this anthology will challenge the idea that the golden era of boxing is over and that the sport is on its last leg, given the celebrations of social, political, and cultural importance of boxing throughout the twentieth century. Nearly every decade of the sport, going back to the inception of prizefighting in the late nineteenth century, has described boxing in some way, shape, or form in these backward-looking terms. This assumption that boxing is dead is rooted in racist and classist mythology, as boxing appears to diminish only if one measures the sport's popularity and vitality based on the interest of white middle-class audiences. Among white working-class and working-class populations of color, boxing is arguably more popular and relevant than it has ever been.

These instances of agency also reveal how those with the least power in this sport are often the fighters themselves. As social actors who do not own arenas, boxing networks, or the buildings in which they train, professional boxers' journeys into the ring are often characterized by stories of austerity, racism, individualism, resilience, and exploitation. Unlike Major League Baseball or the National Basketball Association, professional boxing in the United States is not centrally governed, meaning there is no national regulatory commission overseeing the sport and thus making boxers among the most vulnerable to manipulation in this sports industry. Furthermore, since they are classified as independent contractors, professional boxers have no access to comprehensive work benefits and protections and are not covered by federal labor standards (Mondragón, Valenzuela Jr., and Hernández 2024). Still, many boxers have used the few instances of agency available in the industry: press conferences, weigh-ins, and ring entrances. Studying these sites of resistance and performance directs our attention to disparities not meant to be seen and to irregularities in the narrative of individualism and democracy that permeate the representation of boxing in the United States. Almost all of the most famous boxers in the sport's history, from Jack Johnson, to Joe Louis, Sugar Ray Robinson, and Muhammad Ali have used the occasion of press conferences, ring entrances, and fashion choices to demand justice and claim important affiliations and identities. More recently, Claressa Shields, a world champion boxer who has held titles in five different weight classes, enters the ring for every fight with a blue-streaked braid intended to raise awareness of the ongoing struggle for a basic human right: clean water in her hometown of Flint, Michigan (Matthews 2019). These examples and others point to a larger history where boxers and their support systems have refused and resisted the hegemony of boxing. The power of these acts and their importance is because boxers stand outside the collective wealth that influences the structures of economy that holds sway over earning power.

The boxers who are interviewed and discussed in this anthology have discovered how to represent themselves and their communities in powerful ways. In ring entrances, weigh-ins, fashion politics, soundscapes, and persona, boxers from severely marginalized communities have resisted the economies of exploitation and commodification that characterize the sport, often in ways overlooked by commentators, scholars, and sometimes even fans. This book is about instances and performances of agency and resistance in boxing. Studying these sites reveals how power is exerted, enforced, and created by the people who finance and manage the industry and by the boxers who train on reservations, local gyms, in garages, or fight in renown arenas.

The power and importance of boxing should not surprise anyone, given the place of boxing with America. Boxing has always had an influence and power that extends beyond the confines of the ring. In other words, popular cultural productions outside of boxing have been heavily influenced by this sporting culture. This is evident in the popularity of boxing in Hollywood motion pictures. Since the nineteenth century, films have brought to life endless stories about down-and-out, left-behind, and marginalized working-class people who rise from the ashes to become champions.[3] In the realm of American literature, boxing has served as a source of narrative inspiration to essayists, novelists, journalists, and poets such as Norman Mailer, Ernest Hemingway, Ralph Ellison, George Bernard Shaw, Joyce Carol Oates, and Luis J. Rodríguez. These well-known writers have used boxing as a common theme and analogy for working-class struggles, as recognition for a person's success in an economic market that is not intended to empower all people.[4] In both literature and film, these stories have largely celebrated white male protagonists.

Boxing references, metaphors, and stories are also found in the expressive cultures of music. From Bob Dylan's "Hurricane" to the recent examples in rap, boxing soundscapes have emerged, focusing on stories of racial injustice that Black and Brown working-class men have fought to overcome in the quest to fulfill the promises of the American Dream. Dylan's "Hurricane," for example, is a protest song about former professional boxer Rubin "Hurricane" Carter, who was released from prison in 1975. Carter was wrongfully arrested and convicted of a triple homicide in 1967. This song, which addresses racism, profiling, and the prison system, is one of many boxing songs about dissent, resistance, and fighting injustice. In Jay-Z's "Some People Hate," the rapper states: "Think they Ali and shit / I roll with the punches so I survive / I bob and weave, move my feet from side to side / I'm back, stronger than ever surprise surprise / They try to take me out the game but I's alive" (Preezy 2017). With creative and intentional use of boxing phrases like "roll with the punches" and "bob and weave" and using Muhammad Ali as an inspirational subject, Jay-Z is rhyming and using metaphors to highlight evasiveness, avoidance to the attacks from structural forces and oppressions, one's ability to be flexible, and the power of resilience, survival, and staying alive.

Boxing has also served as a source of inspiration across other sports. Black tennis and golf champion Althea Gibson noted that her father taught her to box as a child: "He would box with me for an hour at a time showing me how to punch, how to jab, how to block punches, and how to use footwork" (Lansbury 2022, 78–79). For her dad, teaching her how to box became a vehicle for him to work through the disappointment of not having a boy; for Althea, these lessons would be important, as it "would toughen her up," all while developing the athletic prowess that would propel her onto the tennis court (79). Evident in its importance within popular culture and its centrality in our memories, boxing is always about more than the fight. Boxing shapes our sense of collective identity ("the fighting American spirit") and the stories we tell about communities.

Although not distinctively "American," the sport of boxing is indeed a site for the promulgation of narratives of American exceptionalism. Endless narratives and stories about disciplined work ethics, romanticized representations of working-class struggles, hypermasculinity, homosocial spaces, muscular Christianity, and an adherence to strict rules of progress and respectability are commonly found in how the sport is promoted and marketed. As in other American sports, boxing stories in mass culture function to reaffirm ideologies of white supremacy and race as biology. The cultural production and consumption of "America" is often located in representations of upward mobility. The ideology of American meritocracy, for example, is primely located in boxing. It is packaged as the idea that if a boxer works hard enough, then they too can achieve financial security and fame. However, within the hypercapitalist and neoliberal brutal economy of boxing, this reality is scarce and reserved for the superstars of the sport. Despite this somber reality, boxing is nonetheless a place where we can locate stories and moments and acts of agency, resistance, dignity, and visibility for the unheard, marginalized, and left-behind. This is true whether they are stories of professional and amateur fighters or those who use boxing as a launching pad for successful athletic careers, or those who find their voice and power through the sweet science. Peirce Egan (1999), a British sportswriter who wrote about English bare-knuckle fighting during the nineteenth century, is often cited as the originator of the term "the sweet science." Carlo Rotella and Michael Ezra (2017) argue that this term doesn't fully capture the history or nature of boxing. They contend that "bittersweet science" is a more fitting descriptor of boxing, given the violence, physical dangers, the despair, heartache, and the horrors that define the business side of the sport.

And whether one likes the sport or not, boxing has impacted and reached everyone in our society in some way. Within this collection, Rudy Mondragón argues that "we all have boxing stories," because boxing and society are not separate but, rather, are intertwined political worlds that are mediated by social, cultural, and structural forces.

Boxing is a political world where race, gender, and nation matter. In this world, racial capitalism and the commodification of Black, Brown, and working-class bodies anchor the industry's organization, while creativity and oppositional performance by the athletes, like Deontay Wilder, create subversive narratives of community and dissent. In this regard, the boxing ring is, as we have noted, about more than knockouts, winning, or losing: It is a space where boxers of color, queer boxers, and white female boxers have leveraged their contextual visibility to challenge white supremacy, capitalism, heteronormativity, and patriarchy. In other words, we theorize the sport of boxing as a metaphorical and material site of political struggle, contestations, resistance, dissent, and liberation.

Rings of Dissent draws attention to and emphasizes the cultural politics and performances of marginalized boxers to reveal structures of power and practices of agency that are always in play in boxing. The book is not an exhaustive historiography of boxing but aims to provide alternative stories that complement and enhance the rich stories found in popular culture about iconic figures like Muhammad Ali, Joe Louis, Joe Frazier, and Mike Tyson. The collection is guided by the following key questions: To what extent are boxers engaging in performances of rebellion and dissent? What forms of dissent can we excavate in boxing? What do these manifestations of dissent reveal about the past, present, and future?

The contributors to this volume reveal how communities of color use the sport, practice, and locations of boxing as sites of dissent where new understandings of power, race, gender, culture, identity, and capital are created. These new understandings are important as they add substance to and bridge the interdisciplinary fields of ethnic studies and critical sports studies. There is power in sport, so a deeper examination of boxing and dissent is well past due.

Fighting Oppression: Boxing's Heritage

Through a series of essays and interviews, we remix Howard Bryant's (2018) idea of "full dissidence," demonstrating that for communities of color boxing exists as a space of ceaseless dissent, opposition, and navigation of the structures of violence and dehumanization, no matter where it occurs. "To be black is to be a dissident," writes Bryant. "Dissidence can never be a place of origin but is rather a destination, a conclusion after the long journey that faith" in the system "is no longer an option and was probably never a particularly good one in the first place. It is the realization that our conventional strategies and solutions have been, if not illegitimate, then failures of mission. It is a break with the mainstream and finding comfort living outside of it" (1–2). To be a fighter who comes from the margins of society, socially and economically, and participates in a financially lucrative and exploitative sporting industry is an act of dissent. And to be dissident in boxing means a declaration of rejection and imagining and manifesting new ways of being. This is what the authors of *Rings of Dissent* are concerned with presenting in this anthology.

Rings of Dissent finds inspiration in previously edited anthologies on boxing that emphasized histories of power, race, class, gender, and sexuality.[5] Yet, absent from this rich body of work is an in-depth interrogation of the sport and complex performances of dissent situated within their proper historical and sociopolitical contexts. Evident by its place within American folklore, boxing is about more than a fight in the ring. It is bigger than its world titles, a single competition, or a legendary fight night. Boxing is more than columns of Red Smith and Dick Young, of *Wide World of Sports* and *Friday Night Fights*, of pay-per-view and breaking news on SportsCenter. It is more than romanticized and celebrated stories of fighters, those who persevered, who came to embody the American Dream, the rugged individualism that purportedly defines American exceptionalism. Its power and cultural importance extends beyond Ralph Ellison and Joyce Carol Oates, Bob Dylan and Jay-Z, and *Rocky* and *Creed*. *Rings of Dissent* draws connections between broad conversations around intersectional politics of resistance, disruption, and interruption and the more intimate interpretations, expressions, community formations, and family histories of boxing.

Building on the work of Howard Bryant, as well as Theresa Runstedtler (2012) and Louis Moore (2017), this collection situates boxing not only as a site of sport, politics, and capitalism but also as a space of resistance, where enactments of refusal are deployed by boxers. One of the earliest boxing dissenters is the great Jack Johnson of Galveston, Texas. Runstedtler (2012) argues that Jack Johnson, who was also the first Black heavyweight champion of the world, was a "rebel sojourner" who traveled in search of opportunities to compete as a boxer. Her examination of boxing offers a deeper look on how the sport and Johnson's life intersected with discourses of race, gender, religion, social class, and body culture at the beginning of the twentieth century. Moore similarly looks at how working-class Black men used boxing as part of a larger struggle for freedom and justice. Through their displays of hegemonic understandings of manhood and dignified forms of labor, boxers challenged anti-Black racism (Moore 2017). The work of Bryant, Runstedtler, Moore, and others, including Lucia Trimbur (2013), William C. Rhoden (2007), and David Remnick (1999), informs our conceptualization of dissent in boxing as a multifaceted process of creating oppositional views, ideas, pedagogies, and performances that challenge and disrupt hegemonic and structural power. Through voice, sartorial choices, alternative performances, and occupying the ring itself, *Rings of Dissent* demonstrates the many ways that boxers exhibit agency and dissent at every step and shine a light on the contradictions in boxing that reinforce and reinvent dominant structures.

Rings of Dissent is also interested in the untold stories and performances of underappreciated and under-studied boxers. Common are the tales of Joe Louis, Muhammad Ali, Mike Tyson, and Julio César Chávez, which this book aims to deviate from in order to highlight the performances of resistance by a handful of important and overlooked boxing dissenters. In this manner, this anthology builds on the work of Erving Goffman (1959) and Diana Taylor (2003), whose conceptualizations of performance serve as a guide for our collective understanding of the boxing sportscape. Performance, as a methodological tool, allows for the analysis of stories, narratives, and complex subjectivities of fighters all while locating historical and contemporary moments of dissent and resistance. Goffman defines performance as "all the activity of a given participant on a given occasion which serves to influence in any way any of the other participants" (36). These influential performances can be found in multiple boxing spaces and events—from local boxing gyms to press conferences and weigh-ins, face-offs, and mega-fights and ring entrances. This anthology analyzes these boxing events, among others, as performances that are filled with the deployment of multiple identities and are, as Diana Taylor argues, "rehearsed and performed daily in the public sphere" (3). This includes the daily rehearsed and performative moments of dissent.

Beyond the major icons of sport known for their athletic activism and performances of resistance, *Rings of Dissent* privileges the stories of fighters who have not received much attention regarding dissent. It examines these boxing figures and accompanying events and the meanings behind their daily acts that are performed within the public spaces of boxing. Describing the Muhammad Ali and Ken Norton fight of 1976, for example, Ishmael Reed (1976) writes, "The Heavyweight Championship of the World is a sex show, a fashion show, scene of intrigue between different religions, politics, classes; a gathering of stars, ex-stars, their hangers-on, and hangers-on assistants." Reed's description is significant not only to the Ali and Norton fight but to all boxing matches and events, as they all consist of complex performances situated in different sociopolitical and sociohistorical moments, which require a tailored analysis to locate moments of dissent that have never been discussed until now.

While the history of boxing is one of storied fighters and epic battles of dissent and resistance, it is also a tale of Americana: a space of corruption, greed, big money, racial capitalism, organized crime, white supremacy, homophobia, and sexism. Jeffrey T. Sammons (1988) and Gerald Horne (2021), for example, have interrogated these very tragedies within the context of boxing, demonstrating how boxing reflects broader societal history. Their examination of boxing begs the question, Why does the sport of boxing exist to this day? This question is still relevant in the twenty-first century, given that boxing is structurally designed to recruit fighters who come from marginalized racial backgrounds and low socioeconomic standing to fill its pool of working boxers. Boxing has continued to be this space, albeit with contradictions, conflicts, and even possibilities. Sometimes explicit, as evident by participation in social movements, embracing rhetoric that challenges white supremacy during a weigh-in performance, or part of the hidden transcript, boxing offers tools and a space of opposition.[6]

None of this is to say that boxing provides the perfect panacea; whether with its embrace of hypermaterialism, violence, and misogyny, among other things—its American exceptionalism—boxing has always been a space of hegemony and the reinforcement of power. It is messy and contradictory, a metaphor for marginalized communities that are ripe for exploitation and disposability. It is also a rich site to excavate performances of agency and dissent that challenge power and dominant structures. As academic researchers and scholars, we cannot be so conformable with quickly dismissing this potential.

More Than Ali and Kaepernick: Resistance beyond Raised Fists and Bended Knees

The history of boxing is defined by the ubiquity and entrenched nature of resistance and opposition. Boxing has always been a place where the marginalized and the left-behind have fought for a place at the table. *Rings of Dissent* is a representation of this understanding and what race and sport sociologist Ben Carrington (2013) calls the critical paradigm of sport, which is an effort to theorize and situate sport "as a site of contestation, resistance, and creative freedom." Part of our examination of boxing as a site of political struggle, contestation, dissent, and creative freedom responds to Cathy van Ingen's (2003) call to academic action about how relations of race, gender, and sexuality are produced, negotiated, and contested in sporting social spaces, and her assertion that the critical study of sport can unveil the creation of counterspaces infused with resistant possibilities. As a project building on the critical paradigm of sport and examining under-studied spaces of dissent in boxing, the objective of *Rings of Dissent* is to locate and expand on a history of resistance in boxing. In reading the sport of boxing critically, this anthology elevates significant examples of cultural productions, counternarratives, and counterspaces that have been curated by professional boxers (McDonald and Birrell 1999).

Resistance in boxing has taken many forms, among them breaking through color lines and glass ceilings; leveraging success to individual and communal empowerment; and being heard and seen. While Jack Johnson's refusal to submit to the rules and demands of white supremacy (Runstedtler 2012), and Muhammad Ali's courageous stances against racial injustice and the violent Vietnam War (Remnick 1999) are well known, the everyday and ordinary performances of resistance during press conferences and weigh-ins, of refusing to "shut up and fight," in refusing to play one's role, are often not taken seriously and erased from the public imagination. Yet, in the ring entrance, for example, boxers, especially those from severely marginalized communities, have deployed fashion politics and soundscapes not only to spotlight injustices outside the arena but also to resist the brutal economies of exploitation and commodification that characterize the sport, often in ways overlooked by commentators, scholars, and fans.

Scholars like Theresa Runstedtler, Lucia Trimbur, Louis Moore, T. J. Desch Obi (2009), Dave Zirin (2005), and José M. Alamillo (2020) have changed the discourses on boxing and performative, symbolic, and material forms of resistance. Their works examine boxing and resistance in the context of race, labor, religion, gender, styles of fighting, antiwar politics, and immigration. *Rings of Dissent* enters this history, shining a spotlight on how Black, Brown, racially minoritized men and women boxers and their respective teams have leveraged the ring, and the power that surrounds it, to speak truth to power. This collection not only highlights the history of resistance but also expands how we see sporting politics, what we see as a site of resistance. The essays included within this collection reflect on the different ways that boxers have used the ring and their bodily place within this space to be legible and in the process speak truth and offer disparate forms of dissent.

The boxing performances we examine in this volume are an enactment of democratic imaginaries and often offer a sense of collective dignity and hope. For subordinated and vulnerable communities, resistance often needs to be disguised. Boxers, who generally come from vulnerable and marginalized backgrounds, also require subtlety and strategic and calculated approaches when it comes to dissent, given the risks, and especially the economic structure, of boxing.[7] We invoke Robin D. G. Kelley's seminal anthology, *Race Rebels* (1996), here, to underscore our understanding of performing dissent in boxing, as we recognize that the meaning and impact of boxers' performances happen in relation to the social, historical, and political moment. Kelley, who builds on the work of James Scott (1990), argues that political acts "do make a difference, whether intended or not" by the performances of dissent enacted by the boxers who are examined in this text (8). Whether fighters intentionally create counternarratives and counterspaces is not where we draw the line. The emphasis and focus of this book comprise an examination of the social context that renders these actions and performances of dissent as politically significant.

These instances of agency also reveal how those with the least power in this sport are often the fighters themselves. As social actors who do not own arenas, boxing networks, or the buildings where they train, professional boxers' careers are often characterized by stories of austerity, racism, individualism, sexism, abuse, despair, powerlessness, and exploitation. They are alone in a world that shows little concern for their safety, security, and financial futures. Boxing is a sport that has no official governing sanctioning body, minimum salary, health care, nationwide pension plan, or financial literacy for boxers, making these workers among the most vulnerable to manipulation and corruption in the sports industry. Yet, in absence of those governing powers, rules governing dress, policies about how to stand during the national anthem, or respectable behavior are virtually nonexistent in the world of boxing. Not surprisingly, boxing has a long tradition of resistance and refusal, of challenges to the structures of broader injustices.

Many boxers have relied on the few instances of agency available in the industry: press conferences, weigh-ins, and ring entrances. Studying these sites of resistance and performance directs our attention to disparities not meant to be seen and to the irregularities in the narrative of individualism and democracy that permeate the representation of American boxing. Yet, such oppositional performances are not limited to the past or to the most famous boxers in history. *Rings of Dissent* is interested in how symbolic triumphs over white supremacy and American authority are articulated in and outside of the boxing ring, particularly in times of great oppression. In the late nineteenth century, Frederick Douglass described the importance of Peter Jackson, a "West Indian boxer, who was the first Black heavyweight of note to fight white opponents in the United States" (Bloom and Willard 2002, 1). Douglass praised Peter Jackson as a role model, as a freedom fighter: "Peter is doing a great deal with his fists to solve the Negro question" (1). For John Bloom and Michael Nevin Willard, the pride expressed by Douglass highlighted the power of sports within a larger struggle for racial justice: "Sports have become a critically important terrain on which most racialized groups have contested, defined, and represented their racial, national, and ethnic identities" (1).

Fast-forward to April 2001, when Yemeni-English boxer Naseem Hamed entered the ring to vie for the vacant International Boxing Organization World Featherweight Championship title. Following the ring entrance of Marco Antonio Barrera, Hamed's entrance commenced from behind the audience on its own built stage modeled to resemble the pillars of a *masjid*. The sounds of the *takbīr* filled the arena as several fans to the left of the stage raised a keffiyeh, signaling a time for prayer. The words

"Allah" and "Muhammad" were brightly illuminated as Hamed stepped onto the stage amid a pyrotechnic and sonic display that transformed the MGM Grand in Las Vegas from a boxing arena into a mosque for nearly a minute. Hamed, in leopard-print boxing trunks with "Islam" in block letters at the belt line, raised his arms in prayer and walked to the front of the stage before being lifted into the air and set down near the ring. One spectator threw a cup of beer at him as he descended. Though Hamed lost this fight, his ring entrance constituted a sonic and visual disruption of business as usual, temporarily transforming the arena by centering his faith tradition in ways that mainstream audiences were unaccustomed to seeing. Yet Hamed's ring entrance could not have occurred just five months later, after what has now become commemorated as 9/11.

In 2014, fighting on the same night against different opponents, boxers Raymundo Beltran and Evgeny Gradovich both expressed a unique solidarity to direct the audience's attention to the forty-three students who went missing from Ayotzinapa Rural Teachers' College in Iguala, Guerrero, Mexico. Beltran attached the number "43" to the front of his boxing trunks, while Gradovich, also known as "The Mexican Russian," entered the ring with a *charro* sombrero adorning the same number after his trainer Robert Garcia encouraged him to take action.[8] In an interview conducted by Rudy Mondragón, Beltran shared details about his decision to make a political statement by putting "43" on his belt line instead of using the belt as ad space to sell to a sponsor. 4Sparring.com, which was a company at the time, had expressed interest in purchasing the front belt-line ad space on his trunks, but Beltran was transparent with the representatives of the company and informed them that the front belt line was going to be used to raise awareness and honor the lives of the forty-three missing students. Had he agreed to sell it as ad space, which is a way for fighters to make extra money in addition to their fight purse, Beltran said, "That one [would've] paid me $10,000 . . . I took a chance to let it go, but they [4Sparring.com] supported [me] because of my motive and they liked that and still supported me . . . It was not about the money."[9] This was a powerful announcement about how boxers continue to invite spectators to imagine a world where high-profile athletes hold state and national governments accountable for corruption, police violence, and transparency. Along with boxers themselves, Black and Brown, LGBTQ, first-generation citizens, and undocumented fans participate in a practice of public praise and critique on these occasions. This public commentary creates spaces of felt meaning and belonging in a public sphere largely controlled by white men and heteropatriarchal narratives of nation.

In this book, we show how boxing is a site where a kind of democracy of visibility and participation can be made possible between fans and fighters. We do this in the tradition of boxers like Orlando Cruz, the first openly gay fighter to compete for a world title. Cruz dedicated his July 15, 2016, fight against Alejandro Valdez in Kissimmee, Florida, to the forty-nine victims, family members, and survivors of the June 12, 2016, Pulse nightclub shooting that took place in Orlando. Jim Buzinski (2016) of *Outsports* reported that prior to the start of the fight, "Cruz and his opponent Alejandro Valdez joined the crowd in silence as the ring bell was struck 49 times to honor each of those killed." Four of the victims were also friends of Cruz. Fans took to Twitter to express their reactions and appreciation for Cruz's prefight actions. User name @POOLSHARKQUEEN2 tweeted, "@ The Kissimmee Civic Center watching #OrlandoCruz Representing Us, More importantly the Families of the Victim's of Pulse #weRunited." Someone with the user name @gaystarnews also tweeted, "#OrlandoCruz wins for victims of #PulseShooting." Cruz's impact spread all the way to Greece as @MEN_gr tweeted, "Auto #OrlandoCruz #StopHomophobia #MEN_gr #Gay_Greece." Cruz's actions specifically demonstrate a powerful statement against homophobia and violence toward LGBTQ communities.

These examples are just a few of the many stories that embody a rich tradition of sporting resistance in the sport of boxing. The stories in *Rings of Dissent* focus on boxers' unexpected public interventions and the ways they exhibit their autonomy in relation to their social, political, and historical context. The contributors to this collection also recognize the significance of the fans who cultivate community and are empowered through the successes of their favorite fighters. In sum, boxing matters and this sporting culture has a plethora of meanings to those who participate and contribute to it.

Blow by Blow: Purpose and Scope

Rings of Dissent convenes scholars, commentators, activists, artists, and boxers to examine the ways that the sport of boxing has critiqued predominating ideologies of power. It not only interrogates how politics operate within and beyond the ring while revealing the agency and power of boxers themselves, but it also builds on the critical paradigm of sport by centering questions of inequality, exploitation, and resistance within the analysis of boxing (Carrington 2013). We situate this book on dissent in boxing within a history of sports writing that, while extensive, remains peripheral in many of the fields whose scholarship is most closely associated with marginalized communities. We intend for this book to emplace boxing as a locus of contestation, resistance, and creative freedom as it intersects with power, gender, sexuality, citizenship, immigration, indigeneity, and performance. We are concerned with how boxers navigate the neoliberal hypercapitalist sports industry that benefits from the idea that boxers are pawns and human commodities. By examining boxing through the critical paradigm of sports, the scholars, writers, activists, thinkers, artists, and teachers have come together to present new ways of listening, reading, analyzing, interpreting, and writing about boxing and how it reveals boxers' power to animate substantial political interventions.

Rings of Dissent is not simply a collection of essays and interviews; it is a collection of histories, voices, and experiences; it is a collection that spotlights the varied ways that boxers not only engage with their sport but also navigate the scripts and structures that govern their experiences through boxing. In this collection, each contributor illustrates that boxing exists as a space, tool, cultural production, and vehicle to perform dissent and resistance and as a contested site where boxers navigate dominant structures of race, ethnicity, gender, sexuality, immigration, and class. As the editors of this volume, we emphasize that performances of dissent in boxing are not homogeneous acts. They look different and are often hidden from plain sight and require careful meditation in deconstructing, analyzing, and representing these important interventions. As such, the readers of this anthology have the power to select the essays they want to engage with that deal with boxing, dissent, and resistance. Readers can jump from body chapters to informal interviews with a professional boxer, social justice hip-hop artist, ESPN commentator, and critical sports journalist.

We begin with Louis Moore's "Passing and Prizefighting: Ralph Dupas's Fight to Be White," which examines the racial landscape and sportscape of the early twentieth century, highlighting the profound ways that boxing operated as an arena to reinforce racial policies in and out of the ring. Moore reveals how boxing became a space of racial formation by establishing who was empowered to fight. The struggle over civil rights, over white supremacy, would define America throughout the twentieth century (and still persists). Boxing was no different. Moore highlights the story of Ralph Dupas, whose history of racial "passing" culminated in a different sort of fight: a legal challenge to his classification as Black. In order to fight, he had to prove his whiteness. His story, and that of so many other Black boxers, reveals that the history of boxing has always been about more than title fights, fierce jabs, and vicious uppercuts; the racial fabric of America is central to the history, as are the ways that Black boxers have both resisted, dissented, and leveraged the ring in the face of white supremacy.

The next two chapters focus on professional boxer and Home Box Office (HBO) *True Detective: Night Country* co-star, Kali "KO Mequinonoag" Reis. Chapter 2 is the first of five conversations where the editors engage in discussions with those outside of the academy whose work within and beyond the ring is crucial to understanding the politics and possibilities of boxing. As the editors, we sought to include the voices and experiences of people whose connection to boxing highlights the importance of boxing as a site of identity formation, resistance, community formation, and dissent. These conversations expand our understanding of discourse, challenging the privileging of scholarly essays at the expense of other voices, experiences, and methodologies. The beauty and power of these conversations is that we see how boxing bridges innumerable conversations, histories, and themes. This interview consists of a conversation between Mondragón, Johnson, and Reis, who is a Two-Spirit Black Indian woman who has held world championship titles in two weight classes. In their conversation, Reis discusses her early life and introduction to boxing, the parallels between her ring entrance and powwows, her mixed-race identity as a Native Black Two-Spirit woman, and becoming the first female (along with Cecilia Brækhus) to be on a televised HBO fight card. Her visibility, existence, successes, and performance of her culture in her ring entrances is dissent and a refusal to perform in ways that appease the white male and settler colonial gaze.[10] Just as boxing became a source of power and opposition to the persistent anti-Indigenous racism, Reis's approach to boxing demonstrates the powerful ways she not only navigates but also refuses the racist and gendered expectations that regulate her life and the lives of so many others.

In chapter 3, "'Fighting 4 All Nations': Boxing and the Indigenous Heritage," Kyle T. Mays reflects on the importance of Reis's career, offering a larger context for understanding both her words and her accomplishments. For Mays, Reis and countless more Indigenous boxers are "using one's agency—in this case, the body—to offer counternarratives to how Indigenous people are supposed to be. It is a critical reflection of Indigenous identity that is not tied to the white imagination but, rather, moving beyond it." Boxing is never just a sport. The story of boxing is one of marginalized communities asserting identity, challenging confinement and surveillance, and otherwise dissenting from the scripts of white supremacy. In Mays's reflection of Reis's conversation, he emphasizes that boxing allows people to express themselves through the use of a combat sport that allows for a momentary possibility of anticolonial struggle and resistance.

Chapter 4 is the second interview-based chapter, which features a conversation between David J. Leonard and Jessica Luther, an accomplished journalist, commentator, and scholar of gender and sports. In their conversation, Luther further pushes our understanding about gender and boxing, reminding us to think about how gender and race shape the stories we tell about boxing, boxers, and ourselves as fans and consumers. She challenges us to think about our gaze and how that gaze can reinforce yet also disrupt the hegemony evident inside and outside of the arena.

For chapter 5, we go back to the first half of the twentieth century, with José M. Alamillo's "Down, but Not Out: Mexican Prizefighters and Struggles against US Immigration in the 1930s." Alamillo explores how US immigration law and the practices of the boxing industry shaped the experiences of Mexican and Mexican American boxers in the 1930s. Whereas so much of the narratives surrounding boxing deploy a Black/white paradigm in examining the history of the sport, especially in the pre–civil rights movement era, Alamillo tells the story of Mexican boxers before World War II. While these boxers faced dehumanizing rhetoric, abusive treatment, and scapegoating that mirrors the racism and xenophobia that persist in the twenty-first century, these boxers challenged the subjugation through hidden forms of resistance and strategic performances of visibility. This chapter points to the historic foundation for ongoing discussions of both the criminalization and demonization of athletes of color and the ways that boxers have leveraged their platforms inside of sports to challenge endemic white supremacy.

In chapter 6, Roberto José Andrade Franco brings us into the late twentieth century with "The Great Off-White Hope," which offers an important intervention alongside a discussion of race and the career of Oscar De La Hoya. Challenging those who argued that "boxing is dead," a relic of a sporting past, Andrade Franco reflects on how such narratives privilege the experiences of middle-class white America, thereby erasing its cultural, political, economic, and social importance within communities of color. "Boxing, often considered dead by white, middle-class standards," he writes, "survives, in part, by manufacturing its own hope that a boxer will emerge and through charisma, skill, and proper marketing attract an entire country." As evident in the storied career of De La Hoya, boxing is neither dead nor losing its significance as both a sport and a site of racial formation. The performances of identities, alongside the athletic performances in the ring, exist as a site of dissent. So do the gazes and histories that fans bring into the arena.

Whereas Alamillo's chapter explores the ways that US immigration law and practices of the boxing industry shaped the experiences of Mexican and Mexican American boxers in the 1930s, Rudy Mondragón's "'Yo Soy José De Avenal': The Deployment of Expressive Culture in Disruptive Ring

Entrances" (chapter 7) is a contemporary examination of how a Mexican American world champion boxer uses their celebrity platform to advocate for immigrant communities in the United States. In this essay Mondragón challenges a rethinking of multiple narratives around sporting protest and demands a reckoning of the politics of dissent employed by boxers in a post–Muhammad Ali sportscape. Mondragón examines the September 14, 2018, ring entrance of José Carlos Ramírez, a world super lightweight champion. By situating Ramírez's ring entrance as a space where subtle and fluid performances of dissent and resistance to dominant ideologies and power structures can be found, Mondragón demonstrates how this boxer uses expressive culture to amplify a "Pro-Immigrant and Proud" political message intended as a counternarrative to Donald Trump's nativist and anti-immigrant "Make America Great Again" slogan. This chapter not only challenges the erasure of boxing from narratives of sporting resistance but also introduces the ring entrance space as an analytical unit that is ripe for critical interrogation. The connective tissues between boxing and activism (boxing as activism), between boxing and sartorial choices, and between boxing and other forms of popular culture, including music and one's entourage, are on display in this chapter as well as throughout the collection.

While the emphasis on individuality, braggadocio, performance, and battling are central to each endeavor, we are reminded that hip-hop and boxing afford spaces of creativity, resistance, and community. Chapter 8 is the third conversation, this one between Mondragón; Johnson; and hip-hop artist, activist, boxing enthusiast, and founder of 1Hood Media, Jasiri X. Here, they discuss the themes of self-confidence and self-belief that are central to boxing and hip-hop and how expressive culture can be used by boxers to perform dissent alongside social movements. To see resistance in boxing only through professionals leveraging their visibility, successes, and the platforms of ring entrances, interviews with the media, and sartorial choices is to ignore the profound ways that boxing, and sports in general, offers a myriad of tools of resistance.

This is what Priscilla Leiva (chapter 9) and Lucia Trimbur (chapter 11) demonstrate in their examination of boxing gym spaces. Leiva's "Why Gyms Matter: Boxing and the Struggle for Los Angeles," shows how the boxing gym exists not only as a space for personal empowerment, survival, and racial formation but also as part of a larger fight to protect communities of color from divestment, removal, and gentrification. Often celebrated as a vehicle for the American Dream, as a tool for America's poor to pull themselves up by their bootstraps toward stardom and financial success, Leiva demonstrates how boxing and the boxing gym exist as sites for communal resistance. In other words, urban boxing gyms exist not only to produce champions but to offer others an opportunity for community and a space of personal empowerment. Found between Leiva's and Trimbur's chapters is a conversation between Mondragón, Johnson, and Khnum Muata Ibomu (previously stic.man), an award-winning hip-hop artist, activist, platinum producer, and published author, who makes up one-half of the legendary hip-hop duo called dead prez. In this conversation, Ibomu tells his story about his introduction to boxing and the ways the sport informs and is connected to the RBG Fit Club. RBG Fit Club is "a holistic lifestyle movement" and brand that incorporates boxing and centers on wellness and healthy living.

In chapter 11, "Solidarity or Sanction: The Moral Economy of the Urban Gym," Lucia Trimbur takes readers back into the gym space to highlight the powerful ways that boxing gyms serve both trainers and gym members to find personal solace. In other words, she reveals how and why gym members rearticulate well-being while living in an economy of scarcity outside of the boxing gym. Her focus on Brooklyn reminds readers about the powerful place of boxing with the histories of cities. The story of boxing is not simply a story of bodily agency and domination over one's opponent but also one of developing a "moral economy," in regulating and controlling space in the face of surveillance, hyper-policing, and a powerful state. Through the development of relationships and a community of like-minded pugilists, Gleason's Gym, like its counterparts across the nation, is a refuge from their lived realities. As Trimbur notes, "The gym exists as a place where those who are frustrated, excluded from full citizenship by criminal records, and unable to meet the expectations of dominant society can create work, perform the work, and be recognized for that work." Chapter 12 is a conversation between Mondragón and former ESPN television personality Max Kellerman, one of the foremost experts on boxing. In this conversation, Kellerman reminds us that boxing offers important lessons about the political economy of boxing, including how boxing relies on narratives and stories to market the theatrical spectacle of the sport. He also discusses the exploitative nature of the boxing industry and the fighters who have navigated this terrain.

Following Mondragón and Kellerman's conversation is a creative and provocative meditation on fandom, Blackness, masculinity, and Floyd Mayweather Jr. In chapter 13, Javon Johnson, with "'Sincerely, These Hands': Mayweather, Money, and Masculinity," reflects on how we consume boxing in complex and contradictory ways. Using boxing icon Floyd Mayweather Jr., Johnson invites readers to think about new approaches to theorizing Black masculinity, building a case, round by round, about the possibilities of supporting Mayweather despite his laundry list of vile actions. In arguing for his own continued love for Mayweather, which is symbolic of the complex choices some people make in their quest to fight back against the pernicious violence of white supremacy, Johnson advances a necessary conversation about Mayweather, boxing, fandom, complexities of Black masculinity, and intersectional politics. This final chapter in *Rings of Dissent* highlights the messiness and complexity of dissent that is found in boxing. As scholars, researchers, and fans of boxing, we can unapologetically celebrate it while also interrogating and problematizing the neoliberal hypercapitalist and exploitative structures of this sporting industry.

The Final Face-Off

As we finished writing, millions of people were confined to their homes because of the ultimate opponent: COVID-19. Never mind the boxing cliches, no amount of training would prepare to battle this destructive opponent. COVID-19 has taken so much from so many: It has taken thousands upon thousands of lives. It has destroyed families, taken jobs, and left the world's economies in ruins. It has stripped away our institutions, our places of gathering and community formation. Sporting arenas stood quietly, deserted monuments memorializing a time when many people gathered without fear of a virus providing the ultimate knockout. Before the pandemic, however, most boxers were already working multiple jobs in order to make ends meet. Like many marginalized and low-wage workers, fighters were not fighting during the pandemic, but they were nonetheless working, finding creative ways to generate income even though gyms were temporarily closed. It was not simply the loss of money, the fears of gathering, or the loss of the ring and arena as communal spaces but a loss that disproportionately affected communities of color: With so few designated public spaces of congregation, the loss of a space that brings meaning and joy can be devastating for a working community that invests so much time and faith in the power of boxing. And, unfortunately, many boxing gyms, spaces of congregation, even closed their doors permanently.

And as the pandemic continued to be a persistent reality, we have also witnessed the terror of war escalate. On February 24, 2022, Russia invaded Ukraine, re-escalating the Russo-Ukrainian conflict. This indefensible invasion in Ukraine, led by Russian president Vladimir Putin, has not only violated international law and prompted serious violence, but it has also resulted in the unnecessary deaths of thousands as well as displacing families. Both retired and current professional boxers of Ukrainian descent have taken up arms and joined their country's military defense.

Vitali and Wladimir Klitschko were some of the first to publicly denounce the invasion and join the fight, followed by current world champion boxers Vasiliy Lomachenko and Oleksandr Usyk. Putting a temporary hold on their professional boxing careers, Lomachenko and Usyk took up arms and made calls to end the war via their social media accounts, which are followed by millions of people around the world. These actions demonstrate the ways in which boxing and global politics are not separate entities but intertwined societal realities where boxers use their celebrity platforms to make a difference. This was equally visible during the 2024 Olympics, which we reflect on in our coda, from the ways that athletes stood in protest against the brutality faced by the Palestinian people to the transphobia, queer antagonism, and bigotry directed at Imane Khelif and Lin Yu-ting. Both boxers, who secured gold for Algeria and Taiwan, respectively, were subjected to global bigotry, used as political pawns by those who are comfortable when sports descend into politics as long as it done so in the name of white supremacist, heteronormative, patriarchal power (ESPN 2024; Zirin 2024).

The cultural and political articulations of value and dissent by the boxers we present in *Rings of Dissent* feel even more significant within the present historical moment. The essays that follow will demonstrate the many ways boxers exhibit agency and creativity and perform dissent at every step. These essays also highlight contradictions and complicated representations in boxers' performances: Navigating an exploitative and hypercapitalist industry can sometimes lead to unwitting reinforcement and reinvention of oppressive paradigms. Yet the stories found here also have the power to remind us that boxing lives within each of us; we all have been affected by boxing. It lives within the histories we share, the legacies we hold on to, and within our own memories.

From fighters to fans, from activists to artists, boxing exists as a means to tell stories about others and ourselves. To be a scholar and fan of boxing is also to acknowledge the central place of the sweet science in Black, Latinx, Indigenous, and resource-poor communities, and to understand the multiple layers of race, gender, nation, immigration status, and capital that constitute its representation and function as a public sport. It is to see the long-standing linkages between the world of boxing and stories of resistance and dissent. It is to see refusal and opposition not simply in the jab or in the most visible articulations of protest but in the everyday spaces of boxing where demands to be seen and heard are articulated. Boxing has long served as an instrument of, an ideological buttress against, and a barometer of white supremacy, misogyny, homophobia, and other forms of injustice. It is our hope that in the stories of resistance, we find hope and possibility that has been dampened in the midst of COVID-19; the Russian invasion of Ukraine; the persistent rise of fascism in the United States and elsewhere; and the continued brutalization of the people in Gaza, the West Bank, and Lebanon. Boxing is not simply a reminder of the human spirit, of our abilities to preserve and dust ourselves off in the face of adversity, but a place where the marginalized and disenfranchised have found ways to not only battle but to also reimagine what is possible. Knowing there are countless examples yet to be studied, *Rings of Dissent* offers thirteen rounds—unique and powerful essays—about boxing, performance, and rebellion.

Notes

1. D Smoke, "Black Habits I," February 6, 2020, track 7 on *Black Habits*.

2. At the weigh-in for their July 16, 2016, fight, Deontay Wilder and Chris Arreola stood next to each other with signs that read "His Life Matters" and arrows pointing at each other. This action was a demonstration of racial solidarity between Black and Brown people and in support of the Black Lives Matter movement. Later, leading up to his February 22, 2020, rematch with Tyson Fury, Wilder spoke with boxing journalist Radio Rahim on the racial double standards that existed between him and Fury. He specifically talked about how Fury's struggles with mental health and drugs were represented by the media with sympathy and care, whereas, if the roles were reversed, Wilder argued, people would say he was a "drug addict" because "I come from a different world."

3. See Body and Soul (1947), The Ring (1952), The Great White Hope (1970), Rocky (1976), Raging Bull (1980), Ali (2001), Million Dollar Baby (2004), Cinderella Man (2005), The Fighter (2010), Creed (2015), Hands of Stone (2016), and Bruised (2021), to name a few. Also see Zak Wojnar et al., "The 15 Greatest Boxing Movies of All Time" (2016) for additional examples. Boxing movies have a long history going back to the first prizefight film, between James J. Corbett and Bob Fitzsimmons in 1897. At that time, fight pictures were used to destigmatize the sport and turn it into legitimate entertainment. For more, see Dan Streible, Fight Pictures: A History of Boxing and Early Cinema (2008).

4. The works of authors Ralph Ellison and Luis J. Rodríguez are important to note here. Ellison's *The Invisible Man* (1995) starts with a horrific story about battles royal, a violent fight involving multiple fighters who are pinned against each other until only one stands alone. Ellison shows how this was a source of entertainment for white wealthy men at the expense of young Black men who were stripped of their humanity, dignity, and immersed in a dangerous environment. Rodríguez's *Always Running* (2005), an autobiographical book, talks about his experiences with boxing and frames it as a sport that Chicanos had a great deal invested in because it provided them, as well as Black youth, with a sense of belonging and community.

5. David Chandler's *Boxer: An Anthology of Writings on Boxing and the Visual Arts* (1996) examines the tensions of boxing and art and explores the link between the sport and artistic world, providing essays that look at boxing and masculinity, class, eroticism, and race. Similarly, Bill Hughes's *Come Out Writing* (1991), George Kimball and John Schulian's *At the Fights* (2011), and Pierce Egan's *Boxiana* (2014) each bring forward the "best writers" of the sport for enthusiastic fans of boxing and literature. Gerald Early's *The Muhammad Ali Reader* (2013) offers thirty writings about Ali from the perspectives of authors, athletes, and social commentators who spoke to the controversies and charismatic boxer-activist. Finally, Carlo Rotella and Michael Ezra edited *The Bittersweet Science* (2017), which brings scholars, journalists, and former fighters to produce a composite in-depth look at boxing through profiles of superstar fighters, boxing agents, and first-person accounts from the fighters themselves.

6. At the weigh-in for their July 16, 2016, fight, Deontay Wilder and Chris Arreola's "His Life Matters" performance on July 15, 2016, is a good example of this. And in 2014, during the weekend of the Amir Khan and Devon Alexander fight in Las Vegas, Andre Berto and other Black boxers wore, and attempted to pass out, "I Can't Breathe" and "Hands Up" T-shirts to protest and raise awareness about racial violence. They experienced opposition by the event organizers for their act of dissent.

7. Boxers are often engaged in what James Scott calls *infrapolitics*, which are "the silent partner of a loud form of public resistance," daily confrontations, evasive actions, and stifled thoughts that often inform organized political movements. As Robin D. G. Kelley suggests, these subtle and calculated acts are worthy of examination because "the political history of oppressed people cannot be understood without reference to infrapolitics" because the daily acts and performances "have a cumulative effect on power relations." This builds on the seminal work from James C. Scott, *Domination and the Arts of Resistance: Hidden Transcripts* (1990).

8. Robert Garcia (retired professional boxer and current trainer) in discussion with Rudy Mondragón, September 2019.

9. Raymundo Beltrán (professional boxer) in discussion with Rudy Mondragón, February 2020.

10. For more on this, see Rudy Mondragón, "Boxing Ring Entrances as Insubordinate Spaces: A Disruptive Oral Herstory" (2023).

References

Alamillo, José M. 2020. *Deportes: The Making of a Sporting Diaspora*. Rutgers University Press.

Bloom, John, and Michael N. Williard. 2002. "Out of Bounds and Between the Lines: Race in Twentieth-Century American Sport." In *Sports Matters: Race, Recreation, and Culture*, edited by John Bloom and Michael N. Willard, 1–10. New York University Press.

Bryant, Howard. 2018. *The Heritage: Black Athletes, a Divided America, and the Politics of Patriotism*. Beacon Press.

Buzinski, Jim. 2016. "Gay Boxer Orlando Cruz Dedicates Win to Victims of Orlando Gay Bar Shooting." *Outsports*, July 18. https://www.outsports.com/2016/7/18/12210942/gay-boxer-orlando-cruz-dedicates-win-orlando-pulse-shooting.

Carrington, Ben. 2013. "The Critical Sociology of Race and Sport: The First Fifty Years." *Annual Review of Sociology* 39: 379–98.

Chandler, David, ed. 1996. *Boxer: An Anthology of Writings on Boxing and Visual Culture*. Institute of International Visual Arts.

Early, Gerald, ed. 2013. *The Muhammad Ali Reader*. HarperCollins.

Egan, Pierce. 1999. *Boxiana; or, Sketches of Ancient and Modern Pugilism, from the Days of the Renowned Broughton and Slack, to the Championship of Cribb*. Adegi Graphics LLC.

Ellison, Ralph. 1995. *The Invisible Man*. Vintage International.

ESPN. 2024. "Lin Yu-ting Joins Imane Khelif with Olympic Gold amid Gender Dispute." August 10. https://www.espn.com/olympics/story/_/id/40810760/lin-yu-ting-joins-imane-khelif-olympic-gold-amid-gender-dispute.

Goffman, Erving. 1959. *The Presentation of Self in Everyday Life*. Knopf Doubleday.

Horne, Gerald. 2021. *The Bittersweet Science: Racism, Racketeering and the Political Economy of Boxing*. International Publishers.

Hughes, Bill. 1991. *Come Out Writing: A Boxing Anthology*. Edited by Patrick J. King. Queen Anne Press.

Kelley, Robin D. G. 1996. *Race Rebels: Culture, Politics, and the Black Working Class*. Free Press.

Kimball, George, and John Schulian, eds. 2011. *At the Fights: American Writers on Boxing: A Library of America Special Publication*. Library of America.

Lansbury, Jennifer H. 2022. *A Spectacular Leap: Black Women Athletes in Twentieth-Century America*. University of Arkansas Press.

Matthews, Wallace. 2019. "Blue-haired Olympian Claressa Shields Fights for Flint in Latest Daring Challenge." *New York Daily News*, February 27. https://www.nydailynews.com/sports/more-sports/ny-sports-claressashields-christinahammer-20190226-story.html.

McDonald, Mary, and Susan Birrell. 1999. "Reading Sport Critically: A Methodology for Interrogating Power." *Sociology of Sport* 16, no. 4: 283–300.

McFarlane, Nyree. 2020. "The Meaning behind Deontay Wilder's $40,000 Black Mask and Cape." *The National*, February 23. https://www.thenationalnews.com/lifestyle/fashion/the-meaning-behind-deontay-wilder-s-40-000-black-mask-and-cape-1.983124.

Mondragón, Rudy. 2023. "Boxing Ring Entrances as Insubordinate Spaces: A Disruptive Oral Herstory." *Kalfou: A Journal of Comparative and Relational Ethnic Studies* 9, no. 2. https://tupjournals.temple.edu/index.php/kalfou/article/view/625.

Mondragón, Rudy, Abel Valenzuela, and José M. Hernández. 2024. "Down but Not Out: Labor Struggles for Professional Boxers in California's Ring." *UCLA Latino Policy and Politics Institute*, 1–18. https://latino.ucla.edu/wp-content/uploads/2024/05/Down-but-Not-Out-Labor-Struggles-for-Professional-Boxers-in-Californias-Ring.pdf.

Moore, Louis. 2017. *I Fight for a Living: Boxing and the Battle for Black Manhood, 1880–1915*. University of Illinois Press.

Obi, Desch. 2009. "Black Terror: Bill Richmond's Revolutionary Boxing." *Journal of Sport History* 36, no. 1: 99–114.

Preezy. 2017. "20 Great Rap Lyrics for Die-Hard Boxing Fans." *XXL Mag*. January 24. https://www.xxlmag.com/news/2017/01/rap-boxing-lyrics/?utm_source=tsmclip&utm_medium=referral.

Reed, Ishmael. 1976. "The Ali-Norton Fight: The Man Who Knew Too Much." *Village Voice*, March 31.

Remnick, David. 1999. *King of the World*. Knopf Doubleday.

Rhoden, William C. 2007. *Forty Million Dollar Slaves: The Rise, Fall, and Redemption of the Black Athlete*. Crown.

Rodriguez, Luis J. 2005. *Always Running: La Vida Loca: Gang Days in L.A.* Simon & Schuster.

Rotella, Carlo, and Michael Ezra, eds. 2017. *The Bittersweet Science: Fifteen Writers in the Gym, in the Corner, and at Ringside*. University of Chicago Press.

Runstedtler, Theresa. 2012. *Jack Johnson, Rebel Sojourner: Boxing in the Shadow of the Global Color Line*. University of California Press.

Sammons, Jeffrey T. 1988. *Beyond the Ring: The Role of Boxing in American Society*. University of Illinois Press.

Scott, James C. 1990. *Domination and the Arts of Resistance: Hidden Transcripts*. Yale University Press.

Streible, Dan. 2008. *Fight Pictures: A History of Boxing and Early Cinema*. University of California Press.

Taylor, Diana. 2003. *The Archive and the Repertoire: Performing Cultural Memory in the Americas*. Duke University Press.

Trimbur, Lucia. 2013. *Come Out Swinging: The Changing World of Boxing in Gleason's Gym*. Princeton University Press.

Van Ingen, Cathy. 2003. "Geographies of Gender, Sexuality and Race: Reframing the Focus on Space in Sport Sociology." *International Review for the Sociology of Race and Sport* 38, no. 2: 201–216.

Wojnar, Zak, Mary Kassel, Aryanna Alvarado, Eli Morrison, and Lilo Navratil. 2016. "The 15 Greatest Boxing Movies of All Time." *Screen Rant*. https://screenrant.com/best-boxing-movies-ever-rocky-creed/.

Zirin, Dave. 2005. *What's My Name, Fool? Sports and Resistance in the United States*. Haymarket Books.

Zirin, Dave. 2024. "We Must Defend Imane Khelif." *The Nation*. August 5. https://www.thenation.com/article/society/imane-khelif-olympics-paris-boxing-transphobia/.

1

Passing and Prizefighting

Ralph Dupas's Fight to Be White

LOUIS MOORE

When the white fans saw Ralph Dupas's 140-pound frame sitting in the stands for that night's heavyweight contest between Joey Rowan and Crowe Peele, they erupted into a loud cheer. They had come to see Peele, a former Louisiana State University football player who was climbing the ring rankings as a white hope, but before the main event, these four thousand white "balcony fans" got caught up in a racial drama. Dupas, a local welterweight, had recently been outed as Black, and now he had to fight this charge in court. Those cheers were a signal from the white fans that they supported Dupas in his fight to be white; he was one of *them*. That night, their support brought tears to his eyes. "It was the most applause I ever got," Dupas said. He added, "The fans won't be let down by me Monday night."[1] Monday night? That was his upcoming fight with Vince Martinez, which was still a week away. The next morning, however, Dupas had a bigger battle. He had to go in front of the New Orleans boxing commission and prove he was white.[2] In Louisiana, a state that had been swept up in a hate-filled hurricane of White Citizens' Council (WCC) politics, determining Ralph Dupas's race was a fight for the meaning of whiteness and a battle to keep the races separated (Pascoe 2009; Davis 2001; Williamson 1980; Baker 1964; Magnum 1940).

In the Jim Crow South, boxing operated as a tool to reinforce racial policies in and outside of the ring. In a sport that supposedly showed off manhood, Black men, no matter how good they were, could never be seen as being equal to white men. And this meant marking clear lines of racial distinctions. A white fighter could fight a Mexican. A white fighter could fight a Filipino. But a white man could never fight a Black man. Too much was at stake.

Prizefighting, more than any other sport, assumed a level of equality and meritocracy. Men fought in the same weight class, with the same size gloves, and fans refused to watch fights deemed mismatches. The ring, in other words, assumed equality. And the best man won. But just separating the races was not enough for Southern fans and promoters. For the first half of the twentieth century, Southern promoters used battle royals, where Black fighters, including young boys, were blindfolded and forced to battle in the ring for the pleasure of white audiences. These demeaning affairs were meant to reinforce the absolute powerlessness that Black people had. In short, white Southerners saw Black boys and men as a joke. But by the turn of the century, outside of the South, fight promoters started to allow Black men a chance to fight for championships, and soon Black boys born in the South, like Jack Johnson, Tiger Flowers, Henry Armstrong, Beau Jack, and Joe Louis, won world titles and became symbols to Black folks that if given a fair chance in society, Black men were whites' equal.

After World War II, every major sport started to integrate. Black men could be seen on the diamond, the hardwood, and the gridiron competing with whites. Northern newspapers wrote about the quickening spirit of American democracy and started to champion these momentous integrated occasions. In the 1950s, this integration spirit of sports finally made its way down south. First with college football. Then came minor league baseball. At the same time, the US Supreme Court ruled that the South had to integrate its public schools. White Southerners feared that since sports integrated, they would have to follow the law and integrate schools. So they dug in deep—no schools or sports.

Whiteness was a property that had to be protected at all costs. As scholar Cheryl I. Harris (1993) contends, "In ways so embedded that it is rarely apparent, the set of assumptions, privileges, and benefits that accompany that status of being white have become a valuable asset that whites sought to protect and that those who passed sought to attain—by fraud if necessary." "Whites," she further explains, "have come to expect and rely on these benefits, and over time these expectations have been affirmed, legitimated, and protected by the law" (1713). In New Orleans, a city with a public reputation as having a racially mixed heritage, protecting the property of whiteness meant outing the most popular white fighter in the area, Ralph Dupas, as a Black man.

By examining Ralph Dupas's legal battle to be white from 1957 to 1960, this chapter explores the fragility of whiteness.[3] At a moment when most Black people stopped racially passing because the walls of Jim Crow segregation were crumbling, Dupas stood his ground (Hobbs 2014). In

Louisiana, however, Dupas had no legal standing. He was born to Black parents. Instead of allowing the state to define his racial status based on the blood in his veins, Dupas fought his battle on the idea that he possessed social whiteness determined by his ability to live publicly as a white prizefighter.

Dupas's resistance from race laws, however, was not a dissent from Jim Crow. Rather, his public passing and battle to maintain white status was an attempt to maintain the status quo. He resisted the legal definition of whiteness. Instead of trying to tear down the walls of Jim Crow, he fought to make sure he benefited from their existence. Being white gave him access to better schools and housing, and in the ring it also meant he made more money than his Black counterparts. Dupas was not going to relinquish those privileges and immunities, even if, as he said, it cost him every penny to get "this mistake cleared up."[4]

How to Pass

At some point in the 1930s, Peter and Evelyn Duplessis decided they would rather be poor and white than poor and Black. Racially ambiguous but light enough to pass as white, they finally acted on their plans in October 1935 after their son, Ralph, was born in Plaquemines Parish, a town that rested at the end of the Mississippi River roughly sixty-five miles from New Orleans. It is not clear why they waited until that moment. Maybe they had been denied white racial status on Ralph's birth certificate by the local vital records keeper, Lucretia Gravolet, who had a reputation for overruling suspect whites who wanted legal white status on their certificate. Maybe they simply wanted a new life that avoided Jim Crow. Whatever the case, this was not a hasty decision. Every detail leading up to that moment and thereafter was planned with the recognition that one day they, or their kids, could be outed as being Black.

Their first step was to move to New Orleans, a city where nobody knew their histories but also a place where racially ambiguous folks like them blended in. They changed their name from Duplessis to Dupas. They moved into a white neighborhood. They had Ralph baptized at their neighborhood Catholic church, and then they had him marked as white in church records. They had eight more children after their move, and all eight were marked as white on their birth certificates. And all of their kids attended white schools.[5]

Whiteness, however, did not protect them from poverty. Based on the 1940 census, Peter, who had a fourth-grade education, had not worked in roughly thirty-five weeks when the census enumerator stopped by their house in March. In fact, he had worked for only six weeks in 1939 and earned a total of $50 working on a shrimp boat. This figure was way below the median income of $956, but their whiteness was the value they sought.[6]

Young Ralph, however, wanted more. The teeming poverty he faced made him risk the lie. While most people passing shied away from a public existence for fear of exposure, Dupas chose to live his lie publicly, and in 1950 he turned professional at the age of fourteen.[7]

The Rise of the Native Dancer

Despite being so young, Dupas had immediate success in the ring and quickly became a hometown favorite. Dubbed the "Native Dancer" by a local sports editor, a nickname that was as disrespectful as it was descriptive, the lightweight (135 pounds) Dupas used a slick defensive yet optically boring style to befuddle his opponents, with constant head movement and counterpunches. Seldom was he the aggressor. He was content to win rounds on his way to a victory rather than taking a chance scoring a knockout. But this strategy left his fate in judges' hands. Sooner or later, if he was not going to be the aggressor, he risked losing a close contest as he did in July 1956, to lightweight contender Kenny Lane. He learned his lesson.

After the Lane match, Dupas changed his style and started to come forward. He scored knockouts in three of his next five fights and thoroughly dominated his other opponents. The press and his fans took note. Before Dupas's March 4, 1957, bout against lightweight Ray Portilla, a Mexican American fighter from Houston, Art Burke of the *New Orleans States* declared, "Dupas is confident and even cocky on the outcome promising another of his 'aggressive fights' which he will try to end 'as soon as possible.'"[8] Dupas did not get the knockout, but he used his "new style of 'go in there and hit 'em'" to shred Portilla.[9]

Next up for Dupas was the Italian American Vince Martinez, a welterweight in line for a shot at the 147-pound crown. Their catch-weight fight—they agreed to fight at 145 pounds—would be Dupas's biggest fight and the most financially successful battle in New Orleans history to date.

At twenty-one years old, Dupas seemingly had everything. He had bought his parents a house. He was married to his high school sweetheart. He had business investments, two houses, a new car, a boat, and was a top-ranked boxer. But he also had "Black blood" running through his veins, and in Louisiana that meant trouble for a white man.

His Greatest Fight

With his racially ambiguous features, there had always seemed to be something different, not quite white, about Dupas, but until 1957 nobody had publicly acted on their suspicions. In 1952, when he was sixteen, the city denied him a white birth certificate, but that went no further than a simple rejection. Somehow, even without proper paperwork, the state allowed the teenager to fight as a white man. The following year, the city's vital statistics director changed the birth certificates of Dupas's siblings and removed their white designation, a legal right the director had under state law and a common practice in Louisiana (Dominguez 1986). But there is no indication of why this happened. In 1956, before his November battle with Siegfried Burrow, somebody told the local boxing commission that Dupas was Black. The boxing commission, however, allowed the fight to continue and did not make these charges public. After that charge, Dupas had two more local fights in 1957 without any racial objections. But then, in late March, leading up to his encounter with Martinez, the rumors about his race bubbled up to the surface. A concerned citizen from Plaquemines alerted the boxing commission that Ralph Dupas was not a white man born in New Orleans but rather a Black man born Ralph Duplessis in Plaquemines. Dupas tried to play it off as jealousy, saying, "Nobody questioned I was white until I was making big money as a fighter. I went through grammar school and high school and was always accepted as white."[10] But this was not jealousy. This accusation came from formidable opponents, the White Citizens' Council.

Led by state senator W. M. Rainach, the WCC came into existence in Louisiana in January 1956 as part of a racist Southern strategy to fight integration in the wake of the US Supreme Court's *Brown v. Board of Education* decision. Rainach said he formed the council in order "to protect and preserve, by all legal means our historical southern social traditions in all their aspects."[11] With a goal to preserve their so-called white rights through legal channels, Rainach worked to organize other segregationists across the state, parish by parish. Led by Judge L. H. Perez, a noted "expert authority on, and exponent of segregation," Plaquemines, Dupas's true birthplace, quickly became a WCC stronghold.[12] With voters from Plaquemines and other parishes, the council took over state politics and immediately started to implement segregationist laws, including the sports segregation bill passed in July 1956.

Louisiana's sports segregation bill, HB 1412, was a law that intentionally used segregated sports to slow down the quickening pace of integration. In

Louisiana, professional and college sports had slowly started to integrate after the *Brown* decision, and the WCC believed that if sports continued on this path, schools would be next. Integrated sports provided proof that society could integrate and that Blacks and whites could stand side by side on equal footing. If sports could do it, then the schools could too. The bill, signed by governor Earl Long, banned the mixing of Black and white athletes on the sports field, from training together, and integration in the stands (Moore 2017). When passed, the *Plaquemines Gazette* celebrated the law as "more than a major victory for the white patriotic citizens of the state who have banned together in a common cause to protect the people of Louisiana and more especially the future generations."[13] The same folks who passed the sports segregation bill also tried to stop Dupas, as his presence mocked everything the segregationists stood to protect. That could not go unchallenged.

In March, ten days before the Martinez match, the segregationists officially charged Dupas with being Black. Because the charges came from state lawmakers, and not ordinary citizens who might have a grudge, the boxing commission had to reevaluate whether Dupas could fight a white opponent. To determine his fate, the commission had an open hearing for both sides to make their case. The complaint from Rainach and Anthony Ciaccio, the state registrar of public health, claimed that the postmistress from Plaquemines Parish in 1935, Lucretia Gravolet, verified that Dupas was born Ralph Duplessis in Plaquemines to parents Evelyn and Peter Duplessis. They also presented his original birth certificate marking him as Black.

In Louisiana, the state gave public employees who kept vital statistics full authority to determine one's race, even after death. The property of whiteness, Cheryl I. Harris argues, is the "absolute right to exclude." Harris notes, "The possessors of whiteness were granted the legal right to exclude others from the privileges inhering in whiteness; whiteness became an exclusive club whose membership was closely and grudgingly guarded" (1993, 1736). In Plaquemines, postmistress Lucretia Gravolet wielded the power to grant or deny whiteness to local citizens. One woman who worked with Gravolet stated, "Sometimes parents would tell me they were one race and Mrs. Gravolet would tell me another."[14] Gravolet marked Dupas as Black. Twenty-two years later, she was so sure of her ability to determine race that she stood up in court, pointed at Dupas, and yelled, "You are a Negro. I know you are a Negro. Now put me in jail if you don't like it."[15] Nobody sent her to jail. Dupas told friends that he was so humiliated by the charges that he planned to leave the city.

Dupas came to the initial hearing with a host of evidence to prove his social white status. He had his mother testify to his race. He brought his parent's old white neighbor in New Orleans, who claimed she was the midwife when he was born on Mandeville Street in New Orleans, not Plaquemines. He also had his baptism record that marked him as white, along with records showing his other siblings had white birth certificates, including his brother Tony, who was also a pro boxer. He even had one of his former high school teachers, Miss Tomney, testify that he was "a wonderful boy who got to the top through hard work."[16]

For the commission, however, the decision to decide Dupas's racial fate was too much of a burden to bear. For one, they believed in their own judgment to determine one's race. They were not ready to mark Dupas as Black because they had always known him as white. Second, the commission had to weigh the legal implications of their decision. If they marked him white and were wrong, Dupas could sue them for libel. But if they allowed him to fight as a Black man against a white opponent, they could be charged with violating the sports segregation bill. Finally, there was too much money at stake. Contracts had already been signed, and thousands of people had bought their tickets for what promised to be one of the most attended boxing events in city history. The fight had to go on, and thus for the time being that made Dupas a white man. After the ruling, Dupas told a reporter, "Man, that's a lot better. I'm ready now for what I feel will be my biggest ring test." Dupas, as one headline claimed, had won his "Greatest Fight."[17]

The whole ordeal motivated Dupas in the ring. After the commission's ruling, he claimed, "There's no stopping me now."[18] He also told reporter Pete Baird, "I'm really going to make a good fight. I never will forget how the people gave me the okay the other night (at the Peele–Rowan fight) and I'm not going to let all my friends down." Baird predicted, "Now he feels so grateful that I believe he will go out there and slug away trying for a kayo [a knockout]." He also concluded that if Dupas was willing to risk all his money on being white, he would "risk his life" to win the boxing match.[19] Art Burke of the *New Orleans States* argued that the case might have brought Dupas unwanted attention, but it also made him a box-office draw. "The way Dupas came out of the racial hearing won him many new friends in the fight business," Burke noted, "and it is expected to reflect in his pay envelope next Monday."[20]

As predicted, the fight broke local records for attendance and money. In the ring, Dupas unleashed a physical viciousness. "I had been in a number of court hearings before the Martinez fight," he declared, adding, "I was determined to take it out on someone, and it turned out to be Martinez. If it hadn't been for this, I may never have beaten Martinez. But that night I was determined."[21]

At All Costs

Despite the ruling, the WCC continued to put pressure on the boxing commission. Three weeks after the Martinez bout, the commission demanded Dupas show them a birth certificate. Instead of producing a birth certificate, Dupas, whose only real birth certificate marked him as Ralph Duplessis and Black from Plaquemines, sued New Orleans for a delayed birth certificate that marked him as white. Dupas now staked his legal claim to whiteness on a lie that the city did not originally send his family a birth certificate and thus must send him one with his correct racial designation.

His new line of attack, however, forced the city to change their tactics too. After Dupas sued New Orleans, local officials were so desperate to defeat Dupas and prove he was Black, they changed city records. Naomi Drake, New Orleans's recorder of vital statistics, who years earlier had erased the white status of the Dupas children on their birth certificates with no explanations, went back into the records again and changed the racial status on Dupas's paternal grandfather's death certificate from white to Negro. This change effectively made his grandfather, father, and Dupas Black. When asked in court why she did that, Drake said she was just being "honest."[22]

Racial passing came with a price. For some, it meant leaving one's Black family and community behind for fear of being outed. For Dupas, he had to pay in dollars for the property of whiteness (Roediger 1999). To maintain his racial status, Dupas vowed to spend every penny he had. In August 1957, as his case against New Orleans went to trial, he told the local press, "I have two homes, one paid for, a boat and a car and I'll sell them all to fight this thing. It's already costs [*sic*] me $1500." He continued, "You have no idea the tortures I've gone through since these charges were made. I've been living a nightmare."[23] The specter of having to live as a Black man in the Jim Crow South scared him. If he lost this fight, he might have to give up his marriage, family, and career. Thus, for Dupas, the fight to be white was worth the price.

Passing and Precedence

Dupas had precedence on his side. More than sixty years before Dupas, New Orleans fighter Andy Bowen (1868–1894) took up the fight to be white (Fleicher 1939, 236–38). Bowen's career coincided with an increase in anti-Black legal restrictions that ultimately ended with the Supreme Court codifying Jim Crow with the *Plessy v. Ferguson* decision (Golub 2005). As a boxer, Bowen gained national renown for being one of the top lightweight fighters and was frequently called the "lightweight champion of the south" by local papers, a name that represented his whiteness in a Jim Crow city (Fleicher 1939, 236–38). Back then, newspapers never failed to mark a fighter's race designation. And Bowen did all he could to make sure folks knew: in the ring, he tried to assure his whiteness through his ring attire and often wore a belt that intertwined the American flag with the Irish flag.[24]

Despite his assertion about his heritage, rumors constantly flowed about Bowen's race. On a few occasions writers outside of New Orleans referred to him as a Creole, octoroon, colored, or mulatto, and some writers made remarks about his Negro blood. As early as 1890, for example, a writer for the *Duluth Times* described him as a "pleasant but course-looking fellow, with a very dark skin showing plainly the little negro blood in his veins."[25] Despite these references to his possible racial heritage, most writers treated him as white.

When white people stepped out of line, Bowen was quick to put them in their place. In 1891, for example, he went after the pocketbook and reputation of the Audubon Club of New Orleans for treating him as a Black man. In that year, Bowen negotiated a match with the club to battle the tough white fighter Austin Gibbons. As the date for the fight approached, however, Bowen pulled out of the contest to protest club members questioning his race, leaving the club to deal with refunding tickets and paying for Gibbons's return trip to New Jersey.[26]

The following year, a *Chicago Herald* writer described Bowen as "colored," which prompted a swift response from Bowen's manager. His manager wrote to the *Chicago Inter Ocean*:

> In order to set at rest at once this report I think it only just and right to correct these misstatements through the papers of Chicago. New Orleans is my place of birth, and having resided there all my life I have had every opportunity of knowing Andy Bowen, and claim to know something about his birth and parentage. I think this is a gross injustice done him and deny positively that Bowen has a particle of the negro blood in his veins. Mr. Bowen's mother is alive in New Orleans and of the pure Irish race. As to his father, the facts are uncontradicted that there is not one drop of the negro blood in his veins. It has been thoroughly discussed by us New Orleans people and the facts in the case set at rest any doubt or suspicion.[27]

Lamenting the injustice of a white man being called Black, and testifying to Bowen's Irish heritage, his manager definitively stated Bowen's claim to whiteness. Understanding their "gross injustice," the *Herald* backtracked on their statement and issued an apology. Titled "In Justice to Andy Bowen," the paper said, "In justice to Bowen it should be stated that published statements as to his color were erroneous. He is neither an octoroon nor a negro, but a pure Caucasian, his dark skin being due to the southern climate in which he has lived since his birth and which he rarely leaves."[28] For Bowen, establishing his whiteness was necessary, considering that Louisiana had started a legal campaign of racial segregation. The same year Bowen and his manager challenged the Chicago press, Homer A. Plessy challenged Louisiana's segregated railroad cars. Unfortunately for Bowen, his life ended early in 1894 when his head hit the floor after being knocked out in the eighteenth round against George Lavigne.

Then in 1949 the Docusen brothers (Bernard, Regino, and Maxie) won the right to be legally half white and half Filipino, a very important dual distinction that clearly marked them as not Black. Much like Dupas, the Docusens had started out as white fighters only to have their careers derailed when a government official charged them with being Black. The legal action against the Docusens commenced in 1945 when the state refused to give the youngest brother, Maxie, a boxing license that marked him as white. The state argued that his parents were marked as "colored" in the city's records. The commission then deduced that if his parents were colored, then so too were Maxie and his brothers.

Being marked as Black would have changed the Docusens's fistic fortunes. Bernard was one of the top fighters in the world, and his success had been financially rewarded as he grossed upward of $10,000 a fight at his peak.[29] For comparison's sake, in 1947, when top-rated Black fighters Sandy Saddler and Joe Brown fought in the city, Brown, a New Orleans native, earned only $495.[30] To retain their white status, the Docusens sued. For them, timing was everything. In a 1946 case, a judge had ruled that for Filipinos, "colored" did not mean Negro (Dominguez 1986, 34–36). That distinction made all the difference, because the state's segregation statutes were aimed at Black people. With legal precedent on the fighters' side, in 1949 the city reversed their decision about the Docusens and stated that their mother was white, and their dad was Filipino and therefore not Black. As their attorney Monk Zelden noted, "This means the Docusen brothers can fight anywhere in the United States."[31] Eight years later, Zelden represented Ralph Dupas.

For the Dupas case, Zelden tried to expand the meaning of whiteness. In a city like New Orleans that had, as one Black writer put it, "the blackest white folk and the whitest black folk on earth," it was important to see whiteness as something more than just the absence of Black blood.[32] Since both of Dupas's parents had birth certificates and records that marked them as Black, a fact that made it hard for Dupas to claim whiteness, Zelden centered on the fighter's social claims to whiteness. Zelden had white neighbors testify to the family's whiteness. He presented parish records that marked them as white, and he showed birth certificates that marked all of their kids born in New Orleans as white, arguing that the employee who had marked the Dupases as white thought they were white—meaning they socially passed and thus had legal status. Zelden also pointed out that Dupas had boxed as a white man. The lawyer demonstrated that Dupas attended white schools. He argued that Dupas married a white woman and reasoned that Dupas lived in a white neighborhood. In essence, Zelden simply followed the path that Peter, Evelyn, and Ralph had been laying for twenty-two years as they resisted the state's legal definition of race. They lived as white people, so therefore they were white. The argument worked.

On October 30, 1957, Judge Rene A. Viosca, the same judge who ruled in the favor of the Docusens in 1949, ruled that the city of New Orleans had to award Dupas a white birth certificate. The judge argued that the city had demonstrated that Dupas's parents had changed their name from Duplessis to Dupas, but it had not proven that Dupas was Black. He argued that the Dupas family's ability to live as white on both sides of his lineage was the reason why they were legally white.

The conclusion relied on an intertwined social and legal understanding of whiteness. The judge noted that Dupas's paternal grandparents were legally treated as white, citing the fact that they had registered as white to vote in New Orleans, were noted as white on their death certificates, and were also handled by white undertakers who handled only white bodies.[33] In other words, once they had declared their whiteness, nobody had challenged them. And for Dupas's mother, the judge noted that she not only had social whiteness, but she also passed the eye test. Evelyn Dupas "appears to be a white woman. Her hair is straight, and her complexion is not dark," Judge Viosca avowed. Her white appearance, he argued, had allowed her to register her kids as white under the watch of Henry Lanauze, the former register of births for New Orleans, known for his "careful scrutiny." Judge Viosca also added, "Mrs. Dupas has been accepted as white from the time she entered the City of New Orleans." He contended that the city had failed to "establish beyond a reasonable doubt that relator [Dupas], a man who ha[d] been commonly accepted as Caucasian, [wa]s in fact of colored ancestry in either his maternal or paternal lineage." Upon hearing the judge's ruling, Dupas told the press, "It's the best news that ever could have happened for me, my wife and my family." His mom, Evelyn Dupas, fainted.[34]

Dupas, however, had to pay for his privilege. He was white, but he was financially broke. As Peter Baird noted in his weekly New Orleans *Picayune* boxing column, "Ralph Dupas being officially declared white is the big news in local boxing, of course. Now Ralph will start fighting again, and probably will take on any logical opponent brought in, because that litigation over the past five years [months] has cost Ralph a pretty penny." As one anecdote in the press alluded, after he won his court battle Dupas did not even have enough money to buy a ten-cent Coke.[35] Dupas disputed the latter claim and told the a local writer that he and his wife were financially sound, for they had a new modern home with electrical appliances, other property investments, and an annuity that would pay him fifteen thousand dollars a year after he turned thirty-five.[36] It appears, however, that before the case, Dupas had invested most of his winnings and did not have cash on hand. With no liquid cash, he had to fight. He immediately cashed in on his whiteness and agreed to fight Mickey Crawford, an easy ten-round go that netted him seventeen hundred dollars. It was not his best purse, but it was likely money he desperately needed.[37] After his victory, Dupas called out Joe Brown for a chance at the lightweight title. The Brown–Dupas fight was the most anticipated bout in city history. It just could not take place in New Orleans.

To Be Black

Joe Brown was too dark to pass. He had to live the life of a poor Black boy in Jim Crow Louisiana. He never forgot that fact when dealing with Dupas. Born in New Orleans, Brown moved to Baton Rouge at a young age with his mother when his parents divorced. Brown, who grew up in a shotgun-style shack, was an all-around athlete of note in Baton Rouge, even garnering attention from Grambling State and Southern universities in football before taking up boxing. After graduating from high school, Brown entered the navy, where he began boxing and eventually won sixteen fights and the All-Service Lightweight Championship. Upon discharge in 1946, he turned pro. Known as a fighter with devastating power in both hands, Brown liked to stalk his opponent and wait for the right opening before unleashing his bombs. After ten years and at least eighty-two fights, at the age of thirty he finally got his shot at the lightweight championship when he faced Wallace "Bud" Smith in New Orleans.[38]

The Brown–Smith championship, which took place a month after Louisiana passed the state's sports segregation law, was the first championship fight in the state to feature two Black fighters. While some local Black fans wanted to boycott the battle to protest the state law, most opted to sit in segregated seating to root for Brown. It was their first chance to see a local Black fighter in a championship bout. Despite breaking his hand during the match, Brown won the fight. But even with the championship, Brown remained a bitter man. He was a Black man fighting in the South.

Brown's career highlights why Dupas dissented from the state's racial laws. Simply put, Dupas, an inferior fighter, got paid more money because he was a white fighter.[39] For his championship fight versus Smith, Brown earned roughly $7,000, his biggest payday to date, while Dupas's non-championship fight with Martinez in April 1957 had scored him an estimated $11,000. In a 1958 interview with *Jet*, Brown claimed that he earned roughly $10,000 a year fighting; however, he had to travel the globe to get his money.[40] To put this in perspective, Dupas, who mainly fought in New Orleans, made $17,000 in 1955; $8,500 in 1956; and roughly $20,000 in 1957.

If Brown wanted to be paid like a champion, he had to leave the state. While another local Black fighter, Joe Dorsey, fought the segregated system by suing Louisiana to end the sports ban, a battle he would eventually win in 1959, Brown moved to Houston, a fight-crazed city that had segregated seating but integrated fights (Moore 2017, 95–96). And that meant more money, because promoters always paid more for integrated scraps. On this decision, Jim Hall of the African American *Louisiana Weekly* wrote, "The champ is proud of his title and his nation, but ashamed of the small time conniving politicians which have disgraced the fair name of Louisiana with its white supremacy (Hitler) laws."[41] His fight with Dupas on May 7, 1958, in Houston, Texas, would earn Brown roughly forty thousand dollars. Dupas, however, had some unsettled business before he could fight Brown. He had to win an upcoming bout against Ramon Fuentes, and then he had to fight another battle in court.

Sports functions as a political space and the WCC wanted to make an example out of Dupas. Just when Dupas thought he had won his right to be white, white supremacists used the courts to maintain their contested claim to white authority. In March 1958, after Judge Viosca ruled in favor of Dupas, the White Citizens Council fought back, getting the attorney general's office to issue a statement designating Dupas as Black and thereby releasing New Orleans from having to issue him a white birth certificate. State lawmakers also suggested that the upcoming Dupas–Fuentes fight on April 7 be stopped because it would violate the sports segregation law.

Although he worried about the ruling, Dupas stayed calm and confident. While the attorney general's decree seemed like a major shift in the case, the three local white daily newspapers hardly carried a word. "Local newspapermen have failed to comment on the racial status of Dupas," Black writer Jim Hall noted. "In Louisiana," Hall continued, "to touch upon the controversy of racial identity is like picking up a hand full of hot potatoes."[42] Moreover, Dupas was buoyed by the support of white fans. "At first these court battles worried me," Dupas told the press, "but with so many people coming on my side I feel I can't let 'em down and believe me when I say from here on out I'll be fighting as though my life depended on the outcome of each bout."[43] Encouraged by fan support, he told a reporter, "I will win that court battle and also the Fuentes bout and then go to dethrone Joe Brown as lightweight champion."[44] He suggested to another writer, "I want the fans and the public to know I sincerely appreciate their concern in my behalf and promise them they'll be looking at the next lightweight titleholder Monday night."[45] In a unanimous decision, the boxing commission went against the WCC and allowed Dupas to keep his white status. He beat his case. He beat Fuentes. Next up was Joe Brown.

The Brown–Dupas bout was one of the most anticipated fights of the decade, but the battle was a mismatch from the start. For the previous year, Dupas had been campaigning at the welterweight division and fighting anywhere from 140 to 144 pounds. In his fight against Fuentes he weighed 140 pounds, which meant he had a month to lose five pounds while keeping his strength and stamina in order to fight lightweight Brown at 135 pounds. Most experts believed this situation would drain him. Dupas, himself, said he looked like a "greyhound."[46]

Plus, Brown was a far superior fighter. Brown had dynamite in his fists and a chip on his shoulder. Underappreciated by New Orleans fight fans who favored the white Dupas, Brown had been begging for this fight since he had won the lightweight championship in 1956. He had been wronged by racism and was going to take it out on Dupas. There was no way Dupas was getting out of that Houston ring with a victory. As Brown said, "Too many of my friends have spent too many years hearing that Dupas was a better fighter than me. I've got to prove that he doesn't belong in the same gym with me." Brown was so confident in his abilities, he told reporters that if Dupas did not run, he would knock him out inside of five rounds, and if the "Native Dancer" took flight, Brown told the press, "I've got to run him down."[47]

Brown predicted a knockout and followed through. Dupas was down in the eighth round from a terrible combination of punches. Or as J. Don Davis from the *Houston Informer* wrote, "The sad boy who has been fighting with the courts to prove that he is white admitted that he didn't know what first hit him. Joe said he got him with the right." Davis finished his assessment by scolding, "The Sports hate law made it necessary for them to come way over here to see a French Quarter dancer get a real licking by a boy of color who was born in the first of the highlands on the Mississippi in Louisiana."[48]

The Final Fight

A month later, a court stuck Dupas with an unfavorable ruling. The court ruled that the city of New Orleans did not owe him a delayed birth certificate because, as they stated, Dupas was born in Plaquemines to Black parents and thus he was legally Black. Dupas appealed that decision, but in December 1960 the state supreme court rejected his appeal.[49] The lone dissenter, Justice Joe B. Hamiter, argued that New Orleans did not prove beyond a reasonable doubt that "a man who has been accepted as Caucasian, is in fact of colored ancestry in either his maternal or paternal lineage."[50] That same year, Dupas filed for bankruptcy. It turns out, the fight to be white cost him everything.

While not a legal victory to claim whiteness, the justice's words left room for Dupas to socially live as a white man. Dupas won that battle. In other words, despite the court ruling Dupas was Black, the public and promoters in New Orleans treated him as white. At a time when they refused to host mixed bouts, promoters still allowed him to fight white opponents. City promoters even allowed him to fight a white man for the middleweight championship in 1963, and after Dupas won, both major dailies noted that Dupas was born in New Orleans—a fact that was legally wrong but a distinction his parents had been trying to make since 1935, when they fled to New Orleans.[51]

Unfortunately for Ralph Dupas, boxing got the best of him. By the end of the decade, his eyesight had failed him, but to keep making money to avoid the life of poverty he was born in, the one he hoped his whiteness would protect him from, he was fighting while wearing contact lenses. This was a recipe for disaster. In his very last battle, the referee stopped the fight as the onetime champ was on the canvas looking for his contact lens in the ring. Soon he hit rock bottom and could be seen in Las Vegas parks searching for cans to recycle, just to survive, before his brother rescued him and took him back to New Orleans. By then, Dupas was punchy from all the pounding he had taken in the ring, and his memory had started to fail him (Gurtner 1991, 114–16).

In the end, while contemporary Black fighters like Joe Dorsey and Joe Brown fought back against Jim Crow, Dupas resisted racism only to benefit from it. Ralph Dupas dissented from the rigged laws of Jim Crow to better his prospects in life, to improve his family's living conditions, and to enjoy the privileges and immunities of whiteness. That the White Citizens'

Council came at him so strenuously shows the power of sports and how it operates as a political space to regulate race in society. Dupas's fight to pass, and the state's battle to determine his true race, is a remarkable story that highlights how boxing functions as a site for production, alternation, and contestation over racial meaning.

Notes

1. "Martinez Looks Impressive in Opening Drill," *New Orleans States*, April 3, 1957. For information on the Joey Rowan–Crowe Peele bout, see "Rowan Couldn't Hold That Tiger," *New Orleans Item*, April 2, 1957.

2. "Ralph Dupas Wins Greatest Fight," *New Orleans States*, April 3, 1957.

3. This essay heavily relies on the Picayune, New Orleans States, New Orleans Item, Louisiana Weekly, and Plaquemines Gazette to reconstruct the story.

4. Pete Baird, "Hooks and Jabs," *Times-Picayune*, April 7, 1957.

5. The court decisions from October 30, 1957, and June 1958 are online at various internet sites. For newspaper information on the court cases and the Dupas family, see, "Ralph Dupas Wins Greatest Fight," *New Orleans States*, April 3, 1957; "Dupas Martinez Bout on as Scheduled, Is Belief," *New Orleans Picayune*, March 30, 1957; "Ralph Dupas Court Fight May Go Over until Fall," *Times-Picayune*, August 29, 1957; "Dupas Hearing Delayed until October," *Times-Picayune*, August 30, 1957; "Ralph Dupas Case Continued to Oct 1," *New Orleans Item*, August 30, 1957; "Order City to Issue Dupas Certificate," *New Orleans Item*, October 31, 1957; "Records Bared in Dupas Birth Claim Fight," *New Orleans States*, August 25, 1957; "Dupas Attorneys Warn of Hearing 'Fireworks,'" *New Orleans States*, August 27, 1957; "Dupas Vows All-Out Fight on Race Status," *New Orleans States*, August 28, 1957.

6. I accessed this information using the genealogy database My Heritage.

7. For firsthand information on his early career from his first manager, Whitey Esneault, see "First 'Title Shop,' Trip with Ralph for Whitey," *New Orleans Item*, May 4, 1958.

8. Art Burke, "Dupas, Portilla to Clash Here Tonight," *New Orleans States*, March 4, 1957.

9. "Dupas Pressing Attack All the Way," *Times-Picayune*, March 5, 1957.

10. "Dupas Hearing Delayed until October," *Times-Picayune*, August 30, 1957.

11. "Form State Wide Citizens' Council to Fight for Segregation," *Plaquemines Gazette*, February 4, 1956.

12. "Parish Turnout Seen for Citizens' Council Mass Meeting Tuesday Nite," *Plaquemines Gazette*, March 17, 1956.

13. "Athletic Segregation Bill Is Signed," *Plaquemines Gazette*, July 21, 1956.

14. "Dupas Vows All-Out Fight on Race Status," *New Orleans States*, August 28, 1957.

15. "Injunction Hearing Set for Tuesday," *New Orleans States*, March 29, 1957.

16. "Injunction Hearing Set for Tuesday," *New Orleans States*, March 29, 1957.

17. "Ralph Dupas Wins Greatest Fight," *New Orleans States*, April 3, 1957.

18. "Martinez, I'll Lead the Dancer," *New Orleans Item*, April 3, 1957.

19. Peter Baird, "Hooks and Jabs," *Times-Picayune*, April 7, 1957.

20. "Martinez-Dupas Bout Most Publicized in Local History," *New Orleans States*, April 5, 1957.

21. "A Grim Dupas Ready for Busso," *New Orleans States*, August 29, 1957.

22. "Ralph Dupas Case Continued to Oct 1," *New Orleans Item*, August 30, 1957.

23. "Dupas Vows All-Out Fight on Race Status," *New Orleans States*, August 28, 1957.

24. "To a Finish," *New Orleans Picayune*, May 20, 1889; "Andy Bowen's Way," *New Orleans Picayune*, December 23, 1889.

25. "Pugilistic Pointers," *Duluth Sunday Times*, June 8, 1890; "The Bowen Carroll Fight," *Chicago Inter Ocean*, September 15, 1890; "A Hash of Sports," *Omaha Bee*, May 17, 1891.

26. "Why Bowen Withdrew," *Cleveland Plain Dealer*, March 16, 1891.

27. "Murphy Bests Bowen," *Chicago Herald*, February 16, 1892; "Bowen a Caucasian," *Chicago Inter Ocean*, February 17, 1892.

28. "In Justice to Andy Bowen," *Chicago Herald*, February 17, 1892.

29. "South's Best White Fighter Barred; Is Negro!" *Pittsburgh Courier*, July 21, 1945.

30. "Compare Brown with the Greatest," *New Orleans Item*, May 6, 1958.

31. "Docusen Brothers Get Family Status Straight," *Monroe (LA) News-Star*, March 30, 1949.

32. O.C.W. Taylor, "Dupas Asks for a White Birth Certificate," *Chicago Defender*, September 14, 1957.

33. "Order City to Issue Dupas Certificate," *New Orleans Item*, October 31, 1957.

34. "Boxer Ralph Dupas Wins Birth Certificate Fight," *New Orleans States*, October 31, 1957.

35. Pete Baird, "Hooks and Jabs," *Times-Picayune*, November 3, 1957.

36. "A Beer at the Dupas House," *New Orleans Item*, November 16, 1957.

37. "Ralph's Gonna Get a Christmas Bundle," *New Orleans Item*, November 26, 1957.

38. Brown contended that he had twenty fights unaccounted for by *Ring* magazine. See, "Little Joe Louis," *Ebony*, July 1958, 88–94; "Joe Brown Testimonial Is 'Red Letter' Day for Champ," *Louisiana Weekly*, August 30, 1958; "Compare Brown with the Greatest," *New Orleans Item*, May 6, 1958.

39. When asked about paying Black fighters to fight on mixed cards—an integrated fight card that featured segregated fights—Dupas's promoter, Whitey

Esneault, told a reporter, "I am opposed to mixed cards for two reasons: Promoters don't pay the Negro boys the same money they pay the white boys, and No. 2, I have talked to a lot of fans and they are opposed, so if the fans don't want them, neither do I. Fans pay the freight." Pete Baird, "Hooks and Jabs," *Times-Picayune*, April 21, 1957.

40. "The Boxing Champion Nobody Knows," *Jet*, vol. 11, no. 15, February 14, 1957, 52–55.

41. Jim Hall, "Kill Brown-Dupas Bout," *Louisiana Weekly*, March 8, 1958.

42. Jim Hall, "Timeout," *Louisiana Weekly*, April 19, 1958.

43. Bill Keefe, "Viewing the News," *Times-Picayune*, April 5, 1958.

44. "Dupas Vows He'll Beat Fuentes," *Times-Picayune*, April 3, 1958.

45. "Dupas Vows He'll Beat Fuentes," *Times-Picayune*, April 3, 1958.

46. "Brown Choice over Dupas," *Houston Post*, May 7, 1958.

47. "Joe, If Ralph Runs I'll Run Him Down," *New Orleans Item*, May 5, 1958; "If It Goes 15, I'll Be Disappointed," *New Orleans Item*, May 7, 1958.

48. J. Don Davis, "The Champ Waited, Dupas Got It Real Bad," *Houston Informer*, May 10, 1958.

49. "LA Court Bout Lost by Dupas," *Times-Picayune*, December 13, 1960; "Court Rejects Dupas Birth Certificate Plea," *New Orleans States-Item*, December 12, 1960.

50. "Dupas Loses Round in Racial Identity Fight," *Louisiana Weekly*, December 24, 1960.

51. "Ralph Won Crown for Barbara, Debbie," *New Orleans States-Item*, April 30, 1963; "4 Sites Seeking Rematch," *New Orleans States-Item*, April 30, 1963.

References

Baker, Ray Stannard. 1964. *Following the Color Line: American Negro Citizenship in the Progressive Era*. Harper Torchbooks.

Davis, F. James. 2001. *Who Is Black? One Nation's Definition*. Pennsylvania State University Press.

Dominguez, Virginia R. 1986. *White by Definition: Social Classification in Creole Louisiana*. Rutgers University Press.

Fleicher, Nat. 1939. *Black Dynamite: The Story of the Negro in the Prize Ring from 1782 to 1938*. Vol. 4. C. J. O'Brien, Inc.

Golub, Mark. 2005. "Plessy as 'Passing': Judicial Responses to Ambiguously Raced Bodies in *Plessy v. Ferguson*." *Law and Society Review* 39, no. 1: 563–600.

Gurtner, George. 1991. "Ralph Dupas' Biggest Fight." *New Orleans Magazine* 25, no. 12, August, 114–16.

Harris, Cheryl. 1993. "Whiteness as Property." *Harvard Law Review* 106, no. 8: 1707–791.

Hobbs, Allyson. 2014. *A Chosen Exile: A History of Racial Passing in American Life*. Harvard University Press.

Magnum, Charles S. 1940. *The Legal Status of the Negro*. University of North Carolina Press.

Moore, Louis. 2017. *We Will Win the Day: The Civil Rights Movement, the Black Athlete, and the Quest for Equality*. Praeger.

Pascoe, Peggy. 2009. *What Comes Naturally: Miscegenation Law and the Making of Race in America*. Oxford University Press.

Roediger, David R. 1999. *The Wages of Whiteness: Race and the Making of the American Working Class*. Verso.

Williamson, Joel. 1980. *New People: Miscegenation and Mulattoes in the United States*. Free Press.

2

"Fighting 4 All Nations"

A Conversation with Kali Reis

RUDY MONDRAGÓN
and GAYE THERESA JOHNSON

Kali "KO" Mequinonoag Reis is a complex and multifaceted professional boxer from Providence, Rhode Island. Mequinonoag is her Native American name, given to her by her mother, which means "many feathers, many talents." Reis has a mixed-race background that includes lineage from the Seaconke Wampanoag tribe and Cape Verde Island ancestry. She is the first mixed Native American female world champion boxer, having held the World Boxing Council (WBC), International Boxing Association (IBA), and Universal Boxing Federation (UBF) middleweight world titles.

Reis first started boxing at the age of thirteen to cope with trauma and anger issues and did not have many amateur fights due to a lack of opponents and boxing opportunities in Providence. For Reis, boxing builds on her experiences in competing at powwows as a fancy shawl dancer.

• • •

RUDY MONDRAGÓN: Can you tell us what your story and connection to boxing is?

KALI REIS: I was always a rough kid, always wanted to play sports. My mom prayed for a little girl who was into the girly stuff like she was, but I kinda came out the total opposite. I always played sports, was always interested in sports. A friend of my mom's was actually a fighter and that showed me that boxing was close to home. Cliché-wise, my favorite movie was *Rocky*. Every time I saw the HBO emblem, I would think, "Oh, Rocky's coming on," no matter what was coming on. And around age 11 or 12, I was going through some real hard times between my father being in and out, being the youngest of five kids, and then getting taken advantage of by a neighborhood kid. I just needed an outlet. I was always a feisty kid, always fighting with the boys.

I felt alone, so the solo part of boxing felt at home to me, the fact that I didn't have to depend on a team really attracted me. That's kind of where I started with boxing: needing a home, needing an outlet, and just realizing that there was boxing on Rhode Island. And I, at first, couldn't even imagine accomplishing what I have. I did start setting goals early on, but when I first started, I was lucky if I could get around jump-roping without getting distracted, or getting angry, or thinking I knew everything. I just wanted to hit something. And then it turned into "Okay, I'm hitting something, now I'm hitting a person, but there's a whole new world to this, and I don't even realize it's an art." I had to learn to be calm and stay focused; I had to avoid getting angry. I sparred, and I fell in love with it. I got beat in my first fight, but my first sparring session, I beat the other girl up. My initial reaction to that wasn't "Man, forget this, I don't wanna get beat up, I don't like getting hit in the face." It was like, "Yo, how do I figure out how to *not* get hit in the face?" I like hitting, but I don't like getting hit." Strategy-wise, I fell in love with it. And then from there I started having goals, and it was a wrap from there.

GAYE THERESA JOHNSON: I was wondering, what does boxing in the Indigenous community look like in the twenty-first century? As someone who identifies as both Black and Indigenous at once, how does that flow into the work that you do, to boxing itself, and the other way?

KR: I've always had that warrior spirit, and I've always identified as a strong, Native, Black woman, just like my mother. And what I've learned through boxing, and my culture, is that the common denominator in that is balance. You must have balance to practice your culture, to be proud of who you are without feeling the pressures of being who everybody thinks you should be. Balance has to do with boxing being; you're supposed to be this tough person, but you really have to be passionate about your craft. You have to find that balance. You have to be responsible in the midst of chaos. It is important to balance rage with being really calm and collected and cool in the ring. Even though there's tons of things going on in the ring, you have to have that quiet space.

And being an Indigenous woman, fighting for a purpose is a huge thing. It means so much in our culture. There is meaning as to why we do certain things, say things; we may wear a different color, or why we may not associate with people. And there's meaning to why people fight, in general, no matter where they come from. So it just flows together and intertwines.

I have such a bigger purpose to life; it just really matches up perfectly with boxing. And Indigenous people, there's parts of the Southwest that really relate to running, because a lot of times the only way to get messages across from tribe to tribe was running. There are runs for prayers for different causes.

It was hard to find my footing as a kid, just being mixed, being in this area, being kind of the weird kid that's talking to animals. I've always been a loner, so I'm just elated that I actually have a purpose bigger than myself, and it's been accepted throughout Native country. To be accepted by Indigenous Native people as a mixed Indigenous Black woman for what I do, and how I pray for everybody—fighting is how I pray—is so important. It all intertwines, and I like where it's going.

GTJ: I find it's so true, it feels so true and beautiful, what you're saying, because I feel like a lot of people might imagine that the sexism that's in our communities would prevent us from being able to accept or understand what it's like to be a woman boxer who's Indigenous when we have all these other issues with regard to trying to claim rights or claim land, so why you gotta bring this whole thing about being a female *and* a boxer *and* whatever into this sphere? And yet I find some of the most marginalized communities, that's where you find the most acceptance.

Yours is also a story about power and grace that doesn't get told a lot. When you tell that story, it feels like there's so much there. I wonder, who is your community? Who do you claim, and who claims you?

KR: Everybody. I have so many layers. I'm not just into boxing; I'm not just Indigenous; I'm not just Black; I'm not just from Providence; I'm not just a Two-Spirit—I'm a lot of things. And I try to keep it as real as possible. I like to be as transparent as possible with people and not put on this persona. I like people to see most of me—not all of me but most of me—so everybody can relate. I don't want just a boxing audience, I don't want just Indigenous or Black people, or only people from New England.

My mom raised me and always brought me around, no matter our circumstance, around different people—the poorest of the poor, the richest of the rich. I've rubbed elbows with people in mansions, but we couldn't pay bills. But my mom made sure that I knew how to act around whoever I was, and had the respect, and understood my surroundings so I could mingle with these people. I had to speak their language.

I have an audience, people from everywhere. I have elders that I've met at powwows, during powwows, that hated boxing, that don't wanna see women do any combat sports, but they love me. They'll watch me. They're boxing fans now. If I can have that effect, especially on the old-school elders that say, "Our women are supposed to take care of the village, and raise the kids, and wear skirts, and not supposed to . . ." They love me. They know who I am because I keep it very transparent. And more and more different people are just gravitating to the movement, 'cause even though we're all different, they see the core value of why I fight and why I do what I do. Everybody is on the same page; everybody can relate [to] our cause. It's amazing. I would love it to just keep growing. I don't wanna just hit just one audience; it just has to be everywhere.

RM: That's great. In 2018 you were a part of this historic event. HBO had never televised a fight between two women. And you were a part of that historic event. It was so dope that you were a part of that historic event. Can you tell us what that was like, and the importance of this fight for both boxing and for women in the sport when boxing has something like twenty thousand active men and only twelve to fifteen hundred active women?

KR: That moment hasn't set in all the way. I still look back at, as far as viewers; and [in the context of] every fight, like Canelo and GGG included.[1] We had the most views of any fight on any network last year. It peaked at over 1.1 million views. And it was the first time women had ever been on HBO. And it was a good fight, not just 'cause it was me. If I would have watched that and it was somebody else, I would have been just as happy with it. It was surreal. I did have my moment like, "Wow, I'm on HBO," but I had to handle business, and it was just so important for us—not me, us—to perform at our peak so we could show the world. So it wasn't a flop; it wasn't a slap fest like the other fights you fought on HBO. We had a responsibility to ourselves, and for women's boxing in the whole, to come out there and represent boxing. To make a statement so people who don't follow women's boxing or may think women's boxing is a joke, to show 'em. No, we really train, we really fight, and it was really important. I'm glad the fight was so well matched, and it was a great fight. Of course, I would have liked the results to be different, but regardless, it was such a move forward in the right direction for women boxing.

Even though it was such a historic day, I think it still gets a little overshadowed. I think we got our play, we got our representation, but sometimes when you have a built-up fighter like [Cecilia] Brækhus, they focus a little bit too much on the buildup; they should have focused a little bit more on the fact that it's two women. It's not just Brækhus breaking down barriers; it takes two to tango. So that's probably the only thing that I could say that I'm still a little bit butt-hurt about, because when I look at the headlines it still says, "Brækhus was the first woman on HBO," and I'm like, "What, did she fight her shadow? because there was *two* women in there, and it wasn't a one-sided fight." You know what I mean? But overall it was really important, hence the reason why when she tried to pull the whole glove discrepancy thing and was not going to fight me if she had to fight in eights [eight-ounce gloves]; that's why I took it to the chin and I didn't wanna see it not happen at all because she wanted to be a diva about the gloves. I said, "You know what, give me whatever gloves that's gonna get us to fight, give me those." Because she was gonna cancel the whole fight.

GTJ: That was just an incredible decision that you made. Where do you feel like that came from?

KR: I could have said, "Nah, man, nah, nah," 'cause she was . . . "I'm not gonna fight her if we're fighting in eights," and I'm like, "I'm not gonna fight you if we're gonna fight in tens, I'm not . . . I didn't drop down two weight classes to fight you in tens. We're not fighting in pillows." "We're not gladiators." I'm like, "Yeah, we are, we actually are."

My promoter was ready to pack up, go home, and sue everybody. He's a lawyer anyway, so he was like, "We can sue everybody, get on the plane, 'cause technically they messed up your contract; they went against it."

We sat down till maybe 12 o'clock at night, me, my manager, my promoter. And I was like, "I'll fight in the tens. I don't want this fight to fall out. I wanna fight." So we fought.

RM: How did that impact the fight? Were you dealing with [it] right up until your ring entrance?

KR: That's warm-up time, and because of the whole discrepancy, we had to reselect gloves because I had to get a pair of tens. We had to get Cleto Reyes's gloves, the color that I wanted, 'cause I wasn't fighting in anything else. We had to wait for those gloves to be overnight shipped, and then we had to go to the venue, and I wasn't even sure if we were gonna fight because I wasn't sure if we got the gloves. At the venue, we had to do the glove selection again. That took up a good twenty-five, thirty minutes. I usually use that time to get into my space and warm up; I had to rush and didn't really warm up. I had to put my gloves on, do a little of this, stretch, stretch.

GTJ: That is incredible. You go into the ring, and that's where you're warming up?

KR: Yeah, and usually when I get to a venue, I like getting there early. See, I've never been to StubHub Center. It was my first time. There was a lot of firsts that night. So usually I get there, and I peep the crowd. I might even, if I get [there] really early, I'll go in the ring, feel it out, see my surroundings, and then go back and settle. I didn't get to do none of those. The first time I even saw the arena was when they opened up [the] curtain: "Oh, this is what it looks like. This is amazing. Oh, we're walking, okay." That was the first time.

RM: When you shared that story about warming up in the first two rounds, I thought, "Ah." I used to play soccer in college, and one of the things I learned as a kid was that any time you play on a new soccer field, you go and inspect the field, you explore the divots, the potholes, or the uneven pastures to be familiar with the field and get a feel for it. And so that was exactly where my mind went when you told me that story, because that's a huge part of a fight, the warm-up, the mental, and the studying of the terrain that you're about to step foot in.

KR: Yeah. Not one ring is made alike. Some are really bouncy. Some are stiff. Some are really soft—that means that's gonna take your legs out fast. Some are really small like phone booths. Some are really big like football fields.

So when I got in there, they were already singing the national anthem. And I'm touching the ring. Given the caliber of fight, it would have been nice if things went a little bit smoother, but it is what it is. I look back at it now, and I remember every second, every foot of that walkout, every round. I remember it like it was yesterday. It won't leave my mind. And that was such a great experience.

RM: Your ring entrance has always stood out to me. It's so powerful. Can you talk about your ring entrances, the dynamic and significant components found in it, and what they mean to you?

KR: That ring entrance, it's like crescendoing. It started off as an idea and it took some time to manifest. I had a recording of the drums, but every time I go to a powwow, and I hear a live drum, I hear singing. The powwow drum, it just brings me to a really good place. And I love to dance. I don't dance much anymore, because I'm focused on boxing. And the singing . . . what it means and the prayers. Prayer is nothing less than being at peace where you are. It can be anywhere, and just being able to connect to a source of creation. And when I hear that drum, and when I'm in the ring in my good state, I'm in that peace. So the ring entrance; the drum is the heartbeat of our people, and that heartbeat and the drums are the singing, and the ceremony is how we used to set our people off before war, before battle. There was a big celebration. There was a grand entry. There was a lot of preparation for it. So when I decided to start having live drummers and singers, it wasn't just anybody; it was people whose voices I grew up hearing.

When I'm not allowed to have or I'm not able to have live drummers, hearing Northern Cree, I still get something from that state. But having them singing those ceremony songs, or even just a victory song, and having the dancers—especially the jingle dress dances of that healing dance on the beat of that drum—having them pave the way in prayer in the same state of mind before me, it just adds to the energy that I try to create myself. But I can't do it myself. I can go in the ring by myself, but I wanna make this something that everybody can connect to. And as Indigenous people, for everybody, music, song, dance is a universal language, so no matter whether you speak the language or not, you might connect. You can be halfway across the world, but if somebody's playing a good beat then they start moving.

Just that whole walk, having those prayers, and just feeling the energy of the crowd or the dances and the drummers, it just means so much and it gets me in such a good state. I'm focused and I'm ready for battle. It's that combination of that calm chaos.

The more drummers and singers and dancers, the better, I'm gonna end up having eighty dancers one day. When we dance as Native peoples, that is praying to the Creator. We dance for a lot of reasons: We dance to mourn, to celebrate, and to prepare [for] battle. The whole entrance and how it's turning out to being like a grand entry, it gets better every time. It's a nice spectacle to look at for people who don't understand, because they see that energy. I have people that drive up from Virginia just to dance me out because they wanna be a part of that.

GTJ: Yeah, when you say people drive these long distances just to dance you out, it's incredible to me because this is also time travel because of all this history and legacy that is your ring entrance. You're bringing in people to see you in prayer. I also feel like there's this other thing that's happening too where other people get a platform. And other things that people have assigned meaning to and said, "Oh, this is what that is." And you're bringing in saying, "No, this is the active . . . This is what we're doing here. Whether you understand it or not. I'm still doing this. This is me, but it's also a way to show how we're all here in this moment together and all of the identities and all of the histories are here together in this moment." And yet it's also such a moment of focus as you're moving in there. It just seems like so many things at once. But there was one question that we didn't ask yet, which was about your motto about "Fighting 4 All Nations," and you've kind of answered it a little bit, but just why is that important to you?

KR: It is important to, especially as an Indigenous person, and when I say I fight for all nations, of course, primarily I need to fight for all nations and all Indigenous peoples everywhere. But it also means fight for all nations for everybody. We, as Indigenous people and Native people, have been under the radar and neglected and just kind of swept away. We're in the past. And like you said, when I do the ring entrance, it kinda gets people to, "Oh, yeah. We all are here in the same moment. These Natives are still here, we're not in the history book." It's amazing today, I get grown people [who say], "Oh, wow, you're Native. I thought Indians were extinct." I'm not a dinosaur.

I just fight for all nations. All nations, all Indigenous people. There was a moment where I thought, "I fight 4 All Nations." And four, not like F-O-R, but four, four as the four directions. The four directions, complete circle. Fight 4 All Nations. Once people understand that they might be going through something that they can't physically fight for, but I'm fighting for them. They can see somebody who has been through struggles. And I'm fighting through it, fighting for them.

My entrance means a lot. It just gives another platform for me to connect to people, and they know that this is bigger than me. This is a bigger than us. This is we. This is everybody. Fight 4 All Nations. People know what that means and know that this is not a little spectacle. I have a purpose. People see "Fight 4 All Nations" and recognize, "Yeah, we know why she fights. Yeah, we know what she's doing." It's just an easy, quick, drive-through way for people to identify what I do. And they can use that too—"We fight 4 all nations." Yes, we all do. It's not just mine, it's ours.

GTJ: I love that you differentiate between "for" and "four." Because if you're fighting for all nations, it's like you're part of something bigger than you. When you say you "fight 4 all nations," it's really almost instructive. It's like a directive. We need to fight in so many different ways, for so many different things.

Recently, I was reading *There There*. The author, Tommy Orange, describes several powwows. There seems like there's just so many similarities between a powwow and boxing.

KR: Being judged. Audiences. There's all that, yup.

GTJ: Yeah. And then, especially, just watching your entrance, it just made me, "Oh, my God, there's the bridge right there." And seeing the jingle dresses and the . . . There's little fine points that the outside world doesn't get, but I feel like there's a connection between these two spaces, and I don't know if you feel the same way.

KR: It is. Because like I said, I used to be a fancy dancer; a fancy shawl dancer. When you go into powwow, you gotta be best dressed. Not a hair can be out of place; you've gotta play the part. There are rules that people don't even realize. If a piece of your regalia falls off while you're dancing, you're automatically disqualified. You're out. And if it's a feather? Forget it. They will shut the whole powwow down. And you know, with boxers, we gotta be flashy. We have to have the best shoes, new shoes, new shorts, that have to be shiny, flashy. So it's the same thing: I'm being judged. People are looking at me. When you're dancing, you must do your best moves. You gotta be better than the other four girls over there. She's spinning, I'm spinning. You gotta kinda go tit-for-tat. There are big similarities. People with clipboards judging me. We're gonna line up, get judged. There's a winner, there's a loser. It's very, very similar. You got spectators, you got cheering. People are cheering. It's a circle and there's a square circle. So, yeah, it's very similar.

RM: In boxing, you often see the Mexico versus Puerto Rico rivalry amongst other racial, ethnic, and national rivalries. But it compartmentalizes and essentializes it for the sake of marketing and selling a boxing narrative. What you're doing disrupts that whole idea because of its plurality; it's a multination idea versus the idea of one nation against another. You're uniting and you're calling for action to be taken in many ways that people can interpret that as their fight towards making this place a little bit better.

KR: Exactly. And like I always say, you don't have to physically fight; you can wanna fight for change in your community. That's why I'm trying to start this Res-Tour.

GTJ: What is the Res-Tour? When we think about boxing, a lot of times we think about it in urban space. What does boxing look like in Indigenous communities and on reservations?

KR: There are [some reservations that] don't have the resources. They're more worried about getting water, but training brings people together, to get a positive space. A reservation might have a boxing gym, and a couple of used pairs of gloves for twenty kids; they all share everything. It sucks because they think that that's all there is.

I didn't grow up on a reservation. One the reasons I wanna start this Res-Tour is to learn, because people have this perception of Native Americans. People often ask me, "Do you live on a reservation?" "No, never have." I lived on a reservation maybe for a year and a half of my life, wasn't my res, but [then] I lived maybe an hour away from one. And I wanna learn and see what they need as far as resources. I know they need water, they need to rebuild the communities, they need health and fitness awareness, they need people; they need things that speaks to the needs of so kids that are depressed, obese and suicidal. It breaks my heart.

For me, doing a Res is about bringing education to the people in these tribes that might have an idea of boxing but need a little bit more guidance. And then start programs. The ultimate goal would be to have programs in as many tribal communities as I could and then start a West Coast tournament and East Coast tournament. And then every two years or so we have an ultimate tournament that brings everybody together in the name of boxing, in the name of unity.

RM: That's awesome.

GTJ: We sure do appreciate you and your work.

Note

1. Canelo and GGG are the boxing names of professional boxers Saúl "Canelo" Álvarez and Gennadiy Gennadyevich "GGG" Golovkin.

3

"Fighting 4 All Nations"

Boxing and the Indigenous Heritage

Reflections on the Kali Reis Conversation

KYLE T. MAYS

We are living in times of great resistance. From the continued struggle against various forms of settler colonialism and ending the ongoing violence against Indigenous women, queer, and Two-Spirit folks (called Murdered and Missing Indigenous Women), to stopping the ongoing police violence experienced by Black people, Black and Indigenous peoples continue to fight for their lives. And while that fighting is happening on the ground, they are also fighting—literally—in the realm of sport.

Indigenous fighters recognized in mainstream settler society go back at least to the early twentieth century. Before that time, Indigenous peoples engaged in a variety of combat arts, including the Plains Cree martial art, Okichitaw, which is being revitalized today (Reddekopp 2018). Still, even though Indigenous combat arts have existed in the Americas for a long time, settlers consider it rare to see an Indigenous person boxing. They are a part of what historian Philip Deloria has called "Indians in unexpected places." Like Deloria (2004) arguing that "a significant cohort of Native people engaged the same forces of modernization that were making non-Indians reevaluate their own expectations of themselves and their society," so, too, today, Indigenous people engage in combat sports (6). Indigenous peoples demonstrate their idea of modernity in a variety of combat sports today; numerous fighters participate in sports like boxing and the Ultimate Fighting Championship (UFC). For instance, in the UFC there are at least a few fighters with known Indigenous ancestry, including former middleweight and light heavyweight contender Dan "Hendo" Henderson (Walla Walla) and former welterweight champion Johny Hendricks (Otoe). They seemed to have come more prominently into their Indigenous roots after becoming famous (Salsman 2014). This demonstrates that, depending on the sport, their ancestry is not a major part of their promotional identity. More recently, fighters like Jordan Griffin, nicknamed the "Native Psycho" of the UFC, have been making some noise. Gender and race performance have remained a major part of boxing since the early twentieth century (Runstedtler 2013).

Since at least that time, sports for Black and Indigenous peoples have always been about possibility. They could possibly remove the burdens of anti-Blackness and anti-Indianness through their athletic gifts. They could literally beat European Americans with their physical and mental abilities, even for a moment. And while they might have to deal with oppression after the sporting event, they could bask in the fact that they won. They beat *them*. And then they could imagine the possibilities of what might be, in the future. In the previous chapter's interview with welterweight boxer Kali Reis (Black–Seaconke Wampanoag) by Rudy Mondragón and Gaye Theresa Johnson, we see the continuation of what I would call the "Indigenous heritage."

Reis is a Black-Indigenous, Two-Spirit boxer from Providence, Rhode Island. She is an example of what Howard Bryant, in his recent book, *The Heritage: Black Athletes, a Divided America, and the Politics of Patriotism* (2018), calls "the heritage." He argues that contemporary Black athletes have a long-rooted heritage of activism and protest. And while some have not kept up their end of the bargain, others have, albeit in differing ways, with varying results. Reis is an example of an athlete with an Indigenous heritage.

Native boxers like Reis exemplify the Indigenous heritage by asserting embodied sovereignty in the violence of sport. By sovereignty, I mean the embodied assertion of humanity within a Black-Indigenous self and using one's agency—in this case, the body—to offer counternarratives to how Indigenous people are "supposed to be." It is a critical reflection of Indigenous identity that is not tied to the white imagination but, rather, moving beyond it. It means the ability to express oneself as freely as possible (Simpson 2015, 20). It is also using combat as a momentary possibility of anticolonial struggle and resistance. Though the opponent may not necessarily be the immediate source of aggression in the decolonial sense, it does not mean that one cannot express their anger toward oppression within the context of a ring. As decolonial theorist Frantz Fanon (2004) wrote, "At the individual level, violence is a cleansing force. It rids the colonized of their inferiority complex, of their passive and despairing attitude. It emboldens them, and restores their self-confidence" (51). Reis is able to cleanse herself using jabs, crosses, hooks, uppercuts, and movement in the ring. Training the body, mind, and spirit for combat is also a representation of Indigenous modernity.

By Indigenous modernity, I mean the assertion of being an Indigenous person without worrying about how it fits into settler-created stereotypes (and, sometimes, Indigenous-reproduced ideas of *authenticity*). Reis's ability to be Black, Indigenous, and Two-Spirit is about asserting her individual right to have multiple identities, demonstrating the diversity within Indigenous North America. She allows Indigenous and non-Indigenous audiences to deal with her in an "actually existing sort of way, without the discourses of assimilation or authenticity attempting to discredit [her]" (Lyons 2011, 303).

It also illuminates what it means to be a modern Indigenous subject. Too often, as Reis points out in the interview, non-Indigenous people view Indigenous people as relics only of the past, with no relevance to living in the present. Her presence and story demonstrate an alternative: that Indigenous people, Afro-Indigenous peoples, that Two-Spirit Indigenous peoples, can, in fact, move in modern times (Lyons 2010, 21). An example of Indigenous modernity, she also reclaims Indigenous space, reminding us all that, despite "fighting 4 all nations," no one can be free on occupied Indigenous land. She is both paying homage to her ancestors and producing an embodied presence for the future. As Anishinaabe literary scholar Scott Richard Lyons (2010) writes, "We must always admit that space can be modernized. Indian space is never defined by tradition or culture alone because Native people migrate in modern times as well" (21).

Reis is reclaiming space by asserting her identity as an urban Indigenous person. Claiming the urban space is a radical act. Within some Indigenous communities, growing up on the "res" (reservation) is the authentic, true Indigenous experience. Reis disrupts this narrative. She grew up in Providence, Rhode Island, where she continues to live—proudly. While more than 80 percent of Indigenous people in the United States live in an urban context, too often within the settler imagination some believe that Indigenous peoples can only live on reservations. By identifying as urban, she once more challenges the notion that urban space and Indigenous people are incompatible.

Gender and race performance have remained a major part of boxing since the early twentieth century (Runstedtler 2013). Reis is setting forth an Indigenous future, embodying and putting into practice what Michi Saagiig Nishinaabeg writer Leanne Betasamosake Simpson (2017) has called "kwe as method." Simpson writes, "Kwe as method is about refusal. It is about refusing colonial domination, refusing heteropatriarchy, and refusing to be tamed by whiteness" (33). By participating in a combat sport, she is able to assert an Indigenous feminist praxis, uprooting settler colonization and settler patriarchy (Arvin, Tuck, and Morrill 2013, 11). She is using the sport of boxing in order to help Indigenous people, especially youth, to imagine a future free from colonialism. From the ring entrance to the actual performance of boxing, Reis represents the heart of the people and helps us to imagine a Black and Indigenous world where we all can simply be—and be free. Hopefully, we can walk daily, like her ring entrance, to the drums of resistance and love and continue to fight for a future free of anti-Blackness and anti-Indianness together.

References

Arvin, Maile, Eve Tuck, and Angie Morrill. 2013. "Decolonizing Feminism: Challenging Connection between Settler Colonialism and Heteropatriarchy." *Feminist Formations* 25, no. 1: 8–34.

Bryant, Howard. 2018. *The Heritage: Black Athletes, a Divided America, and the Politics of Patriotism*. Beacon Press.

Deloria, Philip J. 2004. *Indians in Unexpected Places*. University Press of Kansas.

Fanon, Frantz. 2004. *The Wretched of the Earth*. Grove Press.

Lyons, Scott R. 2010. *X-marks: Native Signatures of Assent*. University of Minnesota Press.

Lyons, Scott R. 2011. "Actually Existing Indian Nations: Modernity, Diversity, and the Future of Native American Studies." *American Indian Quarterly* 35, no. 3: 294–312.

Reddekopp, Lorenda. 2018. "Toronto Instructor Fighting to Save Indigenous Martial Art." CBC News. November 1. https://www.cbc.ca/news/canada/toronto/indigenous-martial-arts-1.4886563.

Runstedtler, Theresa. 2013. *Jack Johnson, Rebel Sojourner: Boxing in the Shadow of the Global Color Line*. University of California Press.

Salsman, Jason. 2014. "UFC Welterweight Champ Johny Hendricks (Otoe Tribe) Talks to Native News Today about His New Tribal Sponsorship." *NDNSports*, September 4. https://www.ndnsports.com/ufc-welterweight-champ-johnny-hendricks-otoe-tribe-talks-to-native-news-today-about-his-new-tribal-sponsorship/.

Simpson, Leanne B. 2015. "The Place Where We All Live and Work Together: A Gendered Analysis of 'Sovereignty.'" In *Native Studies Keywords*, edited by Stephanie N. Teves, Andrea Smith, and Michelle Raheja, 18–24. University of Arizona Press.

Simpson, Leanne B. 2017. *As We Have Always Done: Indigenous Freedom through Radical Resistance*. University of Minnesota Press.

4

"There Is Just Something Different about Watching a Woman Be Able to Beat the Shit Out of Someone"

Gender, Boxing, and Fandom

A Conversation with Jessica Luther

DAVID J. LEONARD

Jessica Luther is a widely accomplished writer, commentator, and scholar of sports. She has spent her career writing about sports, advancing critical conversations about gender, sexual violence, representation, and much more. Her first book, *Unsportsmanlike Conduct: College Football and the Politics of Rape* (Edge of Sports/Akashic Books, 2018), examines the intersections of the cultures of sexual violence and college football, highlighting how the systemic playbook facilitates and fosters rape culture within and beyond the football arena. Emblematic of her broader work, Luther argues that "the world of sports has a sexual assault problem the same way one can say that Miami has a global warming problem." In other words, while sexual violence plagues college sports, its culture—one that normalizes, sanctions, and facilitates—is not unique. The injustice is not exceptional but, instead, part of a larger ecosystem. Luther's work is a reminder that sports are not an escape but a larger reflection of both injustices and movements of dissent and resistance.

Her work has appeared across the sports media landscape in *ESPN Magazine*, *Sports Illustrated*, *Vice Sports*, *BuzzFeed*, *New York Times Magazine*, the *Texas Observer*, *Huffington Post*, *Bitch* magazine, and elsewhere. Her book (co-authored with Kavitha A. Davidson), titled *Loving Sports When They Don't Love You Back: Dilemmas of the Modern Sports Fan* (University of Texas Press, 2020), is "an exploration by and for conscientious and conflicted sports fans who want to keep watching the sports they love but who also acknowledge the problems with the industry." She also is working on her dissertation about women's basketball in the 1970s at the University of Texas.

While not a boxing fan per se, Luther talked about her desire to watch women box and how gender, patriarchy, and the privileging of boxing as the domain of men fuels this yearning to see women excel whether in the boxing arena or in the press box. During their 2019 conversation, Luther explained to Leonard, "I'm more likely to watch women generally, just 'cause there's like a principle behind it for me. I get emotional about it in a way that I don't necessarily for men's sports. So it's sort of that feeling of like, "I can't believe women get to do this, and we get to watch it." Her progressive politics notwithstanding, she reflects on the nationalist appeal of the Olympics, pushing readers to think about contradictions, fandom, and how and why we watch various sports. This also led to discussion of the media, fandom, and Floyd Mayweather—specifically, why and how media covered Mayweather's history of violence against women. The celebration of violence and hypermasculinity, alongside the disregard for the lives, voices, and experiences of women, contributes to the type of coverage afforded to Mayweather and countless others inside and outside of the boxing arena.

• • •

DAVID J. LEONARD (DJL): You noted that you don't watch boxing. Has that always been the case? And is there a specific reason you don't watch boxing, given that you are both a writer and a scholar of sport?

JESSICA LUTHER (JL): I don't have anyone in my life who watches boxing, so I don't. I never had that kind of connection to it. I was a college football fan because my dad watched football, and I would watch it with him. I'm a huge tennis fan. On some level, I love sports because I like talking about it with other people; I like competition, but I also enjoy the communal aspect of it. I just don't have that around boxing, and I never did. And I think the only time that I would ever watch is in the Olympics. I love watching the Olympics. I also feel like I was watching when Tyson bit [Evander] Holyfield's ear.

Even now I don't have a sense of how you watch boxing. I know for a lot of years it was on HBO, and I didn't have HBO, and I've never done pay-per-view. I just don't even think about it because of lack of access to it. I guess it's on ESPN, or it was. I don't know. It was never a part of anyone's life that I was around, so I didn't watch or develop a connection.

DJL: It seems like the reasons for why you don't have a connection come back to access. In terms of boxing's unique platforms, whether it be pay-per-view or things like HBO and Showtime, there was a lack of regularity in your life, in your community. It never became ritualized like other sports—without a community or person who says, "Hey, let's watch this," or "Let's all get together to watch the fight." That is also about access.

JL: Right.

DJL: So when there are fights going on, big fights that galvanize part of the national consciousness, did it still not connect with you? Given your presence on Twitter, do you notice people having those conversations on social media? Or is that also a place where the community that you formed isn't so engaged in those conversations?

JL: That's a good question. I feel like I do have a sense when things are happening. Certainly, if it's trending, I have a sense of it, and if there's any kind of big build-up so . . . Mayweather, [Manny] Pacquiao, anything like that, I'm aware of. At this point in my life, I wouldn't watch boxing, even if it is a big deal, because the violence is not something that I really wanna watch. I don't know; maybe that is a lie. I probably would watch it with the Olympics.

DJL: So why do you think the Olympics registers differently for you?

JL: Oh, I'm sure it's nationalism, I'm sure that is a part of it. Also, women box. I would be much more likely to watch the women boxing. The boxer I feel like I know the most about now is Claressa Shields, in part because I interviewed her after I watched her documentary and then because of the podcast that I do. She keeps popping up. We kept track of her; we interviewed her for that. I don't know, that's so interesting. I do feel like I have an idea that it's happening, but I couldn't tell you any of the big boxers by name.

DJL: You mentioned Claressa Shields—does that speak to the way that the professional ranks remain a male-dominated space, whereas the Olympics functions kind of in different ways? There's obviously, from Laila Ali forward, a female presence among the professional ranks, yet, in terms of visibility, in terms of publicity, in terms of the spectacle, the Olympics functions very differently in terms of women.

JL: I just think it's interesting when I'm thinking about when I would watch it, when I would even consider watching it. I really don't like the violence of it. I don't like watching mixed martial arts, but I watch judo, though.

I'm more likely to watch women generally, because there's a principle behind it for me. I get emotional about it in a way that I don't necessarily for men's sports. So it's sort of that feeling of like, "I can't believe women get to do this, and we get to watch it." If I was ever gonna watch a cricket match, I would much rather go watch women do it. Even so, I just can't see myself watching boxing and really enjoying it.

DJL: I hear ya. I find it interesting that I'll hear people who are rightly apprehensive at one level and outraged at another level about concussions in football. They are concerned about long-term impact, yet they still can watch boxing. Their acceptance of the brutality is striking. There is a level of normalization. Whereas football it's like, "Oh, no, I thought I was signing up for something else." And with boxing, it's like, "This is what I signed up for. I signed up for brutality."

There's a certain power in seeing women in the ring. Do you think that comes from the breaking down of these male-dominated spaces in general, or is it specific to "Hey, women are dominating this hypermasculine space that is violent at its core," or is it a combination of both?

JL: It matters to me that it's a hypermasculine space. And there was that whole thing with the IOC [International Olympic Committee] claiming they had to wear skirts so that we could differentiate that it was women doing it, because it's confusing to have women boxing. The idea that we had to put them in skirts. That's so telling, as far as how people imagine what the sport is supposed to be and see women as interim performers and that we must make sure that we now distinguish who it is we're watching, so we don't confuse them for men. Like, that's important.

The fact that it's hypermasculine and that women can do it. There is just something different about watching a woman be able to beat the shit out of someone. We have all these gendered ideas of who gets to be that person in our society. And I'm so sorry to say this right now, but *Game of Thrones* is on my brain and everyone's crazy reaction, not wanting to believe that a woman could kill a mythical creature-man that was superpowerful on the show. It's that same sort of feeling. I was up on my feet watching her do that—like, jumped up off the couch. And then, of course, to see people push back, mainly from men: "The character can't do that."

It's that same feeling when you watch Claressa beat the shit out of somebody else, a woman. But just that she has that ability is just so—I don't wanna say it's enjoyable because I don't like the violence—but there is something powerful in taking up a space that women are so not really allowed to do. And she's gotten punished, of course. She's gotten chided for being so vocal about how much she likes to beat up people.

DJL: This is so important. It's not just that the physicality and the violence of boxing is gendered; the relationship between violence and brutality is equally gendered. Race matters as well. We don't talk about male boxers or male fans in this way. We don't criticize them for daring to enjoy brutality.

JL: We expect it from them.

DJL: Yeah.

JL: We expect the talk from men. That's why they do the weigh-in, right? It is part of the show, and included as a performance of masculinity. It's so different when you see women do it. I like it; I like seeing women have that kind of—I wanna say bravado, but then I wanna change it to bravada, tweak it just a little.

DJL: Right. Right, right. We see this similarly in basketball in terms of what sort of play is acceptable. And it seems that you see power in, not just with Claressa Shields, not just with her being a boxer, but how she boxes and how she approaches the ring. Her disregard for these gendered expectations.

JL: In the WNBA [Women's National Basketball Association], when women get in each other's faces, there is a feeling of "Are they supposed to act that way?" We just have this idea of what female athletes should act like. And they are so often criticized if they're not. They're supposed to act like "ladies" all the time.

I love when women are in each other's faces as competitors because they're not supposed to be. This is why I love Claressa. She is what I imagine, what I think of as most boxers to be. She brags about herself, and she's her own hype [wo]man. She does all of that stuff. She's unapologetic about it. And that is what I imagine boxing to be about. It's not surprising to me that people feel like she's not supposed to do that. She just doesn't seem to care, which I find lovely.

DJL: You've written about Floyd Mayweather. Can you talk about the ways that boxing is not only a hypermasculine sport but a space of violence inside the ring and outside the ring? Violence against women. What does the coverage surrounding Floyd Mayweather reveal about the sports media as it relates to boxing and violence against women?

JL: Stephen A. Smith interviewed Floyd Mayweather after he had just gotten out of jail. The interview was like a scripted place of redemption. And yet there was just a total omission of the actual violence, the domestic violence, and it's horrible. Floyd Mayweather's history is terrible. He has really harmed people in his life outside of the ring. We don't live in a society that takes violence against women seriously.

DJL: Right.

JL: It's always then just being negatively filtered through these individual men.

DJL: Right.

JL: Especially in sport. I think too, like, for me as a consumer of these products, I do care whether or not they're harming people and their lives. What does it mean when you feel so invested in a single person, and you care about them, but obviously they do all this other shit that is reprehensible. How do you ignore because they sold you him?

DJL: Right.

JL: Like you said, he's a commodity.

DJL: We have zero expectations for boxing to have any sort of a moral center and therefore we're like, "Oh, there's no moral center here." So the expectations are different.

JL: We tell lies to ourselves to make sense of all of it.

DJL: Yes, mythmaking or the lies and stories we tell about sports and athletes allow us to reconcile these choices and contradictions. This leads to my next question: Why do you think boxing films are so important to American culture? In this moment, maybe even more important than boxing itself?

JL: Yeah, I would, yeah, absolutely, at least in my life, that's for sure. I watch all of them. I very much enjoyed *Creed*. I thought that was a brilliant movie. When I think about boxing movies, I think about the whole narrative of the boxer overcoming. And *Rocky* just typifies all these things. All the things he had to overcome to be great in the ring. We like that narrative. We enjoy the individualism narrative of "If you just work hard enough, if you just run up the steps enough times, you too could overcome."

DJL: The appeal of boxing films and boxing as a sport is as much about the nation as the individual. It fuels narratives of American exceptionalism, about white masculinity. It allows for the staging of stories of a rugged individual who finds success because of work and dedication. Meritocracy is staged in the ring.

JL: We see this through what they do in the ring and all the stuff that leads up to a fight. Success isn't simply about winning. Adonis [Michael B. Jordan] didn't win at the end of *Creed*, but that was okay because he almost did, right? It was the journey, though, to get there that was so effective.

DJL: This is why HBO has developed its reality shows, the 24/7 coverage leading up to fights. These shows highlight the sacrifice and the willingness of boxers to push their bodies to the edge. That is Rocky [Sylvester Stallone] chasing after chickens; it is him training in the snow of Siberia; it is Adonis Creed battling demons or training in the desert. It is about battle against all sorts of obstacles.

JL: Part of what happens in any sports story is people bringing the bits that they already understand about that sport. So part of what you're up against when you're talking about boxers is that we think of it as Rocky. It is not surprising given these cultural narratives, that Stephen A. Smith is going to present Floyd Mayweather going to prison as yet another thing he's overcome. Rather than for someone like me, a conversation about bad choices that he's made or how he reconciles the bad things he's done out of the ring that mirror the things that he gets credit for in the ring.

I wouldn't want to ask Floyd Mayweather about going to jail for domestic abuse. That would not be on the top of my list of something, but if you're going to do it, it cannot be this source of celebration. How can it be an inspiration or a source of power for sport when you hurt somebody?

DJL: At the same time, prison then becomes this benevolent redemptive space. In such a narrative, violence against women and incarceration becomes productive as it leads to discipline and growth. How can hurting others be repackaged as something beneficial to a boxing career? This process erases the harm done to individuals, those who've been victimized. It is telling.

In recent years, various boxers have used their stage to critique the president, to talk about Black Lives Matter, or to protest the injustice of America's immigration policy. And yet that doesn't seem to resonate with our discourse around protest and sports. Do you think that is because of the limited popularity of boxing today? Or is the lack of visibility of these political interventions because progressives see boxing as a problematic and toxic enterprise not worthy of attention or celebration? Or do you think this reflects the relationship between boxing and casinos, in terms of its politics, its one-percent audience?

JL: The media cycle doesn't include them, more than anything. I feel like so much of what we understand about activism today is people that have platforms are ones that already had platforms and then chose to use them and so on. Think about [Colin] Kaepernick. ESPN is deeply financially invested in the NFL [National Football League]. They're gonna report it, they're gonna talk about it 24/7. There's a whole media that exists to talk about those things they have financial interest in. And that's true for lots of athletes, right?

The WNBA has been at the forefront of recent protests, and then they're still rarely mentioned in the conversation. And then it seems normal—like if you're not in the news cycle, you're not really doing anything.

For as much sports media that exists, they're only interested in a very select group of athletes and sports. And boxing, for all the reasons we've been talking about, is not on the cultural radar in the same way, unless it's a big enough fight.

DJL: Oversaturation doesn't guarantee diversity of coverage in terms of sports or opinion!

JL: The lack of attention to boxing also reveals how there's not much threat in it either. They talked about Colin Kaepernick all the time for three years. If Colin Kaepernick did something today, it would make the news cycle, because on some level, he is seen as threatening in a way that other athletes aren't.

DJL: I wonder if the threat that Kaepernick embodies is because he challenges the lie that sports are apolitical. That team sports—particularly football, baseball, and basketball—are these apolitical, post-racial playgrounds. He disrupted that. Boxing has a very different history. From Jack Johnson to Muhammad Ali, from the Olympics to Manny, Floyd, and Conor [McGregor], it is clear how race, ethnicity, nationality, and politics are on full display

JL: Right, right.

DJL: I also think that because boxing is so wrapped up in notions of performance and bravado, in the spectacle around the weigh-in and the entrance, that the politics and the disruptive ethos gets lost. As we don't see the ring as a place of disruption and dissent, we fail to see those boxing trunks carrying a politically progressive message or the disruptive entry song as nothing more than entertainment and performance. It gets downplayed as being simply about shock akin to wrestling.

One of the things that we're talking about in this book is the way that the ring entrance is so important, the way in which it becomes a space for staging identity, staging protests, and telling a story. Can you think of a similar or comparable place in other sports, where the things that happen off the field, or outside the lines, are just as important as what happens during the game or the match? Or is boxing unique in this regard?

JL: You're talking about all the peacock feathers, like putting on that show, okay. Clearly there must be similar happenings in other sports.

DJL: One example I thought of, and it seems to be a relatively recent phenomenon, one that reflects the politics of the league. In the aftermath of the NBA's [National Basketball Association's] dress code, the walk from the car, or from the parking lot to the locker room, feels very similar to the boxing entrance.

JL: Oh, absolutely. Social media adds to its importance as well.

DJL: As with the media; there's a reason the media shows the ring entrance. These are moments where athletes have an ability to navigate and negotiate the demands of the sport to say something about themselves.

JL: That's a very good analogy. The NBA entry has taken on its own sort of life with social media. I see more pictures of basketball players walking into arenas now than I probably do of actual basketball games. And players use this platform for overt political messaging. Sometimes it's subtle, sometimes the messaging is more subtle, but other times not so much.

DJL: Right.

JL: They know that the pictures are going to be taken and put all over social media, so they go through all the trouble of doing it.

DJL: With other sports that we don't get anything similar. Maybe in college football we get the quick shot of the coach leading the team off the bus, which is a different message. Here we see the college coach leading and controlling. We see students who happen to labor on football fields wearing identical pregame uniforms. This is about control and the parading of a powerful coach; with boxing, the NBA, and the WNBA it's about individuality, expression, and freedom.

We see this also with the walkout song with boxing. A political statement—one about identity, expression, and agency. So what would be your song if you were about to enter the boxing or academic ring? What song would you want playing as you were getting ready to battle a group of commentators on ESPN?

JL: The subversive part of me would want it to be Martha Wainwright, "Bloody Mother Fucking Asshole." How do you even do that? I love that song. When I have to get stuff done that is hard, I would do that song on repeat to get myself through it. Maybe Rage against the Machine's "Guerilla Radio." I love that song; gets me pumped.

5

Down but Not Out

Mexican Prizefighters and Struggles against US Immigration during the 1930s

JOSÉ M. ALAMILLO

This chapter examines the relationship between US immigration law, the boxing industry, and the print media in relation to the experiences of Rodolfo "Baby" Casanova and Luis "Kid Azteca" Villanueva, two Mexican prizefighters scheduled to fight in Los Angeles in the summer of 1933. These Mexican prizefighters, however, faced a rigid immigration regime and nativist climate that prohibited their entry into the United States. They endured humiliating border inspections and negative representations that viewed them as racially inferior and an economic threat. The US boxing industry, with its networks of trainers, managers, promoters, and matchmakers, recruited young men from Mexico City to fill Los Angeles boxing arenas with bankable box-office draws. In response to US immigration officials' poor treatment of Mexican prizefighters, boxing promoters, sportswriters, and fans waged a public campaign to demand their release from custody and allowed entry. Ultimately, these prizefighters were allowed temporary admission as "foreign athletes" with a five-hundred-dollar bond and a requirement to remain in the country for six months. Using US Immigration and Naturalization Service (INS) immigration records, boxing periodicals, and newspaper articles, I argue that Mexican prizefighters challenged their own marginality through hidden forms of resistance and "strategic visibility," as well as through activating their boxing networks and political connections and seeking support and solidarity from boxers, fans, and journalists.[1]

Boxed into a Corner: Mexican Prizefighters Refused Entry at US–Mexico Border

When Bert Colima, a popular Mexican American prizefighter, announced his retirement on September 16, 1926, it became headline news in *La Opinión*, the largest Spanish-language newspaper in Los Angeles.[2] The news raised concerns among LA fans and promoters about the future of Mexican boxing. Los Angeles boxing promoters worried about declining ticket sales. A *Los Angeles Times* reporter put it bluntly: "Promoters of California have been trying for years to develop another Mexican boxer who could pack an arena like Bert Colima. It has proven to be an endless chain of disappointments so far."[3] The solution was to recruit boxers from Mexico. "There is gold down in Mexico," announced the *Los Angeles Times* and advised Los Angeles boxing promoter Jack Doyle to "start importing [Mexicans] for the Olympic Auditorium."[4] Even the boxing industry's leading magazine, *The Ring*, commented on boxing's popularity in Mexico: "Our southern neighbor has taken up this boxing business in a serious way and is serving notice on the world that in the future the Mexican must be reckoned [with] in the championship accounting."[5]

By the late 1920s, the rise of the "Mexican problem," combined with the stock market crash, led to stricter immigration policies and increased enforcement along the US–Mexico border, which markedly reduced immigration from Mexico. Nativist groups declared Mexican immigrants a racial problem because of their supposed cultural inferiority, poor hygiene, and lack of education. Even though the 1924 Immigration Act exempted Mexico from the quota system, this did not preclude the US State Department from using administrative means to restrict Mexican immigrants through head taxes, literacy tests, medical examinations, and Border Patrol arrests and deportations, and by enforcing the contract labor ban. Historian Mae Ngai (2014) asserts that the imposition of border control and administrative measures functioned to racialize Mexicans as "illegal aliens." Once settled in the United States, Mexican immigrants faced legislative bills and judicial rulings that attempted to strip them of their rights to become US citizens. To add insult to injury, the 1930 US Census reclassified Mexicans from "white" to "a race all their own," causing discrepancies in immigration registration listings along the US–Mexico border (Molina 2010). The anti-Mexican movement reached its peak in the early 1930s with the mass deportation and repatriation of more than four hundred thousand Mexican immigrants and their US-born children back to Mexico (Balderrama and Rodríguez 2006).

At the same time nativists complained about the supposed "Mexican problem" in the late 1920s, Anglo-American liberals developed an "enormous vogue" with Mexican art, literature, music, and folk culture (Delpar 1992). For example, preservationist Christine Sterling saved Los Angeles Plaza from demolition and created Olvera Street, where tourists can get a taste of Mexican culture (Estrada 2008). Even Hollywood studios looked to Mexico as a lucrative market to produce and distribute films (Gunckel 2015). A fascination with "all things Mexican" also emerged in the boxing arenas of Los Angeles (Alamillo 2020). *La Opinión* sports journalist Ignacio Herrerías defined the situation as follows: "A Mexican boxer is a real gold mine in California, since it has been perfectly proven since the time of Bert Colima that every time he shows up in a stadium around five or six thousand people follow with him with amazing regularity, that is, five or six thousand dollars at the box office" (qtd. in Maldonado and Zamora 1999, 32). Los Angeles managers and promoters considered "Mexican boxing" a sporting event that could draw the biggest audiences and generate a six-figure purse. By cheering for their favorite boxer, fans from distinct regions in Mexico, according to Douglas Monroy (1999), could develop an emergent national identity. Boxing was not associated with Americanization, according to Gregory Rodríguez (1999), but "came to be identified with 'Mexicanness,' with Mexican guts, Mexican spirit, and Mexican victories" (63). This "Mexicanness" was closely tied to public performance, style, and commodification. But this sporting phenomenon, according to Stephen Allen (2017), occurred within a transnational network of prizefighters, promoters, trainers, matchmakers, and fans that linked the boxing worlds of Mexico City and Los Angeles.

In the early 1930s, Luis "Kid Azteca" Villanueva and Rodolfo "Baby Face" Casanova were two Mexican professional boxers hoping to make it big in the boxing arenas of Los Angeles (see fig. 5.1). In Mexico, Rodolfo Casanova was nicknamed "Chango" (monkey) because of his dark skin and Indian features, but in the United States the sports media anointed him "Baby Face" or "Baby" because of his youthful features (Allen 2017; Páez 2000; Talan 1952). Casanova was born in León, Guanajuato, and after his father's death he moved the family to Mexico City in search of work as a street food vendor. Casanova rose from poverty to become a professional boxer at the age of sixteen. He shocked the boxing world when he defeated top-ranked Filipino boxers, first Diosdado Posadas, better known as Speedy Dado, in November 1932 and then Sid Torres in February 1933 in Mexico City. A few months later, his manager, Jimmy Fitten, persuaded the Mexican bantamweight champion to make the journey to Los Angeles to fight for a larger purse. Luis Villanueva also caught the attention of Los

Figure 5.1. Left to right: Alberto Arizmendi, Luis Villanueva, Rodolfo Casanova, and unknown boxer. (Courtesy of the Department of Special Collections of the Hesburgh Libraries of the University of Notre Dame.)

Angeles promoters. He grew up poor in the working-class neighborhood of Tepito, Mexico City, which became famous for boxing gyms and trainers that produced world champion boxers. As a young fifteen-year-old, Villanueva began his professional career under the name "Kid Chino" (curly hair kid) in Nuevo Laredo, Mexico, while he worked as a tailor's apprentice. In 1931 he substituted for another boxer called "Kid Azteca," and after an impressive ten-round win decided to keep the ring name.[6] A year later, he won the Mexican national welterweight championship by defeating David Velasco in Mexico City. The next year, Jimmy Fitten recruited the Mexican welterweight title holder to accompany Casanova in a boxing tour to Los Angeles.[7]

On June 20, 1933, boxing fans waited eagerly for the arrival of Casanova and Villanueva in Los Angeles, but US immigration inspectors denied them entry at the El Paso–Ciudad Juárez border crossing. Inspectors classified them as "alien contract laborers" and held them in custody for violating the 1885 Alien Contract Labor Law (known as the Foran Act).[8] The Olympic Auditorium, LA's leading boxing venue, had scheduled Villanueva to fight Ceferino Garcia on June 27 and Casanova to battle "Young Tommy" (Fernando Opao) on July 11, but now both fighters remained in immigration detention. Also in custody was their trainer, Rafael Torres-Lopez, who, along with Casanova and Villanueva, waited anxiously for a Board of Special Inquiry (BSI) hearing to explain why they should be admitted.[9]

The INS treated migrant boxers as contract laborers because the Foran Act prohibited any company from bringing workers under contract to the United States, except domestic workers. This law helped fuel racist and nativist sentiments among labor unions and native-born European American workers who blamed immigrants for taking their jobs and driving down wages.[10] Although the law exempted skilled workers such as "professional actors, artists, lecturers, or singers," it did not stop nativist forces from demanding stricter laws against foreign entertainers (Schrag 2010). By the 1920s, increased pressure from the US entertainment industry led the Bureau of Immigration to create a "temporary admittance" procedure that sought "to balance the need for foreign entertainment with nativists' and racists' concerns" (Moon 2012). This procedure allowed foreigners to stay temporarily under a five-hundred-dollar bond and a requirement to depart by a specific date, or risk losing the bond and undergo deportation. As immigration regulations became more stringent by the early 1930s, the "temporary admittance" procedure was selectively enforced based on race and nationality. US immigration officials at border crossings and ports of entry sought guidance and instructions from the Bureau of Immigration on how to treat foreign athletes. INS commissioner Edward Shaughnessy reminded district employees about certain sports exempted under contract labor law: "The present policy of the Central office is to hold that aliens applying for admission to this country as professional tennis, football, baseball, hockey and soccer players . . . [pay] a suitable bond to guarantee status and departure."[11] The INS directive did not include boxing, thus allowing immigration authorities more discretion when considering their entry from Mexico.

At the BIS hearing, Casanova and Villanueva testified through a translator that they were making a "pleasure trip to California." According to Casanova, "We are coming to the United States to go to Los Angeles on a vacation. We are coming here to rest." However, when inspectors presented him with newspaper articles announcing their upcoming bouts, they accused the pair of lying under oath. The *Los Angeles Examiner* explained that Casanova had signed a contract with promoter Tom Gallery for three fights: "It is expected the Mexican will work at the San Francisco Dreamland as well."[12] Casanova said he "did not know anything about it" because his manager dealt with contract negotiations. The inspector asked him, "Would it not seem strange to you that a contract for three fights was signed by your American manager and you would not be advised?"[13] Again, immigration inspectors accused Casanova of making "false and misleading statements before this Board." El Paso boxing promoter Joe Corona came to his defense and testified, "Casanova is the most sensational fighter since Jack Dempsey, and they have heard about him all over the world." Corona explained why Casanova had not signed a boxing contract yet: "In these days, in order to obtain publicity for their fighters, the promoters and publicity agents, a lot of times will write things which have not happened or will not happen and are not the truth. I likewise have done so at times, under the guise of 'ballyhoo' to gain publicity."[14] Despite Corona's explanations, the US immigration judge remained unconvinced.

During the second day of hearings, the BSI chairman asked Casanova and Villanueva why they had not obtained proper immigration visas. In fact, both had applied for visas at the US Consulate in Ciudad Juárez, Mexico, but had been denied because "no proof existed that they are professionals."[15] Since they could not obtain a visa as professional boxers, they sought entry as "tourists." When questioned again, Villanueva admitted that they were coming to the United States for boxing matches. Ultimately, the BSI chairman ruled that Casanova and Villanueva should remain "aliens excluded" for perjury and "not in possession of immigration visas in violation of the alien contract labor provisions of the immigration laws."[16] On June 21, 1933, the news that "Prizefighting Is Work" reached media outlets with headlines as "Fight Work; Mex[ican] Champs Barred."[17] While they prepared their appeal, the board approved their parole to Joe Corona, who agreed to host them at his residence in Ciudad Juárez while they waited for the appeal decision.

News about the Mexican boxers' exclusion generated public support from nativists. In a telegram to the US Department of Labor, J. C. Russell urged immigration officials to deny entry to Mexican prizefighters and "Give American Boxers a Break." Russell wrote, "These Mexicans are coming to this country under contract to fight for Jack Doyle and Tom Gallery in Los Angeles and to the detriment of American boxers." He added, "California right now has a surplus of cheap boxers from Mexico, and something should be done to prevent the entry of others." He demanded that US government officials do more to protect white American workers from "alien Mexicans." Russell concluded, "It certainly is not proper in these hard times that good capable American boxers should be made to lie around in idleness, shabbily dressed and without sufficient sustenance, while imported boxers from Mexico get the principal engagements and live in comfort. An American boxer cannot compete with imported cheap trash from Mexico."[18] This nativist discourse characterized white boxers as hardworking and humble, while Mexican boxers were ungrateful intruders into the sport. The power of whiteness in sports, according to David J. Leonard (2017), continues to valorize white athletes at the expense of their black and Latino counterparts.

Mexican prizefighters were considered a threat to the "Great White Hopes" of Texas boxing.[19] The US immigration office in Galveston, Texas, received complaints that Mexican prizefighters were supposedly depressing wages and reducing opportunities for white boxers. W. J. Stephens, a San Antonio boxing fan, complained against the "wholesale passage of Mexican Boxers from across the river at Laredo." He explained that boxing in San Antonio was "in a very bad condition" because the boxing commissioner, in collusion with newspapers and promoters, imported boxers from Mexico for a cheaper price "while the local [white] boys sit around idle." Stephens added, "The promoter used to pay Americans $35 to $50 dollars for semi-finals but now he uses Mexicans on same spot Ten Rounds instead of Eight Rounds for $20 to $30 dollars." He urged the San Antonio immigration office to investigate and offered his help "to put a stop to this violation in trying to give the fans and especially the boxers on our side a fair deal."[20] This racialized language of "cheap" undocumented Mexican workers "stealing American jobs" led to concerted efforts by federal, state, and local officials targeting Mexicans for deportation and repatriation during the early 1930s because of the mistaken belief that they were a burden on the welfare system and stealing American jobs.

According to Natalia Molina (2014), the US immigration regime used racial scripts against Mexican immigrants to deprive them of a sense of belonging in American society. The "Mexican Invaders" and "Deportable Mexican" racial scripts dominated the sports media coverage of Mexican boxing during the 1930s. These scripts portrayed Mexican boxers as a racial threat to the livelihood of white American boxers that could be resolved through exclusion and deportation. For example, a United Press International article, "Mexican Boxers to Invade Los Angeles," that was circulated around the country described Casanova and Villanueva as "two of Mexico's young but seasoned ring warriors that will invade Los Angeles."[21] A *Los Angeles Times* headline did not help their cause by using the language of invasion: "Rival Gymnasiums Squabble over Invading Mexican Boxers."[22] One boxing enthusiast complained to *Ring* magazine that "too many foreigners have come to our shores in hordes, have taken thousands of dollars from us and have given us little in return but trouble."[23] Sports journalists constructed a racial script of "Mexican Invasion" to recast Mexican immigrants as a racial problem and thus justify legislative and judicial efforts to place them on a quota system and deny them naturalized citizenship.

Coming out Swinging: The Public Campaign for Mexican Boxers

In response to the BSI ruling, Casanova and Villanueva appealed to the US Department of Labor for their release and sought help from boxing promoters like Tom Gallery. The exclusion of Mexican boxers was bad news for Gallery, a former silent film actor who was making his debut as a promoter and matchmaker for the Olympic Auditorium. Gallery postponed the Casanova and Villanueva bouts and kick-started a public campaign to pressure the Department of Labor for a favorable ruling. Gallery had lined up two "Mexico City-versus-Manila" bouts expecting to generate huge amounts of profit. These matches were certain to sell out, according to Gallery, because "Mexicans are champions in their nation. The Filipinos hold California titles."[24] Filipino and Mexican boxers were formidable rivals, according to one observer: "The harder they are pressed, the better they fight."[25] Like Mexicans, Filipinos developed feelings of anger fueled by acts of racial hostility and nativist backlash in Depression-era California. Nevertheless, as Linda España-Maram (2006) asserts, "Filipino pugilists sought a legitimate place within organized sport by defying its assumptions about race and ability" (92). To be sure, though, promoters fueled this rivalry by assigning separate seating for Mexican and Filipino fans.[26] The Olympic Auditorium decided to have separate ticket windows for the two groups because "the feeling between Mexican and Filipino fans is at such a high pitch."[27]

Since the border incident threatened a huge loss in revenue, Gallery publicly lobbied to win a favorable ruling. The *Los Angeles Times* reported, "Bringing Casanova and Azteca from Mexico City gave the fights international publicity. [Until] the two Latins got their feet caught in the immigration bridge between Juarez and El Paso. It took extra work to get them on a plane headed for Los Angeles."[28] Furthermore, Tom Gallery enlisted the help of Salvador Baguez, a staff artist for the *Los Angeles Times* and movie actor. Baguez published a drawing of Casanova's somber face next to Villanueva with slumping shoulders, sad face, and strapped fists with no gloves (see fig. 5.2).[29]

The cartoon headline, "On the Outside Looking In," sought to generate sympathy for the Mexican boxers, who were "forced to camp" for ten

Figure 5.2. Luis "Kid Azteca" Villanueva and Rodolfo "Baby Face" Casanova in a cartoon drawing by Salvador Baguez, *Los Angeles Times*, June 22, 1933. (Courtesy of Salvador Baguez and *Los Angeles Times* Staff.)

days while they waited for a final decision from Washington, DC.[30] Baguez published the same drawing in *La Opinión* to generate support from *paisanos* (compatriots).[31] By appealing to both white and Mexican boxing fans, Baguez's drawing sought to generate public support for Villanueva and Casanova. While they waited for their appeal, *La Opinión* called for the postponing of Villanueva's match against Ceferino Garcia because he needed more time to train: "This encounter is important and you should not risk losing."[32] Tom Gallery told the *Los Angeles Times* he was confident that Villanueva could still make the fight if released immediately. Since Villanueva had been training in El Paso, "he saw no reason why the show would not be held."[33]

Gallery used his political connections to convince Department of Labor officials to allow US entry to Villanueva and Casanova. On June 22, he sent a telegram to his former Cathedral College classmate and *Chicago American* reporter Ed Gorey, asking him to intervene. Gorey explained the situation in writing to James Farley, US postmaster general and close friend of President Roosevelt's: "It seems their Mexican manager for some unknown reason listed them as tailors although Gallery has posted $500 bond listing them as boxers and guaranteed their return in the usual manner and custom prevailing on the west coast[;] apparently the difference in listing caused the authorities to detain them. Gallery flew in for a brief visit with me at the fair and plans to fly back Sunday, shall appreciate the favor greatly if anything can consistently be done to straighten out the matter."[34]

Los Angeles Spanish-language newspaper *La Opinión* played an important role in publicizing the border incident. When Villanueva and Casanova failed to arrive on their scheduled day, the newspaper expressed concern and asked the Mexican Consulate office in Los Angeles to intervene. Vice Consul Benjamin Hill immediately sent a telegram to the consulate office at El Paso requesting that "all necessary steps be taken for Casanova and Villanueva and not suffer any delay when subjected to immigration requirements."[35] "Don't the immigration authorities understand how far they have to travel before their match?" complained *La Opinión* sports columnist Rafael Ybarra. "They are making them go around and around and spending right and left on telegrams." He reminded readers of another Latino boxer, who attempted to cross through San Pedro but was detained and forced to sleep overnight on his boat while he waited for an appeal. This, according to Ybarra, illustrates "the cold face and unshakable heart of the immigration authorities."[36] In a separate column, Ybarra blamed the incident on their manager, Jimmy Fitten, who wrongly advised them to come as "tourists" but, rather, "should have stated their [boxing] profession." He accused Fitten of naïveté for failing to understand that "in this country they don't believe there is such a thing as [a] dark-skinned Mexican tourist with decayed suitcases."[37] The pervasive stereotype of Mexican border crossers was traveling for work for America's industries, not for leisure or sports. Even if they had a boxing contract, there was no guarantee they would be allowed entry because of INS reports alleging that Mexican immigrants had been using "fraudulent boxing contracts" to enter the United States. Such reports led US immigration inspectors to further scrutinize those claiming to be boxers and trainers.[38] Accusations of fraudulent contracts served to mark Mexican prizefighters as untrustworthy and suspicious of manipulating the immigration system for their own gain.

Mexico City newspapers followed the border incident with special concern for Casanova and Villanueva. *El Excélsior* questioned why "the popular Mexicans settled for saying they were going for a walk when they knew they were going to fight [in] Los Angeles."[39] They blamed Jimmy Fitten and Tom Gallery for not advising them correctly and offering them a contract and bond in advance.[40] The incident reminded readers about Casanova's first match in Los Angeles, when he battled Filipino boxer Speedy Dado on November 15, 1932, and lost in ten rounds before ten thousand spectators at the Olympic Auditorium. Casanova's defeat led *El Gráfico* to launch a "Stay at Home" campaign for Mexican boxers who are sent to the United States only "to be victimized."[41] One Mexican doctor cautioned against sending Mexican boxers to the United States "until they are ready to defend themselves not only against their opponents but against the maneuvers of referees as well."[42] He suggested, "A Mexican to win in dollar-land must knock out or overwhelm his opponent to win."[43] The "Stay at Home" campaign abruptly dissipated, but it revealed Mexican leaders' increasing interest in developing athletes to compete effectively at the international level. Thirty years later, however, the new head of Mexico City's boxing commission, Luis Spota, prohibited Mexican boxers from fighting in California until they received fair matches, a medical exam, and equal opportunities to fight in both Mexico and California (Allen 2017).

Mexican American prizefighters in Los Angeles heard about the border incident and sought to defend Casanova and Villanueva. Upon hearing about their border ban, Bert Colima called his former manager, Dutch Meyers, to intervene on their behalf by calling US immigration officials in El Paso. Meyers reportedly spent $160 on telephone calls to El Paso, Washington, and Chicago.[44] After retirement, Colima remained close to the boxing world by attending the fights and mentoring younger fighters. His son, Bert W. Colima (2009), recalled how his dad "would go to the Main Street Gym and talk to the boxers and managers about up-and-coming boxers. He would offer his help, or anything else he could do to stay close to the game. Everyone in the gym always received Colima with great affection, greeting him with 'Geeve it to heem Colima' as he entered the gym" (7). The slogan, first popularized by Mexican stage and screen actress Lupe Vélez, an ardent fan of Mexican boxers, revealed how much fans loved to cheer for Colima.

Vélez attended boxing matches at the Olympic Auditorium and Hollywood Legion, frequently occupying a front-row seat where she would stand, yell, and cajole Mexican boxers to knock out opponents. She defended Mexican boxers when they were wrongly denied a victory in the ring. *La Prensa* recounted an incident when Vélez jumped into the ring to hit the referee with an umbrella when her Mexican boxer lost by a technical knockout.[45] Although it cost her a thousand-dollar fine, she earned a reputation as a top fan of Mexican boxers. When Vélez committed suicide with a drug overdose on December 13, 1944, *La Opinión* sports editor Rodolfo Garcia wrote, "The death of Lupe Vélez caused more sensation in the boxing circles of Los Angeles, than in the artistic world where the number one boxing fan reached international fame."[46] Through her attendance at boxing bouts, Vélez expressed nationalist loyalty to Mexico and challenged traditional gender norms. Besides Lupe Vélez, other early Mexican movie stars with Hollywood ties were also boxing fans, including Ramon Navarro, Gilbert Roland, and Anthony Quinn.[47]

The Final Round: Mexican Boxers Allowed Entry

After a week of waiting in Ciudad Juarez, Villanueva and Casanova received approval on June 28 from the US Department of Labor to be admitted as "nonimmigrants" under a sixty-day temporary visa with the standard five-hundred-dollar bond to ensure their return home.[48] The *Los Angeles Times* declared their release "a token of victory over federal immigration authorities."[49] The political pressure on the Department of Labor certainly helped, but so did the public campaign in the newspapers. The Spanish-language press and Mexican American boxers also helped Villanueva and Casanova gain entry. After they won their appeal, they arrived at the Burbank airport to a welcome party. *La Opinión* announced, "Representatives of the fighters, some athletic groups and numerous supporters, will attend in order to welcome them. It is expected that their presence in these parts will inject animation to pugilistic activities."[50]

Upon arrival, Villanueva and Casanova began training at the Ringside Gym in downtown Los Angeles for their rescheduled double-feature match on Tuesday, July 11. Fans congregated around the gym to catch a glimpse of the two boxers. One sports reporter observed, "They have packed the gymnasium day after day to watch the workouts of the Latins."[51] Jimmy Fitten visited the gym to "personally take care of his boys." Ybarra jokingly reminded readers about the old saying, "The master's eye makes the horse fat," meaning that a business owner should look after his investments to ensure success.[52] It was a mixed result, however, as Young Tommy soundly defeated Casanova in ten rounds and Villanueva scored a ten-round decision over Ceferino Garcia before eight thousand fans. One of the loudest fans was Lupe Vélez, who shouted at Villanueva to knock down Garcia.[53] According to *Los Angeles Times*, she was also "doing one of those hot-cha dances as her Mexican idol put the Filipino in his place."[54] With Vélez's cheering him on, Villanueva knocked out Garcia in the third round but got up after a nine count. After ten rounds, Villanueva received a favorable verdict over Garcia.[55]

Because of their negative experience with US immigration authorities, Casanova and Villanueva disliked fighting in the United States (Allen 2013, 47–48). Six months after their detention, Casanova returned for a rematch against Speedy Dado and again was detained at the El Paso–Ciudad Juárez border. Immigration authorities again took their time investigating the "alien status" of the "little Mexican battler."[56] After several days, Casanova received temporary admission for six months after immigration authorities ruled that his profession was "unusual" and "unique."[57] Both Casanova and Villanueva remained living and fighting professionally in Mexico City, where they enjoyed more success and popularity. In 1934 Casanova left Jimmy Fitten, saying Fitten had "mismanaged" his funds and "injured" his health by forcing him to make weights out of his class.[58] After his retirement, a Mexican film titled *Campeón sin Corona* (1946), largely based on Casanova's life story, helped to bolster his image as a role model of Mexican masculinity. Although mythologized as a "champion without a crown," Casanova wrestled with alcoholism, mental health problems, womanizing, and an unstable family situation that ultimately cost him his life (Allen 2013, 48–49).

Conclusion

Rodolfo "Baby" Casanova and Luis "Kid Azteca" Villanueva believed that boxing could lift their family out of poverty. Under the direction of Jimmy Fitten and Tom Gallery, these boxers from Mexico City traveled to Los Angeles to fight in the summer of 1933, but US immigration laws and nativist forces denied them entry. The immigration cases of these Mexican prizefighters reveal how US immigration policy was applied irregularly with administrative discretion and selective enforcement. Nativists and immigration officials racialized Mexican prizefighters as "brown bodies" who supposedly threatened the livelihood of Euro-American boxers. The negative racial scripts of Mexicans as "deportable" and "invaders" in the print media contributed to their immigration problems.

Although the popular media and US immigration regime treated Mexican boxers as a racial and economic threat, the appeal and public campaign waged by prizefighters, promoters, fans, and sportswriters forced their release and temporary admittance. Temporary admittance became an "in-between" category in US immigration law that limited the rights of migrant athletes and sometimes made them vulnerable to exploitation in the boxing industry. Mexican boxers, however, could resist and challenge their own marginality, not necessarily through their public identity but through hidden maneuvers, activating their sporting networks and political connections, and seeking compassion and solidarity from supporters. By making themselves "strategically visible" to fans and sports media, however, Mexican boxers challenged the production of their illegality and deportability.

Professional boxing continues to offer poor and working-class populations a potential path out of poverty. In order to earn more money and world championships, foreign prizefighters need to compete in the United States; obtaining a temporary visa is not easy. They often need financial and legal assistance and a sponsor to post an insurance bond. Although Mexico has produced a long line of champion fighters, very little is known about their historic struggles with US immigration and the country's boxing industry. Mexico has long been a supplier of boxing opponents for US boxing. The dark side of the sport is that many promising boxers accept fights for less money and are exploited by unscrupulous promoters and matchmakers. The consequences have sometimes resulted in permanent injuries and death. Take, for example, Fernando Ibarra, a mediocre boxer from Piedras Negras, Coahuila, turned professional and started going to the United Stated to box, earning four hundred dollars per fight, until a single punch from a tougher opponent left him with a permanent brain injury. The fight promoter and matchmaker denied any wrongdoing. The Mexican newspaper *Reforma* accused the United States of using their country's boxers as "cannon fodder" (Zarembo 1999). The newspaper comment was reminiscent of the 1932 "Stay at Home" campaign for Mexican boxers. We must move beyond romantic narratives of the US and Mexican boxing industry to examine how racial discrimination, immigration, and labor problems shaped the experiences of Mexican prizefighters.

Notes

1. "Strategic visibility," according to Thomas Carter (2011), "is informed both by public understandings and awareness of a migrant group's social identities, which are positioned accordingly within local contexts and the degree to which the individual in question is visible to relevant authorities, sport and state, who interests help to shape migrant's movements" (17–18).

2. "Bert Colima Se Retira de los Rings," *La Opinión*, September 16, 1926, 8. Bert Colima was the most popular Mexican boxer in the 1920s, attracting standing-room-only crowds from Vernon Arena in Los Angeles to the Plaza de Toros in Mexico City. For additional information, see Bert W. Colima 2009.

3. "Ring Test for Mexican Boxer," *Los Angeles Times*, November 6, 1932, 21.

4. "Gold Found in Mexico Boxers" *Los Angeles Times*, November 6, 1932, E6.

5. Harold Joyce, "Hot Tamales from Mexico," *The Ring*, May 1933, 30.

6. Talan, *En El 3er. Round*, 115–19. See also Lew Eskin, "The Amazing Kid Azteca," *The Ring*, May 1959, 26.

7. Born to a Mexican mother and Jewish American father in Oakland, California, Jimmy Fitten was a former professional boxer turned trainer, manager, promoter, and matchmaker in Mexico City. Fitten was considered the "Tex Rickard of Mexico" because his publicity skills resembled that of boxing's first great promoter, who made boxing into a million-dollar business. See Marco Antonio Maldonado and Ruben Amador Zamora, *Pasión Por Los Guantes: Historia del box Mexicano I, 1850–1960* (Clio, 1999), 46–47; Alan Ward, "On Second Thought," *Oakland Tribune*, April 1, 1956, 10; Paul Lowry, "Fitten Trains Mexicans," *Los Angeles Times*, June 23, 1933, A10.

8. "Mexican Boxing Champs Are Refused Admittance to U.S.," *Lubbock Morning Avalanche*, June 21, 1933, 22; "Casanova and Azteca Still Being Held," *Los Angeles Times*, June 23, 1933, 13.

9. The Board of Special Inquiry is a board set up by the commissioner of immigration to investigate immigrant exclusion cases. Transmission of Records on Appeal, June 24, 1933, file 55836/955, p. 1, Records of the Immigration and Naturalization Service, RG 86 (National Archives, Washington, DC); hereafter, INS Records.

10. Alien Contract Labor Act of 1885, Ch. 164, §1, 23 Stat. 332, 48th Congress, Feb. 25, 1885. http://library.uwb.edu/Static/USimmigration/23%20stat%20332.pdf.

11. "To All Districts Immigration and Naturalization Service from Edward Shaughnessy, Acting Commissioner," April 6, 1937, file 55880/500, INS Records.

12. "Gallery Closes Casanova Bout," *Los Angeles Examiner*, June 18, 1933, 4.

13. Board of Inquiry Testimony of Rodolfo Casanova-Mendez, June 20, 1933, file 55836/955, INS Records.

14. Board of Inquiry Testimony of Jose Corona, June 21, 1933, file 55836/955, p. 12, INS Records.

15. Board of Inquiry Testimony of Rodolfo Casanova-Mendez, June 21, 1933, file 55836/955, INS Records.

16. Memorandum to Board of Review by G. C. Wilmoth, District Director of Immigration, El Paso District, June 26, 1933, file 55836/955, INS Records.

17. "Prize Fighting Is Work, Judge Rules," *Nevada State Journal*, June 21, 1933, 21; "Fight Work; Mex Champs Barred," *Montana Standard*, June 22, 1933, 10.

18. Western Union Telegram to Secretary of Labor from J. C. Russell, June 23, 1933, file 55836/955, INS Records.

19. The racialized term "Great White Hope," coined by Jack London, urged white American boxers to fight against Jack Johnson and other Black boxers

who were dominating the heavyweight divisions during the height of Jim Crow in the early 1900s.

20. W. J. Stephens to District Director Immigration, Galveston, Texas, March 28, 1935, file 55880/500, INS Records.

21. "Mexican Boxers to Invade Los Angeles," *Bakersfield Californian*, June 16, 1933, A8.

22. "Azteca and Casanova on Spot, Rival Gymnasiums Squabble over Invading Mexican Boxers," *Los Angeles Times*, July 7, 1933, A11.

23. *The Ring* 5, no. 5 (1935): 3.

24. "Classy Boxers Open Olympics," *Los Angeles Times*, July 11, 1933, A9.

25. "Juan Zurita Favor[ed] over Gene Espinoza in Hollywood Ring Battle Tonight," *Los Angeles Times*, January 18, 1935, A12.

26. "Kennedy May Referee Casanova–Dado Battle," *Los Angeles Times*, November 9, 1932, 26.

27. "Kennedy May Referee Casanova–Dado Battle," *Los Angeles Times*, November 9, 1932, 26.

28. "Classy Boxers Open Olympics," *Los Angeles Times*, July 11, 1933, 23.

29. Salvador Baguez, "On the Outside Looking In," *Los Angeles Times*, June 22, 1933, A9.

30. "Scrappers Still 'Out' at Border," *Los Angeles Times*, June 22, 1933, A9.

31. "El Martes Se Enfrentaran Los Paisanos," *La Opinión*, July 9, 1933, 7.

32. "Es Probable Que Se Pida Una Prorroga," *La Opinión*, June 22, 1933, 7.

33. "Olympic to Hold Show if Azteca Freed Today," *Los Angeles Times*, June 24, 1933, 5.

34. Ed Gorey to James Farley, Western Union Telegram, June 22, 1933, file 55836/955, INS Records.

35. "Son Esperados Hoy Azteca y Casanovita," *La Opinión*, June 20, 1933, 7; "Los Pugilistas Estaban En El Paso Ayer En La Noche y Son Esperados en Breve," *La Opinión*, June 21, 1933, 7.

36. Rafael Ybarra, "Marginando," *La Opinión*, June 22, 1933, 7.

37. Rafael Ybarra, "Marginando," *La Opinión*, June 23, 1933, 7.

38. "Fraudulent Boxing Contracts," file 56251/138, INS Records.

39. "Por No Decir La Verdad Casanovita y Azteca No Pueden Ir a California," *El Excelsior*, June 21, 1933, 4.

40. "Se Les Niega La Entrada a Casanova y Kid Azteca," *El Excelsior*, June 22, 1933, 4.

41. "Mexico's Fistiana Has Wail, Boxers Victimized in Dollar-Land, Invaders Urged to Stay Home," *The Californian*, November 18, 1932, 7.

42. "Mexican Ring Aces Robbed in U.S. Claim," *Santa Ana Register*, November 18, 1932, 12.

43. "Boxers Given Timely Advice," *San Bernardino County Sun*, November 19, 1932, 5.

44. Western Union Telegram to Secretary of Labor from Dutch Meyers, June 16, 1933, file 55836/955, INS Records.

45. "Muchos Han Sido Pugilistas y Después Actores de Cine," *La Prensa*, June 29, 1941, 12.

46. Rodolfo Garcia, "Esquina Neutral," *La Opinión*, December 17, 1944, 4.

47. In his autobiography, Quinn (1972, 148–57) recounts how he himself became a boxer and befriended Mexican boxers. Fighting under the name "Tony Quinn," he won nine welterweight fights and earned twenty to thirty dollars per fight, until he got knocked out by an African American boxer. He retired early from the sport because he lacked "a killer instinct." It is interesting to note that Quinn used his brief boxing career to deliver a remarkable performance as a boxer in the 1962 film classic *Requiem for a Heavyweight*.

48. US Department of Labor, "Report of Execution of Department Decision," June 29, 1933, file 7001/3385, INS Records. See also "Ring Stars of Mexico Due Today," *Los Angeles Times*, June 29, 1933, A11.

49. "Mexican Boxing Stars Arrive in Los Angeles," *Los Angeles Times*, June 30, 1933, 37.

50. "Young Casanova y Kid Azteca Llegan How en Aeroplano, Se Les Prepara Una Recepcion en el Aeropeurto," *La Opinión*, June 28, 1933, 7.

51. "Casanova, Azteca Primed to Repel Filipino Foes," *Los Angeles Times*, July 9, 1933, D2.

52. Rafael Ybarra, "Marginando," *La Opinión*, July 7, 1933, 7.

53. "Siguelo . . . Siguelo . . . Gritaba Lupe Vélez," *La Opinión*, July 14, 1933, 4.

54. "Kid Azteca New Mexican Title Threat," *Los Angeles Times*, July 13, 1933, A9.

55. "Azteca Floors Garcia to Cop Wild Ring Go," *Los Angeles Times*, July 12, 1933, A9.

56. "Immigration Authorities Again Halt Baby Casanova," *Los Angeles Times*, November 20, 1933, 11; "Casanova Is Here en Route to L.A.," *El Paso Times*, November 19, 1933, 14.

57. "Immigration Authorities Again Halt Baby Casanova," *Los Angeles Times*, November 20, 1933, 11; "Casanova Is Here en Route to L.A.," *El Paso Times*, November 19, 1933, 14.

58. "Mexican Army Man Will Run Babe Casanova," *Nevada State Journal*, July 21, 1934, 5.

References

Alamillo, José M. 2020. *Deportes: The Making of a Sporting Mexican Diaspora*. Rutgers University Press.

Allen, Stephen. 2013. "Boxing in Mexico: Masculinity, Modernity, and Nationalism, 1946–1982." PhD Diss., Rutgers University.

Allen, Stephen D. 2017. *A History of Boxing in Mexico: Masculinity, Modernity, and Nationalism*. University of New Mexico Press.

Balderrama, Francisco E., and Raymond Rodríguez. 2006. *Decade of Betrayal: Mexican Repatriation in the 1930s*. University of New Mexico Press.

Carter, Thomas F. 2011. *In Foreign Fields: The Politics and Experiences of Transnational Sport Migration*. Pluto Press.

Colima, Bert W. 2009. *Gentleman of the Ring: The Bert Colima Story*. Magic Valley Publishers.

Delpar, Helen. 1992. *The Enormous Vogue of Things Mexican: Cultural Relations between the United States and Mexico, 1920–1935*. University of Alabama Press.

España-Maram, Linda. 2006. *Creating Masculinity in Los Angeles's Little Manila: Working-Class Filipinos and Popular Culture, 1920s–1950s*. Columbia University Press.

Estrada, William D. 2008. *The Los Angeles Plaza: Sacred and Contested Space*. University of Texas Press.

Gunckel, Colin. 2015. *Mexico on Main Street: Transnational Film Culture in Los Angeles before World War II*. Rutgers University Press.

Leonard, David J. 2017. *Playing While White: Privilege and Power On and Off the Field*. University of Washington Press.

Maldonado, Marco, and Rubén Zamora. 1999. *Pasión por los Guantes: Historia del Box Mexicano, 1895–1960*. Clío.

Molina, Natalia. 2010. "In a Race All Their Own: The Quest to Make Mexicans Ineligible for U.S. Citizenship." *Pacific Historical Review* 79, no. 1: 167–201.

Molina, Natalia. 2014. *How Race Is Made in America: Immigration, Citizenship, and the Historical Power of Racial Scripts*. University of California Press.

Monroy, Douglas. 1999. *Rebirth: Mexican Los Angeles from the Great Migration to the Great Depression*. University of California Press.

Moon, Krystin R. 2012. "On a Temporary Basis: Immigration, Labor Unions, and the American Entertainment Industry, 1880s–1930s." *Journal of American History* 99, no. 3: 771–92.

Ngai, Mae M. 2014. *Impossible Subjects: Illegal Aliens and the Making of Modern America*. Updated ed. Princeton University Press.

Páez, Pino. 2000. *A Solas En El Altar: Vida de Rodolfo Casanova 'El Chango'*. Edamex.

Quinn, Anthony. 1972. *The Original Sin: A Self-Portrait*. Little, Brown.

Rodríguez, Gregory. 1999. "Palaces of Pain—Arenas of Mexican-American Dreams: Boxing and the Formation of Ethnic Mexican Identities in Twentieth Century Los Angeles." PhD Diss. University of California San Diego.

Schrag, Peter. 2010. *Not Fit for Our Society: Nativism and Immigration*. University of California Press.

Talan, Raul. 1952. *En El 3er. Round*. Editore.

Zarembo, Allan. 1999. "Taking a Real Beating." *Newsweek*, October 24, 1999. https://www.newsweek.com/taking-real-beating-167956.

6

The Great Off-White Hope

ROBERTO JOSÉ ANDRADE FRANCO

Today, the "boxing is dead" trope that has been around for more than a century continues.[1] For at least a generation, boxing's cultural impact has declined in the United States. Most involved with the sport—from promoters to commentators to fans—have offered opinions on what would restore the popularity boxing last enjoyed when Mike Tyson was a household name. But lost in the urge to resuscitate boxing is the fact that the sport *is* popular, just not with the white, middle-class demographic that marketers covet.

Boxing in the United States has become a Latino, largely Mexican, sport, and this shift was clear in the mid-1990s with Oscar De La Hoya. Despite the boxer playing a vital role in this demographic shift, he has often faced backlash within his own community. When De La Hoya fought Mexican nationals and Mexican Americans who fought, unlike him, with an aggressive, relentless style, that alienation furthered. When he fought Julio César Chávez, a Mexican national hero, some fans of Mexican heritage criticized De La Hoya for what he was not: Mexican enough. What defines that vague description is never clear. As with all identity, it can be situational and contradictory.

Boxing continuously fights to regain the social relevance it once had. Part of the sport's seemingly never-ending quest is to find a boxer who can appeal, once again, to the white, middle-class demographic. De La Hoya understood this, and he recognized his unique position in this quest. He embraced his role in it all, explaining that he fought for more than just "Hispanics." In a sport and country that in the mid-1990s was becoming increasingly Brown, whether or not he understood it, that was De La Hoya's dissent. It earned him millions even if he lost the unanimous support from a community that once protected him.

• • •

It is rare when the term "child prodigy" applies to boxers. Talented musicians, chess players, mathematicians, and even actors receive the label; however, unlike those activities, boxing is violent. And because they are profoundly skilled at violence at such an early age, child boxing prodigies cause discomfort. But as the term "prodigy" evokes excitement and mystery, both of which are a perfect fit within a sport as romanticized as this, some have described boxers as prodigies. Oscar De La Hoya was one of these boxers.

Born to a boxing family in the predominantly Mexican area of East Los Angeles, De La Hoya was a highly decorated amateur forced to spar against professionals to get proper competition. But even *that* was not a given. "[De La Hoya] makes even pros look bad," said the owner of the East LA gym where the eighteen-year-old boxer trained.[2] And like most stories involving prodigies, there was a father who drove and possibly forced his child's ambitions, guiding him toward a lucrative career. That was Joel De La Hoya.

"I wanted him to be somebody," the father explained. "Not like me, working for eight to [ten] dollars an hour. He was a little boy, but he always obeyed me—went to school then straight to the gym. No messing up. Come home and do schoolwork. No booze or girl problems." The son lived up to his end of things for the good of the family, whose future without Oscar seemed bleak. "If I don't win, a lot of things would go away instantly for me," the son said. "I know that. I gotta become champion. I gotta win every time."[3]

He won plenty. In a city full of amateur boxers who would later turn professional and rank among world champions, De La Hoya was the best. His amateur career culminated in not just representing the United States in the 1992 Olympics but also becoming the face of the team.[4] Young, charismatic, and with movie-star good looks, De La Hoya also had a backstory that made him sympathetic to members of his community. And as he won the boxing gold medal, De La Hoya had everything required of someone tasked with saving a niche sport—but not before he returned home as an Olympic hero.

When De La Hoya returned from the 1992 Olympics, hundreds of fans and admirers waited for him at the airport. "OS-CAR, OS-CAR," they chanted. One admirer held up a sign that said, "Oscar your mother must be so proud."[5] The sign pointed to a promise he had made to his mother, who, when he quit boxing, finding the sport meaningless as she lay dying, told him to stay strong and win the Olympic gold medal. "The last words she told me was win the gold medal for her," De La Hoya recalled less than a year after his mother died from cancer at age thirty-eight. "I told her that's what I'm going to do, and nothing is going to stop me."[6] After he won, De La Hoya honored his mother.[7] He celebrated by holding the United States flag in his right hand and the Mexican flag in his left, symbolizing his country and heritage. The son of Mexican immigrants, a Mexican American living in East Los Angeles, and having gone through the adversity of losing his mother, De La Hoya was an entirely relatable person.

When he appeared at the arrival gate, fans swarmed De La Hoya. They tried to touch him, kiss him, have their pictures taken with him. His smiling father stood close. "In my dreams, I dreamed something like this," he said. "It's very excellent."[8] Many of those who showed up at the airport then accompanied the De La Hoyas in a celebratory caravan made up of hundreds of cars.[9] They joined another large group gathered outside the De La Hoyas' home in the Mexican and Mexican American neighborhood of Boyle Heights. That same year, the neighborhood had seen ninety-seven homicides, 57 percent of them gang-related.[10] But for that night—with the neighborhood decorated with flags, Olympic rings, and signs calling De La Hoya "the pride of East L.A."—those concerns were secondary.[11]

"He's going to be a millionaire," De La Hoya's trainer said. "He's going to be a world champ . . . I know that."[12] These words were more than just an emotional, hollow statement. He spoke with a warranted optimism. All the sacrifice appeared close to paying off, not just for De La Hoya and his family but also for the community that had shielded him. Even neighborhood gang members had protected him. Once, when thieves *accidentally* held up De La Hoya at gunpoint, by the time he returned home the stolen items were on his front porch. The thieves presumably had learned whom they had stolen from when they saw De La Hoya's identification card inside the wallet they took.[13]

In 1992, after winning his gold medal, De La Hoya served as the grand marshal for East LA's Mexican Independence Day parade. There is no account of how the crowd reacted to De La Hoya, but it's safe to assume they showed him the same love and respect as they had a month earlier. Four years later, in the same parade, De La Hoya again served as grand marshal. However, by 1996, despite having become the millionaire and world champion his trainer predicted, people's love and respect had faded.

Although evidence of his growing fame spread beyond the usual boxing world, some parade watchers no longer viewed De La Hoya as "the homeboy who made good, coming back to the place that had nurtured his biggest dreams," as *Latina* magazine described him.[14] Instead, as De La Hoya rode atop a new, shiny red Corvette, some threw eggs and tomatoes in his direction.[15] Someone held a sign asking, "What's Oscar doing at a

Mexican parade?" Another person referred to him as "that *white guy*."[16] De La Hoya could only smile and wave as he dodged the projectiles. He tried laughing it off as best he could. But the reception did not surprise him. "In the rest of America, they love me," he said. "But this little community here, something's wrong with them."[17]

Several things led to the drastic change and rising tension between De La Hoya and his community. One of them was the growing sense that De La Hoya—known as the Golden Boy—had it easy. "The loudest part of the community wanted De La Hoya beaten," explains Tim Kawakami, the boxer's biographer. "He had been handed talent, looks, and a gold medal." And on behalf of those who rooted for him, "the least [Oscar] could do was suffer a little. To feel life the way they lived it. For once."[18]

But life was different for De La Hoya. His opportunities appeared limitless, even in a sporting industry that notoriously abused its workforce. He had awe-inspiring talent. "I'd never seen anything like it in my life," said Robert Mittleman about De La Hoya's deadly left hook. "Excuse the expression but my dick got hard," he said of the first time he saw, in person, De La Hoya throw that punch.[19] Mittleman became De La Hoya's first manager and gave him a one-million-dollar contract, just for the privilege.[20] With that, De La Hoya, unsurprisingly, left the barrio. A growing resentment replaced his physical presence in the place he once lived. It was a feeling that he had not only left but had changed as well and that if he came around and was driving one of his fancy cars—the one with the license plate that read "GOLDMINE"—the difference between them and him was clear.[21] He was young, beautiful, gifted, and rich. He relaxed by playing golf—an upper-class sport associated with being white—and he was maybe even boxing's savior.[22] *They* were something else.

Boxing, often considered dead by white, middle-class standards, survives, in part, by manufacturing its own hope that a boxer will emerge and through charisma, skill, and proper marketing attract an entire country. In the process, that boxer will return the sport to the prominence it enjoyed decades ago. This is boxing's version of El Dorado, a tantalizing reward that justifies searching for something that is not there—or at least not to the extent imagined by everyone who stands to gain financially. Still, once every generation or two, a variety of factors come together and a fighter comes close to fulfilling boxing's eternal dream.

From 1990 to 2000, the US Hispanic population increased by 57.9 percent. Mexicans accounted for 58.5 percent of that growth.[23] Mexicans, Mexican Americans, and, to some extent, other Hispanics have long occupied an ambiguous place within the United States' racial hierarchy—somewhere between the white and nonwhite. Or perhaps, as Laura E. Gómez

(2007) has labeled them, "Off-White" (83–84). Regardless of their racial label, the vast population increase attracted the interest of corporations that tried to appeal to Hispanics with language serving as their marker of social class.

Advertisers saw Hispanics who consumed Spanish-language media as a lower-class audience and those who chose English-language media as comparatively upper class. Charisma and skill remained valuable components, but with the changing demographics, marketing a boxer who was not only talented and attractive but also bilingual became ideal. Hispanics who chose English-language media were a much more attractive demographic.[24] An appeal to both the Spanish and especially the English-speaking audience would be ideal, as it could hypothetically make white, middle-class America reachable. Thus, language became a vital part of the never-ending search for boxing's savior. This is how Oscar De La Hoya became the Great Off-White Hope.[25]

Bob Arum, De La Hoya's promoter, predicted that his fighter's marketability and appeal would be the largest in boxing history this side of Muhammad Ali. "He's bilingual," Arum said of De La Hoya, "an American Olympic star carrying a Mexican flag . . . The demographics are right. The Hispanic market is huge and, to some degree, untapped. They're becoming boxing's core audience."[26] In the mid-1990s, Arum estimated that 35 percent of those who purchased pay-per-view fights were Hispanic households. Arum first said De La Hoya's marketing campaign would be "totally as a Hispanic project"—there would be no attempt to make him a crossover star.[27]

But as De La Hoya's appeal transcended boxing and Hispanic audiences, that strategy changed. And as he moved toward becoming a crossover fighter, he and Arum inadvertently contributed to the notion he had embraced mainstream corporate American values, which were inherently white and middle-class. De La Hoya's ambitions were always beyond boxing, a sport he often claimed to dislike and even hate.[28] It seemed as though he would have rather been an architect, but if he had to fight, then he might as well try to "have big endorsement deals, to cross over to the Anglo market."[29] As De La Hoya claimed, "I don't fight just for Hispanics. I want to break that barrier."[30]

De La Hoya broke that barrier. Corporate offices and advertising agencies all wanted him.[31] During the height of his popularity, outside the ring, De La Hoya had a clothing line—the Oscar De La Hoya Collection, sold through Mervyn's department store.[32] There were talks for him to transition to becoming an actor, and there were even plans to make a made-for-TV movie based on his life story.[33] *People* magazine named him one of the world's "50 Most Beautiful People." "His mild-manners and clean-cut style is giving boxing a much-needed image lift," the magazine reported.[34] This image led to De La Hoya becoming part of the "Got Milk?" advertising campaign. As his popularity exploded outside the ring, inside the ring he was among the most popular and highest-paid boxers, a place usually reserved for heavyweights.

Besides his large corporate backing, De La Hoya also enjoyed a large female fan base. He was good-looking with an image as the "rich, lonely boy in need of mothering."[35] HBO and pay-per-view executives claimed that women influenced 40 percent of all De La Hoya fights ordered.[36] "He's so beautiful. He's perfect!" said one of his many admirers. "He's like Selena. He's the boy Selena!"[37]

But while De La Hoya's popularity soared, some in his community continued to view him as a *vendido*, a sellout. "What was the first thing he did after he came back from the Olympics?" one critic and former high school classmate asked rhetorically. "He moved out of here and went to the Montebello hills."[38] It was not just his physical move that strained relations with his community; De La Hoya also distanced himself politically. He espoused assimilationist politics that furthered his alienation. He refused to comment on California's Prop 187, a ballot measure aimed at preventing illegal immigrants from using state services.[39] De La Hoya did, however, take a political stand on language. "I . . . believe strongly that those who immigrate to this country, regardless of where they are from, should learn English. This is America. The first language is English," he explained in his autobiography, *American Son*.[40]

De La Hoya realized it was almost impossible to return home. No longer welcoming, home became a place where he had to hide. It was a place he avoided, in part, because people increasingly forced him to defend his Mexican identity. It was a conversation that a frustrated De La Hoya could not win:

> I found myself having argument after argument with older people around the neighborhood, always forced to defend myself. "Where were your kids born?" I would say. "Here in East L.A.," they would admit. "So what's the problem?" I would ask. "I was born here, too. My parents are Mexicans just like you." "Don't tell me you're Mexican," they would say. "You're a pocho. You're a gringo." "I'm an American," I would say, my voice rising. "What's wrong with that? I'm the same as your kids." "That's different," they would insist.[41]

Identity is a complicated and, at times, contradictory structure. The difference between the supposed authentic and fake is rarely clear. But for De La Hoya, Julio César Chávez magnified that difference. Chávez's Mexican identity was beyond reproach. De La Hoya was something closer to a "watered-down version of a Mexican."[42] Chávez was Mexico. Chávez was machismo personified. A national hero, Chávez never had the luxury of fighting for free, as one would as an Olympian. Nor would he be part of any "Got Milk?" campaigns. There would be no deals for Chávez with athletic apparel companies, no sponsorships worth seven figures.[43] There was no mention of him as one of the world's most beautiful people. And Mennen Speed Stick could never use Chávez to sell deodorant to the Hispanic market the way they did with De La Hoya, because even if all he had to do was smile for the camera, Chávez "still [stunk] of the streets."[44] Their perceived dissimilarities only augmented when the two fought each other. Their fight, on an early July night in Las Vegas in 1996, had a large but different significance for both. For De La Hoya, it was a pathway to legitimacy. For Chávez, who spoke of retiring as close to a hundred professional fights had worn his body and age had diminished his skills, he needed to fight De La Hoya because it offered the biggest payday.[45] Their fight was, as promoters aptly billed it, one for Ultimate Glory. And it was also a contrast of fighting styles.

The boxer and the brawler are two completely different beings, united only in their mutual belief that their distinctive style is superior to the other. The boxer is a calculating, measured, and patient fighter, manipulating opponents into exposing their own flaws and then pouncing. But a boxer, more than anything, is a chess player who, at their best, looks like a magician who uses the deception to their advantage. They can, as Stanley Crouch put it in *Unforgivable Blackness*, "turn their opponent into an assistant in his own ass whipping."[46]

By contrast, brawlers do not hide their intent. Their strategy is overt aggression. Confident their unrelenting attack will wilt an opponent's desire, the brawler lacks any modicum of finesse. And even if his opposition is technically superior, the brawler knows there is only so much punishment their opponent can sustain before they either quit or abandon their patience and fall into their trap of turning the boxing match into a brawl. Brawlers are an uncomfortable reminder of the sport's savagery and can excite the darkest emotions.

De La Hoya was a boxer. Intelligence would be the basis of his strategy to beat Chávez. "People want to see blood and bruises," De La Hoya explained. "But I'm not going to give them that. I love boxing, but I hate fighting."[47] For his part, Chávez was equally confident he would defeat De La Hoya. "I'm not going to lose," Chávez said. "I have a lot of experience; I know a lot; I can take a hard punch; I have a hard punch; and I have other things—*cojones*."[48]

Chávez, as a brawler, took pride in his aggression. He saw and promoted his fighting style as proof of innate Mexican superiority in boxing. That earned him an even bigger following from the Mexican and Mexican American fan base while also allowing him to claim an authenticity De La Hoya lacked as a boxer who based his fighting on intelligence, not bravado. "Mexican boxing is very aggressive; you go forward with great heart," Chávez said. "The American style is always that you run around, you try to be elusive. The Mexican style is much better. I never tried to be elusive."[49]

As their fight was about to begin, Chávez stood there, relaxed as usual. De La Hoya stood in the opposite corner wearing his usual boxing trunks. They represented both his Mexican and American heritage, despite Mexican officials having threatened to sue him if he entered the ring wearing the flag on his trunks.[50] The announcer introduced Chávez. The crowd loudly approved. He then introduced De La Hoya, who received a mix of whistles, boos, and high-pitched cheers.

Just a minute into the fight, De La Hoya connected with what looked like a harmless jab, the most basic of punches. It opened a gash over Chávez's left eye. Commentators noticed the cut and called it harmless. As the round continued and Chávez's face gradually became covered in blood, the cut became visible to the crowd. They fell into a quiet, anxious state while De La Hoya used the cut as a target. He punched at it, opening it further with each successful connection. With a minute left in the first round, the referee stopped the fight, moved Chávez toward the neutral corner, and had the ringside doctor look at the cut. The doctor allowed the fight to continue, but as it did, the cut grew progressively worse. Finally, in the fourth round, the ringside doctor stopped the fight. De La Hoya, barely a mark on his handsome face, had left Chávez a bloody mess. "*Chinga tu madre*, De La Hoya!" a man yelled from the crowd. "Fuck him," a woman told her friend, also about De La Hoya, "man—fuck him, you know?"[51] The fight for Ultimate Glory was an easy victory for De La Hoya. Too easy.

Before the fight Arum and De La Hoya had assumed that once he beat Chávez, his many fans would naturally change allegiance. "They'll have to love him," Arum said of Mexican and Mexican American fans, "They won't have anybody else."[52] But despite Arum's and De La Hoya's naïve optimism, born of a bloodless economic understanding of popularity, that acceptance never came. Mexican and Mexican American boxing fans had not embraced Chávez because he never bled; rather, they embraced him precisely because he did. Chávez also refused to acknowledge De La Hoya's superiority, saying the cut had occurred during training. Chávez claimed De La Hoya's punches never hurt him. "I didn't even feel his punches," Chávez said. "I just couldn't see because of the blood."[53] An excuse, no doubt, but one he was not alone in making. Chávez's fans also refused to accept De La Hoya and the victory.

"You know, I'm learning how these people are," De La Hoya said about the lack of acceptance. "We call them *la raza*, ignorant. They don't know what boxing is. They don't have the slightest idea what a boxer is. They just want to see blood and guts, and that's all it is."[54] The statement only added to the tension between De La Hoya and parts of the Mexican and Mexican American community.

Boxing is violence. And as deplorable as that is for those who think our society should have advanced past a blood sport's brutality, it will exist as long as there is an "other." When it came to boxing and what they represented, De La Hoya and Chávez were each other's "other." De La Hoya yearned for the respect Chávez had in plenty, even from De La Hoya's family. "When I faced Chávez, the Mexican national hero, there were even times when family members . . . like my father was like, 'Hey, take it easy. He's our guy,'" De La Hoya said.[55] Chávez, on the other hand, resented that his hard-earned respect had not brought the material benefits or mass recognition that De La Hoya possessed. And as De La Hoya's star grew, Chávez further bristled at the notion that the young, pretty, unmacho Mexican American boxer was his equal inside the ring—and maybe even his superior. When neither could get what the other had, they each criticized the other for what they symbolized.

For De La Hoya, Chávez proved that "*la raza*" was too ignorant to appreciate anything other than blood and guts—a pointless machismo. For Chávez and those who identified with him, De La Hoya was the assimilated Mexican American who forgot who he was, becoming less Mexican and more gringo, a *vendido* who pushed the products of corporate America. De La Hoya achieved the mythical American Dream and, in doing so, flaunted it and its attainability in front of those who had long recognized it as, if not outright false, then more of a mirage.

Notes

1. The oldest newspaper article I found proclaiming boxing dead is from January 1895 after the death of boxer Con Riordan in Syracuse, New York. See "Ring Is Done For: Probability That There Will Be No More Gloved Fights," *Hopkinsville Kentuckian*, January 18, 1895, 6, *Chronicling America: Historic American Newspapers*. Library of Congress, http://chroniclingamerica.loc.gov/lccn/sn86069395/1895-01-18/ed-1/seq-6/.

2. Richard O'Brien, "El Mejor," *Sports Illustrated*, October 21, 1991, 68.

3. Michael Leahy, "The Not-So-Sweet Science of Selling Oscar De La Hoya," *Boxing Illustrated*, November 1993, 31, Hank Kaplan Boxing Collection, subgroup 12, series 5, box 28, folder 5, Brooklyn College.

4. Among his amateur accolades, De La Hoya won the National Golden Gloves Championship at age sixteen, was a two-time winner of the US Amateur Championship, a gold medalist in the 1990 Goodwill Games, and USA Amateur Boxing Federation named him their Boxer of the Year in 1991. De La Hoya also had a five-year unbeaten streak. See "Gold Rush '92," *KO Magazine*, October 1992, 31.

5. David Ferrell, "A Ring of Admirers," *Los Angeles Times*, August 13, 1992. http://articles.latimes.com/1992-08-13/local/me-5748_1_de-la-hoya.

6. Mike Dodd, "'Nothing is Going to Stop Me,'" *USA Today*, n.d., Hank Kaplan Boxing Collection, subgroup 15, series 1, box 7, folder 2, Brooklyn College.

7. The death of Oscar De La Hoya's mother became so ingrained in his narrative that even President George H. W. Bush referenced it when he congratulated the 1992 Summer Olympians. Bush stated, "Oscar de la Hoya, he not only brought home the gold, he brought honor to his mom's memory." See "Remarks Congratulating the United States Olympic Team," August 11, 1992, Public Papers, George Bush Presidential Library, https://bush41library.tamu.edu/archives/public-papers/4656.

8. Ferrell, "Ring of Admirers," *Los Angeles Times*.

9. Oscar De La Hoya, *American Son* (HarperCollins, 2008), 20.

10. Brittny Mejia and Kate Mather, "The 'Bad Old Days' in Boyle Heights Are Gone, but for How Long?" *Los Angeles Times*, September 2, 2016, http://www.latimes.com/local/lanow/la-me-ln-boyle-heights-lapd-20160824-snap-story.html.

11. Ferrell, "Ring of Admirers," *Los Angeles Times*.

12. Ferrell, "Ring of Admirers," *Los Angeles Times*.

13. "Your Wallet, Sir," n.d., Hank Kaplan Boxing Collection, subgroup 15, series 1, box 7, folder 2, Brooklyn College.

14. Damarys Ocaña, "Golden Boy: Oscar De La Hoya's Legendary Professional Boxing Career Began with an Emotional Gold Medal Win at the 1992 Olympics," *Latina*, August 2008, 128.

15. George Diaz, "De La Hoya, Vargas Bring Bad Blood," *Sun Sentinel*, September 14, 2002, http://articles.sun-sentinel.com/2002-09-14/sports/0209140008_1_hoya-professional-boxing-audience-mexico-s-proud-inner-circle.

16. Tim Kawakami, Golden Boy: The Fame, Money, and Mystery of Oscar De La Hoya (Andrews McMeel Publishing), 226.

17. Diaz, "De La Hoya, Vargas Bring Bad Blood," *Sun Sentinel*.

18. Kawakami, *Golden Boy*, 227.

19. Vic Ziegel, "Golden Boy," *Playboy*, July 1996, 114, Jack Newfield Papers, box number: 2006-274/170, Briscoe Center for American History, University of Texas at Austin.

20. Steve Farhood, "Golden Boy or Gold Digger? The Damaged Image of Oscar De La Hoya," *The Ring*, April 1994, 23, Joyce Sports Research Collection, box 7, Hesburgh Libraries of University of Notre Dame, Rare Books and Special Collections.

21. Kawakami, *Golden Boy*, 109.

22. De La Hoya's critics used golf as another symbol of his privilege. In playing golf, they perceived De La Hoya as becoming part of the upper class who played on exclusive country clubs where memberships is a mark of social class. "I read an article where somebody said, 'Why should De La Hoya play golf if he's not white?'" De La Hoya said of his critics. "Ridiculous. I play golf because I love it." Apart from the sport's association with the white upper class, there is an "often-voiced charge that golf is a 'faggot sport,' that golfers are unmanly in some sense." Adding to this "unmanly" image, the history of golf includes it being perceived as one of the only sports suitable for Victorian Age women to practice. Sports historian Murray G. Phillips says golf "complemented the cultural image of women that was essentially passive, non-aggressive and non-competitive. By fitting this image, golf did not claim the characteristics of sport that were traditionally masculine." Chávez never questioned De La Hoya's sexuality, but other boxers did. See Justin D. García, "Boxing, Masculinity, and Latinidad: Oscar De La Hoya, Fernando Vargas, and Raza Representations," *Journal of American Culture* 36, no. 4 (2013): 329; Richard J. Moss, *Golf and the American Country Club* (University of Illinois Press, 2001), 3; Murray G. Phillips, "Golf and Victorian Sporting Values," *Sporting Traditions* 16, no. 2 (1990): 128.

23. "The Hispanic Population: Census Brief," US Census Bureau, May 2001, 2, US Department of Commerce Economics and Statistics Administration, https://www.census.gov/prod/2001pubs/c2kbr01-3.pdf.

24. Language plays a vital role in marketing not just to the American audience but to the Hispanic audience as well. In "Racialization, Language, and Class in the Construction and Sale of the Hispanic Audience," América Rodríguez shows how, among advertisers, Spanish was a marker for lower-class audiences, while English targeted elite Hispanics: "Those who by virtue of their choice of English-language media are considered to be of a higher class, to have more disposable income, and therefore to be more attractive to advertisers." See América Rodríguez, "Racialization, Language, and Class in the Construction and Sale of the Hispanic Audience," in *Reflexiones 1997: New Directions in Mexican American Studies*, ed. Neil Foley (University of Texas Press, 1998), 44.

25. In 1908 Jack Johnson became boxing's first African American world heavyweight champion. With that, prizefighting entered the era of the "Great White Hope"—an all-encompassing label given to the white boxer who would defeat Johnson, reclaim the title for its supposed rightful owners and again, and reset the supposed order of racial hierarchy.

26. Leahy, "Not-So-Sweet Science," 29.

27. Leahy, "Not-So-Sweet Science."

28. Donald McRae, *Dark Trade: Lost in Boxing* (Mainstream Publishing, 1996), 345.

29. William Gildea, "De La Hoya Fighting Own Image," *Washington Post*,

June 6, 1996, https://www.washingtonpost.com/archive/sports/1996/06/06/de-la-hoya-fighting-his-own-image/e4b67660-6a47-4f5a-b8fd-79d5f7c48b2a/?noredirect=on&utm_term=.e07386c2c153.

30. Richard Hoffer, "The Pugilist and the Professor," *Sports Illustrated*, June 10, 1996, 84.

31. Tim Kawakami, "Things Starting to Add Up for De La Hoya," *Los Angeles Times*, September 8, 1995, http://articles.latimes.com/1995-09-08/sports/sp-43600_1_de-la-hoya.

32. Oscar De La Hoya vs. Felix Strum program, Hank Kaplan Boxing Collection, subgroup 13, series 1, box 10, folder 3, Brooklyn College.

33. Kawakami, *Golden Boy*, 98–99.

34. "The 50 Most Beautiful People in the World 1997," *People Weekly*, May 12, 1997, 82.

35. Gregory Rodríguez, "Boxing and Masculinity: The History and (Her) story of Oscar De La Hoya," in *Latino/a Popular Culture*, ed. Michelle Habell-Pallán and Mary Romero (New York University Press, 2002), 260.

36. Kawakami, *Golden Boy*, 278.

37. Kawakami, *Golden Boy*, 287.

38. Kawakami, "A Culture Clash: Scorn in East L.A.? Not Much De La Hoya Can Do about It," *Los Angeles Times*, June 6, 1996.

39. Kawakami, *Golden Boy*, 221.

40. De La Hoya, *American Son*, 139.

41. De La Hoya, *American Son*, 133–34. Arturo Madrid-Barela offers one of best descriptions capturing the term's essence. *Pocho* is "a general term to refer to the Mexicans north of the border, whose Mexicanness was suspect. It was not . . . affectionate . . . To be a pocho was only slightly less worse than being a pinche gringo. What Mexican culture we had managed to retain was insufficient as far as they were concerned. They could never understand why we did not speak the language of our fathers and mothers, or of our abuelitos. Our accommodations to American society were traiciones in their eyes, era agringarse." See Arturo Madrid-Barela, "Pochos: The Different Mexicans, An Interpretive Essay, Part I," *Aztlan: A Journal of Chicano Studies* 7, no. 1 (1976): 52.

42. Yxta Maya Murray, "Why East L.A. Hates Oscar De La Hoya," *Buzz*, August 1996, 82, Jack Newfield Papers, box number: 2006-274/170, Briscoe Center for American History, University of Texas at Austin.

43. Jennifer Reingold, "De La Hoya: 'I Can Lift the Name of Boxing,'" *Bloomberg*, July 6, 1997, https://www.bloomberg.com/news/articles/1997-07-06/de-la-hoya-i-can-lift-the-name-of-boxing.

44. Mark Kriegel "The Great (Almost) White Hope," in *At the Fights: American Boxers on Writing*, ed. George Kimball, John Schulian, and Colum McCann (Library of America, 2011), 431.

45. Chávez said that after fighting De La Hoya, for which he earned nine million dollars, he would retire. "There are people coming behind me, pushing

me very, very strongly. That's why I want to retire," he said of the younger generation of boxers. "My time has come . . . I don't know if I'll get to one hundred fights because I'm a little bit exhausted with boxing. I've had a lot of problems with my arms, with my knees. I really don't want to extend myself much longer . . . I am not giving what I used to be able to give. I will fight De La Hoya for a lot of money and then retire." See Kawakami, *Golden Boy*, 219; "De La Hoya and Chávez Pave the Way to a Payday," *New York Times*, February 10, 1996, https://www.nytimes.com/1996/02/10/sports/boxing-de-la-hoya-and-Chávez-pave-the-way-to-a-payday.html.

46. Ken Burns, *Unforgiveable Blackness: The Rise and Fall of Jack Johnson*, Florentine Films Inc., DVD, PBS Home Video, 2004.

47. Hoffer, "Pugilist and the Professor," 84.

48. Stephen Totilo, "Chávez-De La Hoya," *International Boxing Digest*, June 1996, 12, Hank Kaplan Boxing Collection, subgroup 12, series 5, box 29, folder 1, Brooklyn College.

49. Gregory Katz, "When Chávez Fights, Mexico's Honor Is on the Line," *Chicago Tribune*, October 12, 1993.

50. De La Hoya, *American Son*, 131. Nothing came from the threats, but, presumably, officials would sue De La Hoya as according to Mexican law, only the secretary of government can promote and regulate who can use the national flag. See Cámara de Diputados del H. Congreso de la Unión, Secretaría General, Secretaría de Servicios Parlamentarios, "Ley Sobre el Escudo, La Bandera Y el Himno Nacionales. Capitulo Cuarto: Del Uso, Difusión y Honores de la Bandera Nacional, Artículo 8º," http://www.diputados.gob.mx/LeyesBiblio/pdf/213_110518.pdf.

51. Murray, "Why East L.A. Hates Oscar De La Hoya," 119.

52. Hoffer, "Pugilist and the Professor," 84.

53. Hoffer, "Pugilist and the Professor," 84.

54. Tim Kawakami, "De La Hoya Coming to Grips with Less-than-Golden Slights," Los Angeles Times, October 7, 1996, http://articles.latimes.com/1996-10-07/sports/sp-51431_1_de-la-hoya.

55. "Oscar: Chávez Fight Changed Things," ESPN.com, March 6, 2015, http://www.espn.com/boxing/story/_/id/12434436/oscar-de-la-hoya-says-julio-Cesár-Chávez-fight-was-turning-point.

References

PRIMARY SOURCES

Archival Collections

George Bush Presidential Library and Museum, Texas A&M University, College Station, Texas

Hank Kaplan Boxing Collection, Brooklyn College

Jack Newfield Papers, Briscoe Center for American History, University of Texas at Austin
Sports Illustrated Vault

Books and Other Documents

Cámara de Diputados del H. Congreso de la Unión.
De La Hoya, Oscar. 2008. *American Son: My Story*. HarperCollins.
US Census Bureau, 2001.

Videos

Burns, Ken. *2004. Unforgivable Blackness: The Rise and Fall of Jack Johnson.* Florentine Films Inc., DVD. PBS Home Video.
Diego Luna. 2010. *JC Chavez: El Ultimo Heroe Mexicano*. Virgil Films and Entertainment, DVD. ESPN Home Entertainment.

Newspapers

Chicago Tribune
Los Angeles Times
New York Times
Sun Sentinel
USA Today
Washington Post

Magazines

Bloomberg
Boxing Illustrated
Buzz
International Boxing Digest
KO Magazine
Latina
People Weekly
Playboy
The Ring
Ultimate Glory: Official Program

SECONDARY SOURCES

García, Justin D. 2013. "Boxing, Masculinity, and Latinidad: Oscar De La Hoya, Fernando Vargas, and Raza Representations." *Journal of American Culture* 36, no. 4: 323–41.
Gomez, Laura E. 2007. *Manifest Destinies: The Making of the Mexican American Race*. New York University Press.
Kawakami, Tim. 1999. *Golden Boy: The Fame, Money, and Mystery of Oscar De La Hoya*. Andrews McMeel Publishing.

Kriegel, Mark. 2011. "The Great (Almost) White Hope." In *At the Fights: American Boxers on Writing*, edited by George Kimball, John Schulian, and Colum McCann, 419–33. Library of America.

Madrid-Barela, Arturo. 1976. "Pochos: The Different Mexicans, an Interpretive Essay, Part I." *Aztlan: A Journal of Chicano Studies* 7, no. 1: 51–64.

McRae, Donald. 1996. *Dark Trade: Lost in Boxing*. Mainstream Publishing.

Moss, Robert J. 2001. *Golf and the American Country Club*. University of Illinois Press.

Phillips, Murray G. 1990. "Golf and Victorian Sporting Values." *Sporting Traditions* 16, no. 2: 120–34.

Rodríguez, América. 1998. "Racialization, Language, and Class in the Construction and Sale of the Hispanic Audience." In *Reflexiones 1997: New Directions in Mexican American Studies*, edited by Neil Foley, 29–51. University of Texas Press, 1998.

Rodríguez, Gregory S. 2002. "Boxing and Masculinity: The History and (Her) story of Oscar De La Hoya." In *Latino/a Popular Culture*, edited by Michelle Habell-Pallán and Mary Romero. New York University Press.

7

"Yo Soy José De Avenal"

The Deployment of Expressive Culture in Disruptive Ring Entrances

RUDY MONDRAGÓN

Athletic activism and performances of dissent are increasingly prominent in sports. The twenty-first century has seen national anthem protests by professional athletes like Colin Kaepernick in football, Megan Rapinoe in soccer, and Bruce Maxwell in baseball. These anthem protests, refusing to stand during "The Star-Spangled Banner," build on a rich history that includes track star Eroseanna Robinson's 1959 anthem protest, John Carlos and Tommie Smith's 1968 Olympics Black Power salute, and Mahmoud Abdul-Rauf's 1995–1996 NBA season protest (Farmer 2016). A month before Kaepernick's anthem protest in 2016, players from the WNBA's Minnesota Lynx and New York Liberty demanded justice and accountability for Philando Castile and Alton Sterling, both men shot and killed by police.[1] Critical sports journalist Dave Zirin (2016c) notes that in 2010 "the entire Phoenix Suns team wore shirts that read *Los Suns* as a statement of solidarity with Latino people in Arizona threatened by the brutal anti-immigrant bill, SB 1070."

Protests take many forms and challenge a myriad of injustices. At the 2018 French Open, Serena Williams wore a black catsuit, disrupting symbolic and fixed meanings of the tennis "dress," a sporting fashion that reinforces acceptable aesthetics of femininity within the sport. Williams's wearing the catsuit was so politically disruptive that French Tennis Federation president Bernard Giudicelli called the act a sign of disrespect to "the game and place" (Shmerler 2018). Williams's 2002 US Open catsuit had similarly sparked reactions from admiration to disgust, the latter anchored by ideologies that reproduce a hegemonic racialized order in women's tennis (Schultz 2005). All of these instances illustrate the broad spectrum of athletic activism and performances of dissent across sports.

While narrative accounts of activism in the broader sports world proliferate in media and academic literature, they are virtually nonexistent in boxing. Specifically, there is an analytic and narrative void in the critical sports literature in recognizing the successors of Muhammad Ali who have also staged public challenges to racial and many other forms of oppression. Locating the history of activism and dissent in the world of boxing requires alternative interpretations and analysis of the sport. Scholars need to look deeper into the archive of boxing to excavate narratives like that of Sugar Ray Leonard, who in his June 12, 1989, fight against Thomas "Hitman" Hearns entered the ring wearing a white-and-red-striped robe displaying a subversive message. At the time, broadcaster Tim Ryan quickly pointed out the word "Amandla" stitched onto the back of Leonard's robe, yet he incorrectly translated it as "'freedom' in an African dialect."[2] Not only did Ryan miseducate the world on the word's political meaning, but he also reduced the significance of Leonard's efforts, as *amandla* is the isiNguni word for "power" (Dalamba 2012, 312). It was used by the African National Congress and its allies as a rallying cry in resistance efforts against apartheid in South Africa. In call-and-response fashion, "Amandla!" was called out, followed by "*Awethu*!" or "*Ngawethu*!" (to us), the words together forming a South African version of "Power to the people!"

Oscar De La Hoya also had a significant moment of activism. During his ring entrance against Ricardo "El Matador" Mayorga on May 6, 2006, he wore a white headband with the words "No HR-4437." Sponsored by Wisconsin Republican Jim Sensenbrenner, H.R. 4437, or the Border Protection, Antiterrorism, and Illegal Immigration Control Act of 2005, "would have implemented more severe penalties for undocumented presence in the United States, changing it from a civil infraction to a criminal offense, and called for criminal penalties against religious and charitable organizations that provide relief" to undocumented immigrants (García 2013, 72).

Leonard and De La Hoya demonstrate how fashion politics can be deployed in ring entrances to deliver subtle yet powerful messages curated by fighters. (In some cases, political statements can continue during the fight when a boxer's ring attire is adorned with messages and symbols of dissent. This was the case for Leonard, as "Amandla" was shown not only on the back of his robe but also on the front waistband of his trunks.) For minoritized boxers, the role of ring entrances is evident. I have argued that ring entrances regularly serve as ephemeral performative spaces where boxers can address social justice issues, challenge structural and ideological discourses of power, and reimagine a liberated alternative world

(Mondragón 2022). As such, the ring entrance serves as a unique site to examine the ways boxers perform dissent and engage in athletic activism.

Still, critical sports scholars have overlooked the ritual of the ring entrance, a cultural text ripe for interrogation and analysis. Ring entrances have historically been contested sites that reinforce racial, national, gender, and other political and social structures. For example, on the day Jack Johnson became the first Black heavyweight champion of the world in 1908, he entered the ring to the crowd's violent calls of "Nier!" and "Cn!" prompting Johnson to smile, laugh, bow, and blow kisses "at those who yelled the loudest" (Lamb 2016, 1). In April 2018, Pennsylvanian fighter "Lightning" Rod Salka wore boxing trunks in a fabric printed in a border wall of red and blue bricks, with the words "America 1st" stitched onto the front waistband. Facing the Mexican-born boxer Francisco "El Bandito" Vargas, Salka had chosen this fashion to express and reinforce white supremacy and anti-immigrant xenophobia. Although ring entrances can be contested sites influenced by dominant social structures within their historical context, they can also be a space where fighters exercise their agency and perform dissent based on their lived experiences, identities, and expressive culture.

In this chapter, I examine the life and ring entrance performances of boxer José Carlos Ramírez of Avenal, California, who was described by his former promoter, Bob Arum, as "the most socially involved American fighter since Muhammad Ali" (Iole 2018). For my analysis, I draw on news sources; YouTube videos; fieldwork notes from attending Ramírez's September 2018 fight in Fresno, California; and data from an interview I conducted with Ramírez in January 2019. I argue that boxing ring entrances can be insubordinate spaces of subtle and fluid performances of dissent, disruption, and resistance to dominant ideologies and power structures. The following sections include discussions about ring entrances and their performative aspects and deployment of expressive culture. I then share Ramírez's biography, including his early beginnings of working in Central Valley bell pepper fields, which is important in understanding his intentionality in collaborating with the California Latino Water Coalition to support its political efforts and in advocating for agricultural migrant workers. Finally, I analyze Ramírez's ring entrance to his fight on September 14, 2018, which I read as a performance of rebellion and dissent against Donald Trump's anti-immigrant politics.

On Ring Entrances, Performativity, and Expressive Culture

The ring entrance has always been a part of boxing. It is a prefight ritual that provides theatrical entertainment, building up the spectacle of the fight yet lasting only a short time. During these brief moments, boxers creatively express themselves, making themselves marketable and visible to their fans by performing new identities, identifications, personalities, and affiliations. Additionally, ring entrances are spaces where dissent is performed. I have argued that ring entrances can be transformed from a space of spectacle and entertainment into an insubordinate space that can disrupt the social order within and beyond the boundaries of boxing (Mondragón 2022). Feminist scholar Barbara Tomlinson and Black studies scholar George Lipsitz define insubordinate spaces as "sites where people who lack material resources display great resourcefulness in deepening the capacity to free themselves and others from subordination, to imagine how things could be otherwise, and to move toward enacting that vision" (2019, 12). Thus, the ring entrance serves as an ephemeral space of possibilities, where fighters can use their imaginations, creativity, expressive culture, and histories to curate performances of dissent.

But in order to perform dissent in ring entrances, boxers must navigate a neoliberal, hypercapitalist, exploitative, and underregulated sports industry. Zirin (2016b) posits, "No sport has chewed up athletes—especially Black athletes—and spit them out quite the way boxing has." Boxing historian Jeffrey T. Sammons (1990) reminds us that many written accounts show that the first boxers were enslaved Black men, with enslavers pitting their strongest against another for both the "glory of the plantation and sizable wagers" (31). This exploitation of the most vulnerable boxers continues to this day. Their vulnerability lies in how they are classified not as employees but as independent contractors in a sports industry that is not centrally governed and does not provide them with a minimum salary, health care, or pension plan for their risky work.[3] Only a select few, known as the cash cows of boxing, have multi-fight and multimillion-dollar contracts with reputable promoters. This is the goal for every boxer, yet there is little room at the top of the boxing hierarchy. As boxers rise in the rankings, they must build a dedicated fan base and prove their financial worth to promoters. Therefore, carefully calculated performances of dissent are necessary for vulnerable boxers. Speaking on subordinate groups, renowned social scientist James Scott (1990) observes, "Their vulnerability has rarely permitted them the luxury of direct confrontation" (136). For boxers, overt performances of dissent risk their being labeled "difficult to work with" by promoters and the media or being ostracized within an industry that measures a fighter's value by their ability to perform inside the ring as well as entertain a captive audience. Fighters who can no longer perform in the ring in an industry lacking an organizational structure to support them are effectively disposable.[4]

In *Race Rebels*, Robin D. G. Kelley (1996) argues that Black working-class resistance has taken place in multiple forms, such as in rap music, churches, households, poetry, dance halls, and public transit. Kelley's argument can also be applied to sporting spaces, like the ring entrance, as Black and Brown prizefighters use discursive strategies to assert their agency, imagining and performing dissent, dignity, and collectivity. In the public sphere of boxing, fighters use clever and indirect methods in their ring entrances to express themselves. One method is the deployment of expressive culture—specifically, fashion and style, music, and the presence and composition of an entourage. Through expressive culture, multiple messages of dissent can be observed. Boxing is unique in that fighters are not restricted to wearing team uniforms like their counterparts in the National Basketball Association or in Major League Baseball. Fighters can choose their boxing attire, the song playing as they enter the ring, and the entourage accompanying them to the ring. Deploying these forms of expressive culture is a unique type of agency that all fighters have: the ability to express themselves as they see fit. Yet, as boxers perform these expressions, they must continually navigate the reality that ring entrances are part of the neoliberal and hypercapitalist theater that fuels the financial machine of the boxing industry.

Boxing trainer and commentator Theodore "Teddy" Atlas describes contemporary ring entrances as performances of self-celebration tangled within a capitalist reality:

> The ring walk in boxing is part of a tradition, two fighters taking a short but long journey to a place that's dangerous and dark. That's lost now. It's not about introspection or history or tradition anymore. It's about self-celebration and how sensational can we make it. Ring walks today look like a Grammy Awards show because the people who run things have decided that's the way to generate more money. That's the economic reality of the situation, and it doesn't matter whether I like it or not.[5]

Atlas speaks to a critique of the modern-day ring entrance, which, he argues, breaks away from tradition, has become too elaborate, and glorifies the celebration of the individual fighter. Though he is correct that boxers have borrowed showmanship strategies from the entertainment industry, he fails to mention the importance of self-marketing that fighters must engage in to generate a fan base and sell tickets for their fights. Atlas also disregards the power of ring entrances in allowing fighters to author their own stories and center their narratives to express their multiple identities and politics. According to boxing writer Thomas Hauser (2018), Ralph Dupas (see Louis Moore's chapter in the present text), a welterweight fighter from New Orleans who competed in the 1950s and 1960s, walked to the ring while playing blues music. Hauser adds that Muhammad Ali was innovative during the later years of his career, "entering the ring to face Earnie Shavers to the majestic sound of the theme from *Star Wars*." Hauser illuminates the connection between ring entrances and the use of music to signal regional affinities as well as to entertain and excite.

Below the surface of a ring entrance, however, are layers that require a closer reading. For instance, North Philadelphia fighter Bernard Hopkins exemplifies how fighters deploy fashion and style to convey their stories and make statements about what they represent. During his illustrious career, Hopkins was famous for entertaining his fans by entering the ring wearing custom-made masks that represented different personas:

> I had two characters when I was fighting. The first was The Executioner. The second was The Alien. They came to the ring in different ways. The Executioner was angry. The Executioner had a boulder on his shoulder. The Executioner was all about inflicting pain and destruction. Two big guys came out with me wearing masks and boots and carrying swords. The Alien came later in my career and was about, "Look at me. I'm as old as the hills and beating guys half my age." Both ways, I was making a statement.[6]

To understand The Executioner's anger and that "boulder on his shoulder," we must go back to 1984, when seventeen-year-old Hopkins was sentenced to eighteen years in prison.[7] Hopkins was imprisoned during the height of the 1980s' "war on drugs," and while serving his time, he became the state penitentiary champion and realized that boxing offered the possibility of a life beyond poverty and imprisonment.[8] After his early release in 1988, Hopkins made his professional debut in the same year and lost, earning a dismal $350 for his work. He took sixteen months off to reflect on whether he wanted to fully commit himself to boxing. When he decided to continue with the sport, Hopkins "came back with a terror."[9] The Executioner was the alter ego that came after his prison sentence. To embody this persona, he wore a mask, donning it when he eventually captured his first world title, against Segundo Mercado, in 1995. He then went on to dominate the division, amassing twenty consecutive defenses of his International Boxing Federation (IBF) World Middleweight title between 1995 and 2005. In an interview with Hopkins, he said the persona served as a tool of intimidation. He wanted his opponents to be nervous as he walked slowly to the ring, forcing them to have to wait for their eventual execution.[10]

The Alien persona emerged years later, leading up to the fight against Karo Murat in 2013, which was Hopkins's first defense of the IBF World Light Heavyweight title. Hopkins had adopted The Alien nickname before that fight to explain that "aliens don't have years, months, days, or minutes" (Rafael 2013). At age forty-eight, he outboxed his thirty-year-old opponent and won by a unanimous decision. As The Alien, Hopkins was asserting his agency to recharge his marketability in the final stage of his career to stay relevant in the boxing industry and secure future fight contracts. He went on to fight three more times as The Alien before retiring as the oldest fighter in boxing history to become a world champion.

The performances and deployment of expressive culture by Hopkins and the others mentioned previously speak to the ways that boxers' stories, identities, and firsthand experiences are reflected in their ring entrance performances. In the next section, I discuss José Carlos Ramírez's biography and the connections between his identity, lived experiences, and activism, all critical components that inform how he has chosen to step into the ring as an activist-fighter.

Biography of an Activist-Fighter

In *Freedom's Web*, a text about 1990s activism, Robert A. Rhoads (1998) posits that a person's sense of identity and connection to others is fundamental to organizing efforts. Discussing Ramírez's biography and lived experiences helps us to better understand why he uses his boxing platform to advocate for undocumented immigrant workers.

Ramírez was born on August 12, 1992, and raised in Avenal, a small agricultural town in the Central Valley of California. He was born on the eve of the 1994 passing of California's Proposition 187 (later found unconstitutional by a federal district court), an anti-immigrant law also known as the Save Our State initiative, which prohibited undocumented immigrants from accessing health care, public education, and other public services. Both of his parents were born in Mexico and later immigrated to the Central Valley. His mother came from La Piedad, Michoacán, and his father from Baja California.

Ramírez's boxing journey started at the age of seven after his father came home from work one day and had signed him up for boxing lessons (Magagnini 2018). At this point, Ramírez was already playing soccer and baseball, but his father wanted him involved in a year-round sport. A year later, Ramírez stepped into the ring for his first amateur match, slated to take place in Fresno against a boxer from Visalia. He was victorious, and after the fight, Ramírez experienced a new kind of validation from the community. "Fresno was like New York to me," he recalls. "Having my hand raised, and people calling me champion as I walked down from the ring in front of at least four hundred people, it was amazing."[11]

As Ramírez developed his craft as a fighter, he was also being exposed to the harsh work conditions that migrant agricultural workers in the Central Valley endure. Witnessing his industrious family toiling under severe labor conditions and experiencing it firsthand built a foundation for Ramírez's resiliency, political consciousness, and activist identity. Ramírez first started working in the bell pepper fields at the age of fourteen. He was excited because working meant he could financially assist his parents and not burden them with the cost of material items and leisure activities that most teenagers desired.[12] Waking up for work every morning before 5:00 a.m. was a difficult task. Though not easy, it was familiar to Ramírez, who recalls being eight years old and watching his parents prepare for their twelve-hour work shifts.[13]

One workday, Ramírez arrived at the bell pepper fields to start his morning shift before sunrise. By noon, the temperature was north of one hundred degrees, punishing Ramírez and the other workers. That kind of heat takes a toll on people. "Before you know it," Ramírez says, "we slowed down because we [got] tired. Our backs were tired, so we [got down] on our knees now, [to] pick the bell peppers, and then scoot over with our knees, kind of grinding our jeans in the dirt."[14] Moments later, Ramírez heard what sounded like a woman moaning. He looked in the direction of the sounds and saw a woman collapsed, her arms stretched out against the dirt to help break her fall. Ramírez quickly responded by alerting his friend to cover his work area while he assisted the woman. As he comforted her, other workers urgently alerted the driver of the oncoming harvesting machine. When they finally got the driver to stop, the front of the tractor was only a few feet away from Ramírez and the woman. She was sent home, but Ramírez remembers seeing her back in the bell pepper fields the next day:

> She was back the next morning! That's when it helps you build character because you understand that even though these jobs are difficult, [the workers] have this different mentality, because they don't complain. There's no room to complain in their lives. They got a family to feed. She's responsible for someone at home. And that's when my respect really grew as a young guy, for my parents, for anybody out there.[15]

As Ramírez shares this memory, his voice and body language communicate great concern for this woman.[16] His conceptualization of character ties directly to observing the inhuman conditions that agricultural workers are subjected to. In this harsh environment, Ramírez has witnessed the unbreakable, resilient spirit these workers both possess and require. His show of connection with agricultural workers is not a meaningless gesture. Rather, it is rooted in a lived experience that informs his performance of pugilistic activism in his ring entrances as well as outside the ring.

Business-Savvy Boxer: Transforming Arenas into Spaces of Political Mobilization

Ramírez is a significant figure to examine because, as he is performing dissent from his ring entrance platform, he is navigating a neoliberal, hypercapitalist, exploitative, and underregulated boxing industry that recruits boxers from racially and socioeconomically marginalized backgrounds. From an industry standpoint, boxing embraces a neoliberal logic, which David J. Leonard (2017) has defined as focusing on individualism, self-reliance, and free markets that resonate with American exceptionalism and meritocracy. Ramírez leverages the neoliberal logic of rugged individualism that fuels the boxing industry by advocating for himself on the business side of boxing and exploiting the ironies of American exceptionalism. In other words, Ramírez's boxing accomplishments, which are praised under the ideology of American exceptionalism, empower and allow Ramírez to create opportunities to use his celebrity platform to engage in political performances of dissent.

The Avenal pugilist gained national recognition when he represented the United States at the London 2012 Summer Olympics. Although he did not win, Ramírez and his manager, Rick Mirigian, used the momentum generated from competing in the games to negotiate a deal with Top Rank Incorporated, a boxing promotional company. Their pitch to Top Rank was that Central Valley was an emerging boxing market and that Ramírez would be the right candidate to lead its development efforts due to his Central Valley fan base and exposure from the Olympics.[17] After negotiations, Top Rank signed Ramírez on November 14, 2012, to a professional contract that allowed him to co-promote his fights in the Central Valley twice a year over five years.

Before co-promoting the first event, Ramírez and Mirigian took on the tasks of organizing partnerships in the Central Valley, investing their own money to pay for a television licensing fee, and ensuring that Ramírez stayed undefeated in his first six professional fights. Co-promoting allowed

Ramírez not only to share in the profits from his fights but also to increase his fan base, an essential part of the business that supports a fighter's career. For Ramírez, a solid Central Valley fan base would provide an audience for his messages of dissent in his ring entrances.

Ramírez's first co-promoted match in the Central Valley was to take place on November 9, 2013. Co-promoting a boxing event in the Central Valley was difficult, as Ramírez and his team had assumed great risk. Part of the deal that Ramírez and Mirigian had reached with Top Rank was that they would pay the company for the television licensing fee to bring a boxing event to the Central Valley. A major television network rarely takes a chance on a young prospect fighter. According to Article 12, Section 18824 (3), of the California state legislature, the Department of Consumer Affairs' California State Athletic Commission requires a 5 percent fee of the gross price for the sale, lease, or other exploitation of broadcasting or television rights.[18] This fee can range from one thousand to thirty-five thousand dollars. With this fee settled and UniMás—an American Spanish-language free-to-air television network owned by Univision Communications—signed on to broadcast Ramírez's first fight in the Central Valley, Top Rank agreed to co-promote the event.

Ramírez and Mirigian were also responsible for securing the hotel rooms that Top Rank required to accommodate the staff and fighters participating in the event. Rather than using their own money for this expense, Ramírez and his team established partnerships with local hotels, convincing them to invest in Central Valley boxing by providing rooms.[19] On top of organizing local businesses and securing a network to broadcast the event, Ramírez had to continue winning his scheduled fights. In 2013 he won his five remaining fights while working with his team to finalize the business logistics for his November event.

In addition, Ramírez was cultivating a partnership with the California Latino Water Coalition (CLWC). Created in 2007, the advocacy group represents and addresses the concerns of Latinos in farm-related employment, who are often unheard and tend to be the first to lose their jobs when water supplies are reduced.[20] The coalition argues for legislation for improved water infrastructure, governance, and conservation; organizes community events to raise public awareness and gain support; and has helped frame California's comprehensive water infrastructure and supply package. Ramírez was first introduced to members of the CLWC when he started his professional boxing career in 2012. As Ramírez and Mirigian listened to Mario Santoyo, CLWC director and technical advisor, on the *Ray Appleton Show* on KMJ talk radio, it made sense for them to get involved with the organization to help tackle the drought problem in the Central Valley. Ramírez reached out to the CLWC with the intent to learn about the issues and find a way to support its work. Though members of the coalition knew who Ramírez was, they were confused and unsure about what this young man could offer them. In multiple meetings with CLWC members, Ramírez learned they were trying to pass a water storage bill. That bill was Proposition 1, a measure that would authorize $7.12 billion in general obligation bonds for state water supply infrastructure projects, such as public water systems, surface and groundwater storage, and clean drinking water.[21]

On November 9, 2013, Ramírez's first co-promoted match in the Central Valley took place at West Hills Golden Eagle Arena at Lemoore College in Lemoore, California. It was also the first of three fights where Ramírez used his athletic platform to raise awareness and mobilize people toward the water crisis in the Central Valley. Ramírez had created a plan to use his co-promoted fights in the Central Valley to generate momentum and mobilize people to vote in favor of Proposition 1 on November 4, 2014. In his first co-promoted fight, called Fight for Water 1, Ramírez knocked out Erick Hernandez forty-seven seconds into the first round. Ramírez had earned another win, but a larger victory was on the young pugilist's mind:

> Well, the fight united everyone. They saw the momentum of being on Univision Deportes–UniMás being aired nationwide. I was 6-0 being in the main event. It was my first JCR [José Carlos Ramírez] co-promoting with Top Rank at 6-0 in a 3,000-[person] venue, sold out. And people wearing blue shirts—"Fight for Water" blue shirts—that's where Top Rank really saw, "Man, if José filled three thousand people, that's definitely a great start."[22]

Ramírez straddled two distinct yet compatible worlds: boxing's business side and athletic activism. As a prizefighter in a brutal business, Ramírez needed to assure his promoter that he could market himself to develop a profitable fan base, this being critical for the success of any professional fighter. Top Rank was pleased that Ramírez and his team had drawn a capacity crowd and sold closer to thirty-six hundred tickets, according to Mirigian (Elliot 2015). Ramírez's fight also set a Univision television network record for attendance, revenue, and number of sponsors. His business efforts and activism had allowed him to amplify the work of the CLWC to a captive audience he would not have reached without his participation in the boxing industry.

Ramírez has described his activist efforts as "my job," meaning he understood that he could leverage his celebrity power and the entertainment of boxing to organize people in support of Proposition 1. Ramírez's plan was to raise awareness of and educate boxing fans on the bill using the first two co-promoted fights. Intentionally naming the events Fight for Water was not the only action that Ramírez and his team took in their attempt to unite fans. Leading up to Fight for Water 1, for example, Ramírez and Paul Rodriguez, comedian and chair of the CLWC, did a public service announcement together in which they encouraged fans to attend Ramírez's November 9 fight and to join Ramírez and the CLWC's fight to address the Central Valley water crisis.

Inside the arena, a CLWC banner hung above the ring next to the banners of businesses sponsoring the event: Wonderful Pistachios, Sony PlayStation, Top Rank, Tecate beer, Chevron, Tachi Palace Hotel and Casino, and Harris Family Enterprises. The CLWC logo was also on the ring mat, strategically placed in the corners where the fighters sit between rounds. On the night of the fight, members of the coalition and Ramírez's team wore and handed out custom-made blue shirts that featured a photo of Ramírez throwing a straight right punch, the CLWC logo, the date of the fight, and the words "Fight for Water" printed above the fighter's right boxing glove. The shirts were another means to increase visibility and foster solidarity in the name of Proposition 1. Similar strategies and actions were taken for Fight for Water 2, which saw Ramírez knock out Jesus Selig on May 17, 2014 (Elliot 2015).

The goal for his third fight, which took place October 25, 2014, at the larger Selland Arena in Fresno, was to spur his fans to vote in favor of Proposition 1 on November 4. Fight for Water 3 had a sold-out crowd of approximately ten thousand fans (Elliot 2015). This figure was a substantial jump from his first Central Valley fight, which had attracted just over three thousand fans. Less than a month later, Proposition 1 passed with 67 percent of the votes. But more importantly, Ramírez's collective partnership with the CLWC to elevate its political cause had disrupted the neoliberal ideas of individualism and meritocracy in boxing for the mere sake of capitalizing on a fan base for financial gain. This partnering enabled Ramírez to reach a new audience that stemmed from the coalition's network and to inform and mobilize his boxing fans about the water crisis in the Central Valley.

Indeed, this effort of political mobilization did not arise from Ramírez alone. Just as the roots of the revolt of the Black athlete had sprung from the sit-ins, freedom rides, and rebellions in Watts, Detroit, and Newark (Edwards 2017), Ramírez's athletic activism is connected to the historical struggles and legacies of the Bracero Program workers and the organizing efforts of the United Farm Workers, who demanded better work conditions, compensation, and treatment for agricultural workers.

Walking to the Ring in the Donald Trump Era

Central to Ramírez's athletic activism and his creation of insubordinate sporting spaces is the performance of his political convictions and dissent from the sociopolitical structures that emerged during Donald Trump's first presidency. In *The Archive and the Repertoire*, Diana Taylor (2003) argues that performance "constitutes the methodological lens that enables scholars to analyze events *as* performance" (3). Events like civil disobedience, resistance, citizenship, race, ethnicity, culture, and masculinities "are rehearsed and performed daily in the public sphere."[23] In this case, I analyze Ramírez's September 14, 2018, ring entrance as a performance of dissent in opposition to both the United States' long history of anti-immigrant racist nativism and its reinforcement by Trump and his administration.

Before Ramírez's fourth co-promoted match in December against Johnny Garcia at the Save Mart Center in Fresno, Donald Trump had formally announced his candidacy for president of the United States in June 2015. Staged inside the Trump Tower in Manhattan, Trump introduced his "Make America Great Again" (MAGA) campaign slogan and unleashed a racist nativist speech that overtly villainized and dehumanized undocumented immigrants from Mexico, stating:

> When Mexico sends its people, they're not sending their best. They're not sending you. They're not sending you. They're sending people that have lots of problems, and they're bringing those problems with us. They're bringing drugs. They're bringing crime. They're rapists. And some, I assume, are good people.[24]

It was during this speech that Ramírez became aware of Trump's anti-immigrant politics and was prompted to act. Through a fusion of liberal activism and strategic marketing, Ramírez's promoter, Bob Arum, created the No Trump undercard matches as part of the HBO pay-per-view program that set up the main event bout between Manny Pacquiao and Timothy Bradley on April 9, 2016. The No Trump undercard was made up of three Top Rank–signed fighters: Mexican national Gilberto Ramírez and US-born Mexicans Oscar Valdez and José Ramírez. In a *Fox Sports* article, Arum comments on the impact of this event, writing, "The more Donald Trump supporters I alienate, the prouder I am. I know who he's appealing to, and if they're his supporters, let them stay home and not buy my fight" (Dahlberg 2016). As a liberal activist and businessman, Arum took a strong political stand against Trump that also served as a catchy way to bring attention to the Pacquiao–Bradley fight, which media pundits said was proving to be a tough sell (Dahlberg 2016). Ramírez saw an opportunity to make a political statement of his own during the promotion of the No Trump undercard and told the media he was troubled by Trump's plan to build a giant wall and deport millions of undocumented immigrants. He declared that he was "not going to just ignore it. I want to use this fight to deliver a message. If we ignore it, obviously he might get away with what he wants" (Dahlberg 2016).

Ramírez kept his word as he continued to build on the momentum generated from the No Trump undercard to his eventual fight with Amir Imam in New York on March 17, 2018. This was the most important fight of his career as it was his first championship title bout. It was also the first time Ramírez officially dedicated a fight to immigration reform. During a press conference, he wore a refashioned red hat that resembled Trump's MAGA hats, with the distinction that Ramírez's sported in blue and white stitching the stylized words "Pro-Immigrant and Proud." Ramírez won that fight, not only becoming the World Boxing Council (WBC) World Super Lightweight champion but also amplifying his support for immigration reform and dissent from Trump's anti-immigrant xenophobic message.

Six months later, Ramírez's first defense of his WBC title took place at the Save Mart Center. The official attendance for his September 14, 2018, match against Antonio Orozco was 11,102. This number includes the 80 tickets purchased by Harris Family Enterprises for their agricultural workers, who cheered on Ramírez from sections 122 and 123 (see fig. 7.1). As is the case for most champions, Ramírez entered the ring second. His ring entrance lasted no more than ninety seconds, yet it consisted of multiple deployments of expressive culture that coincided with his pro-immigrant-and-proud message. Seated in the media section of the arena, I witnessed Ramírez and his entourage wait patiently at the edge of the tunnel that bridged the dressing rooms to the boxing ring. His entourage consisted of Mirigian, famed boxing trainer Robert Garcia, Ramírez's younger brother, and the Fresno Fuego soccer team mascot.

Also part of the entourage was Chuy Jr., playing the important role of composer and singer of Ramírez's ring entrance music. José Jesús Chávez Jr. was born in Fresno and is the son of the founder and lead singer of Los Originales de San Juan, Jesús "Chuy" Chávez. Chuy Jr. wrote and performed "Yo Soy José De Avenal," a *corrido* that highlights Ramírez's hometown roots, perfectionist work ethic, courageous no-quit spirit, son Matteo Maximiliano, and his mother's hometown of La Piedad, Michoacán.

A corrido is a rich and expressive song narrative of Mexican cultural tradition. According to María Herrera-Sobek (1990), corridos are a popular musical genre consisting of a structured ballad that "lends itself to either a male or a female protagonist" and recounts a story in either the first or

Figure 7.1. Boxing fans and agricultural workers from Harris Family Enterprises showing their support by wearing José Carlos Ramírez hats. (Photo by Rudy Mondragón.)

third person (xviii). Mexican revolutionaries Pancho Villa and Emiliano Zapata are two popular figures memorialized by corridos. The narratives speak about the Mexican Revolution, which lasted from approximately 1910 to 1920. Chuy Jr.'s corrido is a counternarrative, however, that provided a moment of disruption to Trump's racist nativist rhetoric directed at undocumented Mexican immigrants, whom Trump had essentialized as drug smugglers and rapists.

Shana L. Redmond (2014), an interdisciplinary scholar of music and race, posits that music is a method and more than just sound: "It is a complex system of mean(ing)s and ends that mediate our relationships to one another, to space, to our histories and historical moment" (1). For Ramírez, it was important that his fans related and felt connected to him during the duration of his ring walk. The centering of Ramírez's narrative in Chuy Jr.'s corrido intensified the collective pride of the fans who were there to cheer their fighter on. Chuy Jr.'s live performance functioned that night as a framing device that transformed the Save Mart Center into a constellation of collectivity where Ramírez proclaimed his solidarity with migrant (un)documented agricultural workers who had been historically denied their rights and humanity and further dehumanized by Trump and his administration.

As Ramírez and his team waited at the edge of the tunnel for his ring entrance, fans chanted supportive messages reflecting their Central Valley roots—"You can do this shit!"—"From Delano, homey!"—"Avenal, homey!"—"Knock his ass out!" This engagement speaks to how fans actively participate in a boxer's ring entrance performance. Fans erupted in collective joy and pride as the sounds of an accordion signaled Ramírez and his entourage to start their ascension to the ring. The arena was illuminated by moving red lights and the phone cameras of fans capturing the moment. Ramírez's ring entrance lasted a total of one minute and twenty seconds, providing Chuy Jr. ample time to perform the first half of the corrido.

Though "Yo Soy José De Avenal" does not make any statements that directly challenge Trump's politics, the centering of Ramírez's story as a professional boxer who works toward perfecting his craft as a champion, endures a great deal of sacrifices, and continues to move forward functions as a counter anthem to Trump's hateful propaganda, which is intended to destroy and divide communities.[25] The corrido paints a powerful image of Ramírez that ignites a sense of dignity, empowerment, and joy for the fans, who can relate to the themes in the song's lyrics. To the naked eye and lazy ear, boxing can be misinterpreted as an individual sport and corridos as privileging the stories of a single person. Yet the lyrics of Chuy Jr.'s corrido amplify a message that privileges collectivity over individualism, describing Ramírez's success as possible only because of the support he receives from his family and fans.[26] In this way, the sonic element of his ring walk serves as a melodic framing of togetherness despite the forces of division and separation present in the Trump era.

Another expressive cultural element of the ring walk was the fashion and style on display to further dissent from Trump's racist nativist politics. In *The Woman in the Zoot Suit*, Catherine S. Ramírez (2009) focuses on the wartime Pachuca-style politics of the zoot suit. By style politics, she is referring to "an expression of difference via style" (56). During the ring entrance, José Carlos Ramírez and his entourage wore black shirts (see fig. 7.2) that read "Pro-Immigrant and Proud," proclaiming an oppositional message to the anti-immigrant actions spearheaded by the Trump administration, such as the rescinding of Deferred Action for Childhood Arrivals (DACA). To complement this shirt, three members of Ramírez's entourage wore the same red hat that Ramírez had unveiled in his previous fight with Imam, with the words "Pro-Immigrant and Proud" alongside Ramírez's JCR logo (see fig. 7.3). Ramírez defines the slogan:

> It's who we are, that's my team. We're pro-immigrant and proud to be. And that's the overall message that I want to give out to those who have an idea towards immigrants, for those who like to divide people. Because when people are divided, they're less powerful, so to be reminded that they should be proud that they're immigrants, and they come here and are doing something positive.[27]

Ramírez further elaborates on the prominent pro-immigrant-and-proud message deployed in his ring entrance as a collective message that his team embodied, serving as a reminder to stay united and resist division. Together, they conveyed this dissenting message through the deployment of fashion and style, intent on empowering immigrants and challenging anti-immigrant ideologies that prevent the design and implementation of comprehensive immigration reform.

Being pro-immigrant and proud is part of Ramírez's identity. It comes with great responsibility. "When I say pro-immigrant and proud," he explains, "I'm also proud because *my job* is to prove to the groups of people who criticize immigrants, saying that they're all bad people. I'm proud to

Figure 7.2. José Carlos Ramírez's ring entrance on September 14, 2018, the fighter wearing a "Pro-Immigrant and Proud" shirt. (Photo by Rudy Mondragón.)

Figure 7.3. Hat worn by José Carlos Ramírez's entourage on the night of his September 14, 2018, fight. (Photo by Rudy Mondragón.)

say that we're not."[28] Ramírez is aware that his celebrity platform gives him the unique opportunity to challenge divisive anti-immigrant narratives. As an athlete in support of immigration reform, Ramírez leverages the excitement and energy heightened by a ring entrance to strengthen the efforts of activists, organizers, and policy advocates working tirelessly toward meeting the needs of and supporting undocumented people, who were particularly vulnerable under the Trump regime. Ramírez's ring entrances, like his transformation of boxing arenas into spaces of political mobilization for Proposition 1, organize his fans toward a pro-immigrant-and-proud politic aimed at sparking action for immigration reform. He plans to continue doing this work throughout his career. Twenty-seven years old at the time of our interview, Ramírez felt a deep enthusiasm for supporting important political issues rather than simply fighting to make money. "That excitement of helping people," he says, "I've done it in my career, and it's only the beginning. The bigger I am, the more I'm going to do. So if you're tired of me, if you don't want to hear me preach about what I believe in, man, you better get ready because the best thing is yet to come."[29]

Conclusion

Boxing is a political site of dissent. The ring entrance is one space where performances of dissent and oppositional consciousness can be excavated. In analyzing ring entrances, we better understand how fighters create new ways of being and imagining liberation through their deployments of expressive culture. Yet engaging in athletic activism while navigating the boxing industry comes with limitations and contradictions. Ramírez has had great success in the ring, which makes him marketable and profitable to his promoter. At the time of our interview, Ramírez was undefeated, with a record of twenty-three wins and zero losses, which gave him the necessary power and relevance needed to curate dissenting ring entrances. These earned factors allow Ramírez to make political statements and, to an extent, minimize the risks involved for a professional athlete who is directly dissenting against the politics of anti-immigrant racism.

Still, neoliberal multiculturalism and free-market forces are observed here because the boxing industry delights in spinning stories of struggle and adversity to create worthy story lines that build up the value of fighters. Ramírez's fight for immigration reform could be co-opted and packaged as a feel-good story that allows his promotional company to benefit from the ticket sales of fans with immigrant backgrounds. At the same time, continuing to build his fan base, sell out boxing arenas, and win matches facilitates Ramírez's ability to navigate the boxing industry and leverage his fights. In other words, by meeting boxing industry standards of financial success, Ramírez gains a kind of leeway that allows him to curate politically disruptive ring entrances.

In navigating a hypercapitalist, underregulated, exploitative, and brutal boxing industry, Ramírez accomplishes two things. First, he creates opportunities that provide him with the financial means to support himself and his family. As Deborah Vargas (2002) posits in reference to Tejana musical artist Selena Quintanilla:

> One may certainly note the problematic nature of Latina/o artist[s] participating in the increased capitalist exploitation of markets in Latin America, but it would be equally problematic to ignore the complex ways in which agency operates in the lives of working-class Chicanas/os and their justified desire to attain a more comfortable economic life. (230)

Second, Ramírez finds ways to use his fame and celebrity platform to amplify social justice issues. Fans who attend his fights are cheering him on as a boxer, but they are also exposed to his declarations of social problems, like the water crisis issues in California's Central Valley and immigration reform. By deploying expressive culture in his ring entrance to perform dissent, Ramírez transforms boxing arenas from spaces of athletic competition to ones of political mobilization. This expression is possible because the ring entrance space is unique among sports. The fighter is expected to make an entrance, the focus solely on the fighter. Fighters can also wield their agency to choose their attire, select their music, and enter the ring with an entourage or community of their choosing. These factors distinguish the ring entrance as a space of possibilities where boxers can grow their brand and bring attention to political issues.

Ramírez is a fighter who has much in common with Jack Johnson, Muhammad Ali, Eroseanna Robinson, John Carlos, Tommie Smith, Mahmoud Abdul-Rauf, Serena Williams, Colin Kaepernick, Megan Rapinoe, Bruce Maxwell, members of the 2016 WNBA Minnesota Lynx and New York Liberty teams, and other rebel athletes who engage in athletic activism. These are the athletes who challenge the status quo and refuse to shut up and play. Ramírez's acts of dissent, however, are not made hypervisible by the media. Rather, his performances advance solutions to the Central

Figure 7.4. José Carlos Ramírez post-weigh-in on the evening before his September 14, 2018, championship fight. (Photo by Rudy Mondragón.)

Valley's local water crisis and disrupt the anti-immigrant ideologies that are so widespread in the United States.

Resistance in sports should never be limited to performances commodified and carefully re-presented by the media, as those co-opted forms of resistance speak to the very injustices that Ramírez and other rebel athletes aim to challenge in the first place. Rebel athletes fall on the wrong side of acceptable politics in sports, meaning that their performances are not aligned with hyperpatriotism, capitalism, or the military-industrial complex. They are engaged in what Dave Zirin has called resistance politics in sports.[30]

As he continues his career, Ramírez does not plan on stopping this pugilistic activism. For him, there is always some concern about the impact of his political messages depending on his ability to stay undefeated. He knows that fans and the boxing industry are more comfortable with a fighter who scores victories in the ring. But win or lose, one thing is certain: His dedication to political causes will speak louder in retirement than his boxing record.

Acknowledgments

I would like to thank José Carlos Ramírez for sharing his story with me. My sincere thanks to Robert Garcia for opening the doors to his gym, the Robert Garcia Boxing Academy, and for always welcoming me with open arms. I am deeply grateful to Gaye Theresa Johnson, David J. Leonard, Alejandro Prado, Natalie Santizo, and Paulina Rodriguez for their insights, feedback, suggestions, and encouragement. Last, I would like to express my appreciation to the American Studies Association Sports Studies Caucus for honoring me with the ASA Sports Studies Caucus Paper Award at the 2019 meeting for an earlier draft of this chapter.

Notes

1. For more on the listed athletes and their protests, see Dave Zirin, "America Needs to Listen to What Colin Kaepernick Is Actually Trying to Say," *The Nation*, August 30, 2016, https://www.thenation.com/article/archive/america-needs-to-listen-to-what-colin-kaepernick-is-actually-trying-to-say/; Dave Zirin, "This Is What Solidarity Looks Like: Why Soccer-Star Megan Rapinoe Stands with Colin Kaepernick," *The Nation*, September 6, 2016, https://www.thenation.com/article/archive/this-is-what-solidarity-looks-like-why-soccer-star-megan-rapinoe-stands-with-colin-kaepernick/; "Athletics' Bruce Maxwell First MLB Player to Kneel during National Anthem," ESPN, September 23, 2017, http://www.espn.com/mlb/story/_/id/20796662/

oakland-athletics-catcher-bruce-maxwell-kneels-national-anthem; Dave Zirin, "WNBA Teams Show What Black Lives Matter Solidarity Looks Like," *The Nation*, July 11, 2016, https://www.thenation.com/article/archive/wnba-teams-show-what-blacklivesmatter-solidarity-looks-like/.

2. "Thomas Hearns vs Sugar Ray Leonard II 12.6.1989—WBC and WBO World Super Middleweight Championships," posted July 23, 2015, by Classic Boxing Matches, YouTube, https://www.youtube.com/watch?v=wIKpP6FTCVg&t=190s.

3. See Rudy Mondragón, Abel Valenzuela Jr., and José M. Hernández, "Down but Not Out: Labor Struggles for Professional Boxers in California's Ring" (UCLA Latino Policy and Politics Institute, 2024), 1–18.

4. Former featherweight contender Daniel Franco is a good example of this. On June 10, 2017, Franco fought in Iowa and suffered a knockout defeat, resulting in a subdural hematoma and a collection of blood between his brain and skull. He required multiple surgeries and was in a medically induced coma for two weeks. Promoters were required to purchase $10,000 of health insurance for Franco, which was minuscule compared to the $2 million in medical expenses that Franco and his family accrued. Even with 80 percent covered by their family insurance, Franco's father, Al, has bills from his son's injury that total about $12,000 a month. Franco's promoter, Roc Nation, founded by hip-hop artist Shawn "Jay-Z" Carter, is a critical part of the boxing industry and structure that turned its back on the young pugilist. Franco told *Sports Illustrated* that Roc Nation representatives fail to return his calls and emails and feed him empty lies about helping him. In 2019 Franco filed a lawsuit against Roc Nation, alleging the company was negligent for booking him in three fights in a span of seventy-nine days. For more, see Chris Mannix, "Fallout from a Knockout: How One Tragic Night Changed a Boxer's Life Forever," *Sports Illustrated*, June 13, 2019, https://www.si.com/boxing/2019/06/13/daniel-franco-injury-roc-nation-lawsuit.

5. Teddy Atlas quoted in Thomas Hauser, "The Evolution of the Ring Walk: Key Moments That Changed Boxing Introductions Forever," *Sporting News*, November 14, 2018, http://www.sportingnews.com/us/boxing/news/greatest-boxing-ring-walks-music-evolution/xjbud3xfr2bx18ti7r4g8kzpy.

6. Bernard Hopkins quoted in Thomas Hauser, "The Evolution of the Ring Walk: Key Moments That Changed Boxing Introductions Forever," *Sporting News*, November 14, 2018, http://www.sportingnews.com/us/boxing/news/greatest-boxing-ring-walks-music-evolution/xjbud3xfr2bx18ti7r4g8kzpy.

7. See Rudy Mondragón, "*Champs* (2015). Dir. and prod. Bert Marcus. Amplify and Starz. 85 Mins.," *Journal of Sport History* 45, no. 2 (2018): 229–30.

8. Mondragón, "*Champs* (2015)."

9. See "Bernard Hopkins vs. Clinton Mitchell," BoxRec, last modified March 25, 2013, https://boxrec.com/media/index.php/Bernard_Hopkins_vs. Clinton_Mitchell.

10. Bernard Hopkins (retired professional boxer) in discussion with Rudy Mondragón, March 2023.

11. José Carlos Ramírez (professional boxer) in discussion with Rudy Mondragón, January 2019.

12. Ramírez, discussion.

13. Ramírez, discussion.

14. Ramírez, discussion.

15. Ramírez, discussion.

16. This interview was audio and video recorded, allowing me to study changes in speech and tone as well as body language.

17. Ramírez, discussion.

18. "Article 12. Revenue and Fiscal Affairs [18800–18828]," California Legislative Information, accessed July 5, 2024, http://leginfo.legislature.ca.gov/faces/codes_displaySection.xhtml?lawCode=BPC§ionNum=18824.

19. Ramírez, discussion.

20. "About the California Latino Water Coalition," California Latino Water Coalition, accessed March 2, 2019, http://www.latinowater.com/About+Us/About+Us.htm.

21. "California Proposition 1, Water Bond (2014)," Ballotpedia, accessed March 4, 2019, https://ballotpedia.org/California_Proposition_1,_Water_Bond_(2014).

22. Ramírez, discussion.

23. Diana Taylor, The Archive and the Repertoire: Performing Cultural Memory in the Americas (Duke University Press, 2003), 3.

24. "Full Text: Donald Trump Announces a Presidential Bid," *Washington Post*, June 16, 2015, https://www.washingtonpost.com/news/post-politics/wp/2015/06/16/full-text-donald-trump-announces-a-presidential-bid/.

25. Chuy Jr., "Yo Soy José De Avenal," Fresno, CA, September 14, 2018. The following are the specific lyrics in Spanish that I refer to in this section, as performed: "Lucho por la perfección y por ser un gran campeón / Son bastante los sacrificios los que tengo que pasar / Voy a seguir hacia delante."

26. Chuy Jr., "Yo Soy José de Avenal." "Yo tengo mijo Matteo Maximiliano y mis papas / también cuento con mis hermanos, mi mujer y muchos más / que son ustedes los fanáticos jamás podría olvidar."

27. Ramírez, discussion.

28. Ramírez, discussion.

29. Ramírez, discussion.

30. *Shut Up and Dribble*, episode 2, directed by Gotham Chopra (2018), aired November 10, 2018, Showtime.

References

"Athletics' Bruce Maxwell First MLB Player to Kneel during National Anthem." 2017. ESPN. September 23. http://www.espn.com/mlb/story/_/id/20796662/oakland-athletics-catcher-bruce-maxwell-kneels-national-anthem.

Dahlberg, Tim. 2016. "Bob Arum's 'No Trump' Undercard Carries a Message with a Punch." Fox Sports. March 24. https://www.foxsports.com/stories/boxing/column-no-trump-undercard-carries-a-message-with-a-punch.

Dalamba, Lindelwa. 2012. "Disempowering Music: The *Amandla!* Documentary and Other Conservative Musical Projects." *Safundi* 13, nos. 3–4: 295–315.

Edwards, Harry. 2017. *The Revolt of the Black Athlete*. University of Illinois Press.

Elliott, Bud. 2015. "Water Warrior: José Ramírez," *Central California Life*, accessed March 4, 2019, http://www.cencalilife.com/2015/04/20/69210/water-warrior-jose-ramirez.

Farmer, Ashley. 2016. "Black Women Athletes, Protest, and Politics: An Interview with Amira Rose Davis." *Black Perspectives* (blog), African American Intellectual History Society, October 14. https://www.aaihs.org/black-women-athletes-protest-and-politics-an-interview-with-amira-rose-davis/.

García, Justin D. 2013. "Rising from the Canvas: Issues of Immigration, Redemption, Gender, and Mexican American Identity in *Split Decision* and *In Her Corner*." In *Identity and Myth in Sports Documentaries: Critical Essays*, edited by Zachary Ingle and David M. Sutera, 63–78. Scarecrow Press.

Hauser, Thomas. 2018. "The Evolution of the Ring Walk: Key Moments That Changed Boxing Introductions Forever." *Sporting News*. November 14. http://www.sportingnews.com/us/boxing/news/greatest-boxing-ring-walks-music-evolution/xjbud3xfr2bx18ti7r4g8kzpy.

Herrera-Sobek, María. 1990. *The Mexican Corrido: A Feminist Analysis*. Indiana University Press.

Iole, Kevin. 2018. "How José Ramírez Became 'the Most Socially Involved American Fighter since Muhammad Ali'." Yahoo. March 16. https://www.yahoo.com/entertainment/jose-ramirez-became-socially-involved-american-fighter-since-muhammad-ali-184735533.html.

Kelley, Robin D. G. 1996. *Race Rebels: Culture, Politics, and the Black Working Class*. Free Press.

Lamb, Chris. 2016. "Introduction." In *From Jack Johnson to LeBron James: Sports, Media, and the Color Line*, edited by Chris Lamb. University of Nebraska Press.

Leonard, David J. 2017. *Playing While White: Privilege and Power On and Off the Field*. University of Washington Press.

Magagnini, Stephen. 2018. "This Central Valley Boxer Is Fighting for the Title Saturday—and for Immigrant Rights." *Sacramento Bee*. March 17. https://www.sacbee.com/sports/article205387669.html.

Mannix, Chris. 2019. "Fallout from a Knockout: How One Tragic Night Changed a Boxer's Life Forever." *Sports Illustrated*. June 13. https://www.si.com/boxing/2019/06/13/daniel-franco-injury-roc-nation-lawsuit.

Mondragón, Rudy. 2018. "*Champs* (2015). Dir. and Prod. Bert Marcus. Amplify and Starz. 85 Mins." *Journal of Sport History* 45, no. 2: 229–30.

Mondragón, Rudy. 2022. "Boxing Ring Entrances as Insubordinate Spaces: A Disruptive Oral Herstory." *Kalfou: A Journal of Comparative and Relational Ethnic Studies* 9, no. 2: 388–414.

Mondragón, Rudy, Abel Valenzuela Jr., and José M. Hernández. 2024. "Down but Not Out: Labor Struggles for Professional Boxers in California's Ring." UCLA Latino Policy and Politics Institute.

Rafael, Dan. 2013. "Hopkins Otherworldly in Decision Win." ESPN. October 26. https://www.espn.com/boxing/story/_/id/9886458/bernard-hopkins-otherworldly-decision-win-karo-murat.

Rhoads, Robert A. 1998. *Freedom's Web: Student Activism in an Age of Cultural Diversity*. Johns Hopkins University Press.

Sammons, Jeffrey T. 1990. *Beyond the Ring: The Role of Boxing in American Society*. University of Illinois Press.

Schultz, Jaime. 2005. "Reading the Catsuit: Serena Williams and the Production of Blackness at the 2002 U.S. Open." *Journal of Sport and Social Issues* 29, no. 3: 338–57.

Scott, James C. 1990. *Domination and the Arts of Resistance: Hidden Transcripts*. Yale University Press, 1990.

Shmerler, Cindy. 2018. "Serena Williams Shrugs Off Catsuit Concerns." *New York Times*. August 25. https://www.nytimes.com/2018/08/25/sports/serena-williams-shrugs-off-catsuit-concerns.html.

Ramírez, Catherine S. 2009. *The Woman in the Zoot Suit: Gender, Nationalism, and the Cultural Politics of Memory*. Duke University Press.

Redmond, Shana L. 2014. *Anthem: Social Movements and the Sound of Solidarity in the African Diaspora*. New York University Press.

Taylor, Diana. 2003. *The Archive and the Repertoire: Performing Cultural Memory in the Americas*. Duke University Press.

Tomlinson, Barbara, and George Lipsitz. 2019. *Insubordinate Spaces: Improvisation and Accompaniment for Social Justice*. Temple University Press.

Vargas, Deborah R. 2002. "Cruzando Frontejas: Remapping Selena's Tejano Music 'Crossover'." In *Chicana Traditions: Continuity and Change*, edited by Norma E. Cantú and Olga Nájera-Ramírez, 224–36. University of Illinois Press.

Zirin, Dave. 2016a. "America Needs to Listen to What Colin Kaepernick Is Actually Trying to Say." *The Nation*. August 30. https://www.thenation.com/article/archive/america-needs-to-listen-to-what-colin-kaepernick-is-actually-trying-to-say/.

Zirin, Dave. 2016b. "The Hidden History of Muhammad Ali." *Jacobin*. https://jacobin.com/2016/06/the-hidden-history-of-muhammad-ali/. June 4.

Zirin, Dave. 2016c. "This Is What Solidarity Looks Like: Why Soccer-Star Megan Rapinoe Stands with Colin Kaepernick." *The Nation*. September 6. https://www.thenation.com/article/archive/this-is-what-solidarity-looks-like-why-soccer-star-megan-rapinoe-stands-with-colin-kaepernick/.

Zirin, Dave. 2016d. "WNBA Teams Show What Black Lives Matter Solidarity Looks Like." *The Nation*. July 11. https://www.thenation.com/article/archive/wnba-teams-show-what-blacklivesmatter-solidarity-looks-like/.

8

"'I'm the Greatest. I'm the Best.' That Bravado, That's Hip-Hop"

A Conversation with Jasiri X

RUDY MONDRAGÓN and
GAYE THERESA JOHNSON

Jasiri X is a hip-hop artist, activist, boxing enthusiast, and founder of 1Hood Media, a collective of socially conscious artists and activists who use art to raise awareness about social (in)justice. Jasiri X also strives to provide marginalized youth with the tools to create their own narratives and dismantle stereotypes.[1]

He is a powerful artist who leverages his artistry to foster awareness and change. In 2015 Jasiri X released *Black Liberation Theology*, a critically acclaimed album that "has been recognized as a soundtrack for today's civil rights movement."[2] A year later, he became the first independent hip-hop artist to be awarded an honorary doctorate from the Chicago Theological Seminary.

In this 2019 conversation, Jasiri, who is a boxing fan, shares his thoughts on the parallels and connections between boxing and hip-hop culture. Both are expressive cultural forms that allow its practitioners to perform dissent; each requires incredible creativity, self-confidence, and self-belief. His social justice work mirrors the work from so many boxers who enter the ring with intentionality to leverage their platform in transformative ways. Jasiri sees this as a connection to boxing as he works to create socially conscious music with a deeply rooted commitment to action.

• • •

GAYE THERESA JOHNSON: Everybody has a boxing story. What is your boxing story?

JASIRI X: One summer I went to camp and there was a boxing ring. That was the way people dealt with beefs. I remember, me and my friend were like, "Yeah, let's go in the boxing ring." And I remember going in the ring, getting the gloves and stuff put on, and thinking all these things that I was gonna do. Different moves and punches and all this stuff. I remember in my mind I was like, "I'm gonna move to the side and I'm gonna throw a jab and I'm gonna do all of this." I just remember the bell ringing and we just stood toe to toe. It was such, it was like a real rush, to be the only two people in the ring and everybody watching and cheering. But once the bell rung, we just pointed at each other. They then separated us, and that was the end of that. That was my boxing career right there.

It made me respect people that do that for a living and get in the ring and can manage the emotions. I mean because it's a fight. Mike Tyson, who said, "Everybody has a plan until they get punched in the mouth." To be able to stick to a particular plan and a goal and despite all of what's going on around you, it takes a lot of focus and a lot of discipline. It increased my respect and understanding of what is happening in the ring.

RUDY MONDRAGÓN: Some say that sports and boxing can serve as an escape for people. When my friend's uncles first migrated to the United States, they would go to this place in Los Angeles called the Grand Olympic Auditorium. For them, it was an escape from the hard labor they would engage in during the day. At night, boxing was their escape and a way to enjoy themselves. Hip-hop plays a similarly important role. In a way, hip-hop brings people back to reality. Do you see parallels between boxing and hip-hop?

JX: Hip-hop was really the first musical forum that I remember people competing in. Of course, you might argue, "Who sings better, Whitney Houston or Mariah Carey?" But it wasn't like they had sing-offs. People know about Michael Jackson and Prince, and they might have been maybe taking shots at each other, but it wasn't overt. It wasn't like something where you had KRS-One and MC Shan, where it's clear: "We're battling." To me, that history of hip-hop and the battle part of it that, like who's the number one, is what boxing is about. When you look at how Muhammad Ali carried himself in interviews: "I'm the greatest. I'm the best." That bravado, that's hip-hop. That's clearly how MCs stepped into the game and into the forefront: "I'm the best. I'm the greatest around. Can't nobody beat me."

You can draw a line directly from that to hip-hop and to how rappers conduct themselves. I remember when Canibus and Mike Tyson was on the beach and he was in the ring.[3] And LL Cool J had like, "Mama Said Knock You Out." LL was punching on the bag. There's always been that thing of being the best and eliminating all competition to where you had rappers wearing belts or carrying them around to signify "I'm the best and I'm the greatest." Boxing and hip-hop embrace a braggadocious mind-set, the ability to say, "I'm the best" and "I beat you" with proof. We've had different battles where it's like, "Okay, I'm number one now. And I beat you and I'm the greatest MC of all time." Famously recently, where Kendrick Lamar in "Control" named everybody, and it caused such a controversy because he was basically making his claim as the greatest rapper in the moment. I think that is very much kind of parallel to what we see in boxing in terms of you're talking a good game but then getting in the ring and handling your business. You're talking beforehand, getting in the ring, knuckling up, and then talking afterwards.

GTJ: That reminds me of what KRS-One said about his first battle rap in a park: "Yeah, so I'm going, and I'm like, 'Yeah, I'm gonna go, I'm gonna destroy this dude.'" And he goes in there and he does something great, and he said that this guy comes back with the simplest two-liner and just destroyed him. He was like, "My name is Chris, and you smell like piss." And then it was over, everybody was just like, "Oh, that's done." And here he was, he came to, basically, the ring to battle with all this bravado and this performance and rehearsal in his head and yet he's devastated by two lines.

JX: I think we've seen that happen in boxing, where you have a more skilled boxer and then he gets hit. That's the things that makes boxing compelling; at any time, you might get hit with that perfect shot. And even if somebody is more skilled, or a better boxer, there's still an opportunity for that person to land that shot. And if you land that shot and you land it right, it's over.

RM: A defeat in boxing is so different from other sports. If you lose in the NFL (National Football League), you have next week to bounce back. In the NBA (National Basketball Association), you have tomorrow night. In MLB (Major League Baseball), you have a three, four-game series. In boxing, if you experience defeat, you must wait at least two months to get back in the ring. And if you have an injury, you might have to wait a little longer. If you don't have a good promoter or manager, then you might have to wait a whole year. So that arc of redemption, of trying to redeem yourself from defeat, is tremendously difficult for boxers.

JX: I think that goes back to the mental. A lot of times, I think when we look at boxers, we judge them on their physical prowess. We're don't give them credit for the mental preparation that boxing requires. Just like you said, if you wait a year and then you're walking back in the ring, what type of emotions do you have to then try to get revenge? Yeah, so that takes so much discipline, so much focus to go through that training, to go back and then do it all over again. You gotta give it up for them.

RM: I'm most interested in the idea of the Greatest of All Time, the G.O.A.T., because it's in both boxing and hip-hop. I also find it interesting when one claims they're the best. I always tell folks in boxing, if you don't claim you're the best, then it could have some serious implications in your performance because you must have that mindset. But then people will see that as maybe not displaying a sign of humility or being overly arrogant. What do you think about that? What do boxers and hip-hop artists mean when they say, "I'm the best at this"?

JX: I think this goes back to my story, to go on stage with just a microphone, no band. You might have a DJ but it's just you and the mic. You must have a self-belief. With baseball, basketball, and football . . . It's a team.

You could always say, "Yo, man, that was on LeBron [James]. He ain't pass me the ball," or, "Coach ain't put me in."

In boxing it's you versus them.

I'm mostly a solo artist. I gotta get on stage by myself. I have confidence in myself and my ability. When I walk on stage, I think, "I'm the best here. I'll crush anybody." You have to project a level of confidence in yourself. If I don't believe in me, you're not gonna believe in me. So, I gotta come up there with a strong self-belief for you to be like, "Oh, wow, this dude is real . . . He kind of believes in himself."

I feel for a boxer that's the same thing. You're gonna get out there by yourself in that ring, you better believe you're gonna win—even if you look and say, "Oh, this dude's about to get beat up." You gotta have some belief in yourself to walk out there. You're only in shorts and you gotta fight somebody in front of the world. And if you're gonna get knocked down, it's gonna be in front of all these people.

For many when they became an MC, they want to be the best. "Why am I rapping? I'm rapping because I wanna be the best. I wanna be looked at as the best. I want people to recognize me in the lineage of all these legendary MCs." Look at Kendrick Lamar; he's writing to be remembered in history as the best rapper ever. That's the level of seriousness that he's approaching the craft. And to me, this is one of the things that makes him really, really good. He's thinking about legacy. He's thinking about his place in history. And I think to me this is what makes an athlete great. They're looking for historical greatness. It's bigger to them than just "What game did we play?" But like I said, the difference between boxers is that it's just you. You rise and fall based on your own personal ability, and that's very different in most sports.

RM: It's a very vulnerable position to be in.

JX: Bet. You know.

GTJ: I find that it's interesting how you describe that, because a lot of times I've heard artists say, "I got this thing in me and if I don't get it out, I will die. I must create. I have to write. I must perform." And that's the thing that allows you to get up on stage by yourself or to have that belief in you, even if other people didn't have that belief in you. And it sounds like you would make a connection to boxers in that way, with their creativity, because you can't just go up there only on bravado, right?

JX: Yeah, there is a lot of creativity in boxing. Particularly if you look at some of the greatest boxers. People have described them as artists, in terms of how they perform or how they move and the things that they do. To get up on a stage by yourself in front of all these people, just kinda like you said, the vulnerability of it. But it's also like a little bit of craziness. I think the same with boxing. Of course, yeah, you gotta train and do that, but just to wanna do that is kind of weird. And so you do have to be different mentally. It's more than just training or having the skills; you have to have that other thing. What makes a great MC and what makes a great boxer, it's kind of like that other thing, that intangible thing. It's that belief that this is what you were put on the planet to do, having a real purpose. And I think it's that kind of connection to that spiritual thing that maybe puts you on a different plane.

RM: What ring entrance would you say has stood out to you the most?

JX: Whenever I think of a ring entrance, I always think about Mike Tyson because he was so stripped down. He was the dude that was no pomp and circumstance—no robe, black shorts; he had black shoes, no socks. It was so different. To me, it was like underground hip-hop. He's not coming with no flash. He's "I'm here to knock you out and call it a day." And it was like, it played into the mythology of Mike Tyson. And so he was the first boxer I ever saw not take that entrance as seriously. To him, it was a formality. He would walk in to knock you out, add you to the list, and move on. I remember the time where Mike was almost looked at as invincible. And he was really winning fights before they even began because he was coming up there, and it was just like, "This dude is gonna kill everything and everybody." So that was always impactful. But I also remember, I think it was a time where Roy Jones Jr. rapped his own song.[4] For him to rap his own song, that's some bravado right there.

RM: There's a history and a reemergence of the athlete-activist, especially when you think about Colin Kaepernick and Serena Williams. In boxing, however, most people can't name activism in boxing post–Muhammad Ali. Are there any boxers that you feel have taken the activist baton from Muhammad Ali?

JX: Well, I don't think explicitly but look at what just went down with Deontay Wilder.[5] I thought that was a very powerful moment. With 1Hood Media, our whole thing is around how Black men are portrayed in the media. And so you had Deontay Wilder talking about how he, as a Black American boxer, is treated very differently. If Deontay Wilder was a white, heavyweight that was 40-0, he would be everywhere. He'd be on Wheaties boxes; they'd be having little toys of this dude. He's this Black man from Tuscaloosa, Alabama, who has talked about how he's treated better in Europe than in the United States. So I thought that was a powerful moment. I thought that was a very powerful moment, and it made me wonder if he could maybe take that moment and make it something bigger. Kind of like in this moment where athletes are taking a stance and taking stances whether it's [the] Golden State [Warriors] saying, "We ain't going to the White House." Or even LeBron James doing a docuseries called *Shut Up and Dribble*. Kind of silencing the critics. Obviously, this is something that Deontay's thinking about and thinking about it in an intelligent way to see if he could kind of go further along those lines. And so I'll be interested if this rematch happens [against Tyson Fury], if he'll kind of revisit and if he'll follow it up.[6]

RM: Yeah, that's powerful. It makes me think about James "Buster" Douglas, who a month after beating Mike Tyson, appeared at a Senate meeting to challenge George H. W. Bush's plan to cut funds from the Low Income Home Energy Assistance Program. Or in 2016 when Deontay Wilder fought against Chris Arreola, and in their weigh-in, each one of them had a sign that was pointed at each other that read "His Life Matters."

JX: A lot of that stuff, we don't hear about it. I feel like if that clip of Deontay Wilder didn't become a viral moment, we might not have even heard that. And then I think too, maybe as he's getting older, folks start having children and you start seeing the world differently.

GTJ: Yeah, it's interesting too because when we think about legacies of people, especially sports figures, these are different times. This is really a politically conscious time, but there was also kind of a decades-long lead-up to Muhammad Ali being where he was to where there were all these other players around him that were accountable to this commitment. I don't know if the same structure is in place in the same way. It's different. It doesn't mean that it's worse or better, but it's different. And I don't know how much. Do you think about how innovative people are trying to fit themselves into a broader conversation around rights?

JX: I think the difficulty is, like you said, it's changing. I remember at one point I was gonna do an album called "The Revolution Is Dead." I kinda looked at Michael Jordan and the point where being an athlete became so financially valuable that to speak out was like, "For what? I'm getting this money." Even though movements were happening, most athletes wasn't really out there. You would get a Craig Hodges, or you'd get like a Mahmoud Abdul-Rauf, but it wasn't . . . It was kind of like, "Yo, I gotta get this money."[7] And I think in a lot of ways, particularly when you look at hip-hop in the '90s and 2000s, it was very much like that too. It's very much like, "We're dancing, we're getting money." It wasn't about challenging systems. So I think we're kind of moving into a moment where you do have athletes thinking and speaking more consciously about what's happening because of the Black Lives Matter movement. I'm hoping we're gonna see more athletes really taking these strong stances.

I know some folks like Mike de la Rocha are doing important work. Mike recorded something with some athletes, and he was working with Ibtihaj Muhammad, the Muslim sister who's the fencer, and some other athletes and putting them folks together to do different panels and different conversations. So, hopefully, those things are being put in place now.[8]

RM: In the spirit of imagination and creativity, if you were prepping for your fight, like it was your second fight, after the first fight you had at summer camp, how would you curate your ring entrance? What would you do, how would you want to enter the ring, what would you want the world to see?

JX: Yeah, I would make a statement. Like I said, the reason Mike Tyson resonated with me was because it was almost like a statement of where he was from. It was very "no frills." If I'm coming into the ring, it has to be making some type of statement connected to the struggles of my community and my people and what's happening in Pittsburgh. If it was now, I might be in purple because that's the color used to honor Antwon Rose, who was killed by a police officer. I would wanna make some type of statement in solidarity with some type of movement, a struggle that's happening right now. So when you saw it, you would be like, "Okay, this is about this movement and this struggle." My song would be "Who We Be," by DMX. I just feel like I gotta win if that's playing because that song is such a hard song with a pow . . . It's hard and spiritual at the same time, which is one of the things that DMX was able to do, which made him such a great artist. He was able to be gruff and really hard-core but also spiritual. *They don't know who we be*—that's part of the problem.

GTJ: That's wonderful. That's so good.

RM: Yeah. And who would you want in your entourage?

JX: Definitely gotta have my mom there. And I guess probably Muhammad Ali. Who wouldn't want to have "The Greatest"? Although, my favorite . . . Maybe I'll also have to give a shout to my favorite boxer coming up, who was Felix Trinidad, so maybe I'll have some space for "King Felix."

RM: I didn't know you liked Felix like that. Remember earlier when Big Pun and Fat Joe walked him into the ring?

JX: Absolutely. It's two fights that I'll never forget that made me love boxing. One was Diego Corrales [Jr.] and José Luis Castillo, which is the greatest fight of all time. Second is the fight where Bernard Hopkins just totally out-skilled Felix Trinidad. It was just something that I can't forget. Hopkins had such a clear victory. That was the first time I really understood skill, because Trinidad had power in both hands; he was undefeated. But the ring generalship of Bernard Hopkins, I feel like that fight made me a boxing fan to say like, "Wow, by use of his footwork, totally shut Trinidad down to the point where it wasn't even no need for a rematch." He beat him horribly. Those are two fights that always stuck with me.

RM: That was a beautiful fight. When it comes to Hopkins's custom-made Executioner and Alien masks, it's amazing how they are both different personalities. Hopkins describes his Executioner persona as: "It was about crushing you, it was about punishing you, it was about making your day miserable." Later on in his career, he began to see himself as an alien: "I'm not supposed to be here. I'm old and I'm still beating guys half my age."

JX: He's a legendary boxer. Philly representing, you know? When you talk about rapping and boxing, you are kind of defined by where you're from. You know how boxers are representative of their city, where they're from. So it is with hip-hop artists as well.

GTJ: That's a great point. That's true, both are very place specific. No matter where you go in the world, you're always representing where you're from.

JX: In boxing, it's like, "Where are you from?" You know [Mike] Tyson: "That's Brooklyn." It's just like you've become representative. Or particularly youth from small towns, you have that town on your back and whole cities coming out to see you. It's very much like that as hip-hop artists as well.

Notes

1. "Jasiri X One Sheet," Jasiri X: Freeing Minds One Rhyme at a Time, accessed January 16, 2020, http://jasirix.com/?page_id=1411.

2. "Jasiri X Bio," https://www.jasirix.com/bio.

3. This is in reference to hip-hop artist Canibus's "Second Round K.O.," which was released on March 24, 1998, and featured Mike Tyson in the song's official music video.

4. On the night of September 7, 2002, Roy Jones Jr. defended his World

Boxing Council, World Boxing Association, International Boxing Association, International Boxing Federation, International Boxing Organization, and World Boxing Federation World Light Heavyweight titles against Clinton Woods at the Rose Garden in Portland, Oregon. Jones entered the ring second and rapped his own ring entrance hip-hop song, "And Still."

5. During the week leading up to Deontay Wilder's December 8, 2018, fight against Tyson Fury, Wilder was interviewed by Seconds Out reporter Radio Rahim. During the interview, Wilder discussed the double standard of race in the sense that Fury (a white man from England) was humanized for coming back to boxing after dealing with substance abuse problems. Wilder stated that if it had been him with substance abuse problems, he would have been dehumanized and labeled a drug addict. Toward the end of the interview, Radio Rahim asked Wilder what he meant when he said, "Your people have been fighting for 400 years." At that point, Wilder responded to the Black American reporter by saying, "Your people too! I don't have to explain what's understood by that, you know what I mean by that . . . You know we've been fighting 400 [years] and still fighting to this day! To this day!" See "Deontay Wilder BLASTS Radio Rahim in His FACE!" uploaded by Seconds Out, November 28, 2018, https://www.youtube.com/watch?v=h30uTmahNFQ.

6. See the introduction in this anthology to read more about Deontay Wilder's February 22, 2020, rematch against Tyson Fury and the significance of his ring entrance that centered Blackness, Black excellence, and Black pride.

7. After the Chicago Bulls won the 1992 National Basketball Association (NBA) Championship, Craig Hodges and the rest of the Bulls visited George H. W. Bush at the White House. Hodges wore a dashiki during the visit and delivered a handwritten letter to the president in which he addressed his discontent with the administration's handling of minoritized people and the poor. He was also critical of Michael Jordan's apolitical ways and in 1996 filed a forty-million-dollar lawsuit against the NBA, claiming the league blackballed him for his connection to Louis Farrakhan and his critiques of Black athletes who did not use their wealth and influence to assist disenfranchised people. At the time, Mahmoud Abdul-Rauf played for the Denver Nuggets. During the 1995–1996 season, he refused to stand for the national anthem before games. Abdul-Rauf noted that the reason he refused to stand was because the flag symbolized oppression and the United States' long history of tyranny.

8. See "Michael De La Rocha at the 2018 LA84 Foundation Summit on Athlete Activism," uploaded by LA84Foundation, November 29, 2018, https://www.youtube.com/watch?v=KH_rPm_2aEQ.

9

Why Gyms Matter

Boxing and the Struggle for Los Angeles

PRISCILLA LEIVA

The sheer mention of the gloried history of boxing in Los Angeles invokes well-known places such as Grand Olympic Auditorium, Main Street Gym, and Broadway Boxing Gym. The Olympic Auditorium, located at Eighteenth and Grand in downtown LA, drew working-class communities of color and hosted legendary fighters hailing from those same communities. According to boxing historian Gene Aguilera (2018), the Olympic Auditorium constituted part of the "axis of boxing in Los Angeles" (7). After its closure in 2005, however, it became the Glory Church of Jesus Christ. Main Street Gym, located on the edge of Skid Row, was the other line of the axis and epitomized the tough and gritty boxing gym that hosted the likes of Muhammad Ali and Sugar Ray Robinson. It was simultaneously a gathering place for boxers, trainers, and managers who were either fixtures in the LA scene or passing through and the quintessential boxing gym that served as a film location for scenes from *Rocky*. During its more than fifty-year history, Main Street Gym occupied three addresses. But it did not make it to the twenty-first century. It now lives on only in the memories of those who experienced its atmosphere firsthand.

Today Broadway Boxing Gym claims its place as the "last old-school boxing gym."[1] Legendary boxing trainer Bill Slayton purchased Broadway Boxing Gym in South Central LA in 1977 with his earnings from training heavyweight contender Ken Norton. At Broadway Boxing Gym, Slayton trained both professional fighters and young amateurs whom he sought to teach about the sweet sciences of boxing and life.[2] After Slayton's death in 2003, Sauchsee Larkins and her father, Melvin Larkins, bought the building and revamped the gym out of an unwavering commitment to the neighborhood youth. To this day, they are open seven days a week and provide a model of consistency for other gyms seeking to impact their local community. These sites are only three in a rich and constantly shifting landscape of twentieth-century boxing spaces in Los Angeles. Although they may appear simple from the outside, they epitomize the struggles of working-class communities of color as they persevere in the changing city.

This chapter examines how boxing gyms in Los Angeles offer a window into the larger tensions at play in the twenty-first-century city. In his study of how seemingly race-neutral urban sites contain hidden racial assumptions, George Lipsitz demonstrates that lived experiences of race quite literally take place in actual spaces.[3] Following from his invitation to consider the racial politics of seemingly neutral places, this chapter looks to boxing gyms as critical spaces for exploring Angelenos' lived experience of race. At Broadway Boxing, everywhere boxers look, they see the photographs of Brown and Black boxers that trained in the very spaces where they now stand. These images are a history of glory in a city that rarely considers the needs of Black and Brown Angelenos. The remainder of this chapter outlines the challenges gym owners face in contemporary Los Angeles and examine Barrio Boxing and City of Angels Boxing as critical sites of dissent in the neoliberal city. Together, these gyms represent two points in what Gaye Theresa Johnson names the "constellation of struggle," in that they separately engage inequality in the service of an alternate future for the economically and racially segregated city. Newer gyms like Barrio Boxing and City of Angels Boxing do not yet have this forty-year history but honor its spirit by countering urban isolation, fostering community, and employing creative strategies to survive in the city.

Inequality, Gentrification, and the Rise of the Boxing Studio

Historically, working-class communities have sustained the sport of boxing and have been the training grounds for boxing greats. In the 2011 documentary *Born and Bred*, boxing trainer Robert Luna argues that young Latino boxers in LA are not coming out of Beverly Hills because boxing comes from struggle.[4] Rather, East Los Angeles, a central poor and working-class Latinx hub of the city, is the only neighborhood that has produced gold medalist Olympians. Boxing gyms in working-class neighborhoods of color reveal both structural inequalities, such as those between places like Beverly Hills and East Los Angeles, and a politics of resistance in the face of economic and racial disparities.

Because the rapidly changing landscape of Los Angeles and its growing economic disparity exceeds the national average, the region is currently facing gentrification, housing shortages, and rapid urban change (Ong et al. 2018, 4). Income segregation is "highly correlated" with racial and ethnic segregation. This disparity comprises both income and wealth inequality. US Black and Mexican households have 1 percent of the wealth of whites in Los Angeles. Other Latinos have 12 percent. Whereas white households demonstrate a median value of liquid assets of $110,000, Mexicans and Latinos hold only zero and seven dollars, respectively (De La Cruz-Viesca et al. 2016, 6). Landownership remains the primary means by which one can experience class mobility. Yet, in immigrant and working-class communities of Los Angeles, rates of home ownership remain low while real estate speculation and weak rent control protections have placed housing in longtime working-class communities out of reach for residents (Huante and Miranda 2019). Consequently, homelessness in Los Angeles County increased by 75 percent from 2010 to 2017.[5] In this economic climate, boxing gym owners must be creative in order to survive increasing rents and changing neighborhood demographics.

In Los Angeles journalistic pieces and public debates tend to focus on gentrification through the arrival of new residents and businesses, particularly coffee shops, craft breweries, local grocery stores, and, namely here, fitness studios.[6] The opening of such businesses and the influx of new residents are symptoms of larger capitalist logics in which profit takes precedence over the people and needs of existing neighborhoods. This deeper history includes, but is not limited to, racist housing policies, urban renewal programs that have privileged the white suburban consumer, the displacement of communities of color, and a focus on the expansion of private business in lieu of investment in communities of color. In Los Angeles the revitalization and corporate densification of downtown during the 1990s invited redevelopment on the peripheries of downtown in the early 2000s. The Great Recession of 2007, which forced the shutdown of businesses and led to a foreclosure crisis, simultaneously created favorable conditions for real estate speculators and reinvestment.[7] While activists fight for a type of investment that reinforces a neighborhood consciousness and inspires existing landlords and homeowners to make improvements, gentrification comes with the risk of displacement as the economic and racial demographics of a neighborhood shift, particularly when the state does not protect long-term renters (Zuk et al. 2018). In Los Angeles County this combination of revitalization and displacement resulted in a 16 percent increase of gentrified neighborhoods between 1990 and 2015.

The divide between boxing gyms and boxing studios demonstrates the spatial transformations that are characteristic of gentrification.[8] The increasing popularity of boxing as a fitness workout has created a new contested geography of boxing "studios" rooted in privilege, produced by economic forces in the increasingly unequal city. Fitness industry professionals have noted that the boutique fitness studio represents a niche growth in a somewhat stagnant industry. In fact, from 2010 to 2014, boutique fitness studios have grown more than 400 percent (O'Rourke 2015). While boxers will be the first to say that the sport has a long history in Hollywood as a means for celebrities to achieve fitness goals, it is also true that the past couple of years have witnessed an increased mainstream interest in boxing for fitness that has resulted in the opening of many boxing studios. Online blogs and print publications from *Elle* to *Zoe Report* to the *Active Times* have explored boxing as a fitness trend in the past few years.[9] Whereas boxing gyms like Broadway Boxing charge about five dollars per day, boxing studios charge between two and three hundred dollars for ten classes. Boxing studios require reservations, offer cucumber water, feature showers with high-end toiletries, and abide by strict rules that charge you for canceling less than twenty-four hours in advance or arriving late to your scheduled time. In Los Angeles the wealthier areas on the Westside claim the bulk of boxing studios. However, boutique boxing studios and studio gyms that offer a repertoire of classes including fitness boxing have begun popping up in gentrified areas, as designated by the Urban Displacement Project, as well as areas experiencing dramatic change in the last couple of years.[10] These boutique fitness studios and their high price tags in affluent and rapidly gentrifying areas offer a glimpse of shifts within neighborhoods, changing clientele, and distinct differences between boxing gyms and boxing studios.

Since the days of lightweight boxer Art Aragon, neighborhoods east of downtown Los Angeles have produced a number of top fighters and Olympic gold medalists, partly due to a longer history of hefty public and private investment in boxing gyms aimed at addressing issues of "delinquency" for youth. In the early nineteenth century, missionaries and reformers relied on boxing and other sports to instill specific virtues in US urban communities of color and abroad in sites of US imperialism like the Philippines.[11] This use of boxing coincided with California restrictions and City of Los Angeles ordinances that aimed to move the sport away from other illicit activities, like gambling, and to impose regulations and reduce the possibility of fatal injuries (Maram 2006). The formation of the Catholic Youth Organization in 1930s Chicago used boxing as a social work tool to deter from gang violence and street fights. They soon became a national enterprise that included a chapter in Los Angeles and sought to minimize juvenile delinquency with the spiritual and physical discipline that boxing required (Gems 2004). In the 1960s, boxing programs dovetailed with John F. Kennedy's antidelinquency programs that pointed to individual behavior as a cause of inequality. In Los Angeles, public recreation funding for boxing in poor and working-class communities reinforced the idea that individual, not structural, transformation was the key to better outcomes. For example, in 1994 the *Los Angeles Times* featured East LA boxing as a refuge for troubled youth to keep them off the streets and as one of the few pathways to success (Waters 1994). These discourses did not question the systemic racism that led to the social problems that boxing helped youth mitigate. Rather, they placed the onus on the individual to transcend one's circumstances.[12]

While public funding for boxing was rooted in racialized discourses of delinquency and the capitalist belief of picking oneself up by the boot straps, public and private gyms became important sites for community development and dissent. For example, the Cleland House in East Los Angeles changed hands multiple times from private benefactors to public investment from the LA County Sheriff's Department over the course of its history, from 1922 to 2016. For decades, this place created a space for generations of youth to find their strength and belief in self, served as a site for the negotiation of gang truces and proved a training ground for community empowerment as fighters fought its closure in multiple instances. In the 1990s, funding declined. In the aftermath of public cutbacks, privately owned boxing gyms sought to fill the need created by the closure of publicly funded gyms while trying to staying afloat (Mondragón 2018). In this context, private boxing gym owners have fought to keep their doors open while maintaining affordable prices in low-income communities by seeking public and private funding for youth programs. Today, privately owned gyms serving working-class communities are faced with the challenge of thriving in a city with rapidly increasing racial and economic inequality. Conversely, boxing studios rooted in entrepreneurship and boxing celebrity refuse the collective ethos of boxing gyms for individual profit.

As boxers turn to creating their own gyms, they navigate the economic landscape of Los Angeles and create a vision for the impact of their gyms. Places like Barrio Boxing and City of Angels Boxing distinguish themselves from boxing studios and the inequality they represent while creating strategies for survival. When Sergio Ramirez opened the brick-and-mortar rendition of Barrio Boxing in 2016, it was the first boxing gym in the predominantly Latino neighborhood of El Sereno. Located on the eastern edge of the city, this community was previously off the radar until recently, when the views from its hilly topography attracted the attention of real estate speculators and middle-class residents who had been priced out of nearby neighborhoods in the Eastside. Ten miles away from Barrio Boxing, City of Angels, owned by Alex Brenes, is located south of downtown in a neighborhood that has witnessed rapid change in part due to its proximity to the University of Southern California (USC). City of Angels occupies an industrial area across the freeway from the university, which has steadily transformed from a commuter campus to a residential one lacking adequate student housing. For this reason, USC continues to be a key engine of gentrification in the area. Although operating at different scales and in separate parts of the city, Ramirez and Brenes both counter racial subordination and exclusion in Los Angeles (Johnson 2013). While Barrio Boxing engages the hostile conditions that face immigrant and working-class youth, City of Angels uses national flags, USC Greek Life banners, and autograph walls to offer regional community rooted in what Doreen Massey (1994) named a "global sense of place," a consciousness of how the local is linked to the wider world. Together, they reflect a larger pattern of strategies that private gym owners employ to create collective spaces in service of a more equal city.

Barrio Boxing: A Place and an Identity

Barrio Boxing reflects the working-class neighborhood to which it belongs. Located on the main thoroughfare of Huntington Drive, which has not yet reflected some of the more visible signs of gentrification happening elsewhere in El Sereno, the gym is sandwiched between Nueva Esperanza, a Christian storefront church, and Huntington Glass, a commercial and residential glass fabricator. From the outside, the gym blends into the commercial landscape. Metal bars reinforce the windows below a sign that reads "Building champions one day at a time." As you step through the doors, you see that the boxing ring takes up the majority of the space, draped on one side with the Mexican national flag and the other side with the US flag. Around the ring are boxing bags and weights. While some of the equipment was purchased, some was homemade, and other pieces were found and rehabbed to look like new. On the walls are posters of boxing greats like Muhammad Ali, magazine covers, and multiple posters related to the 1952 film *The Ring*, a story of a Mexican American boy who turns to boxing to help his family through hard times. Behind a counter at the front of the space is proof of the gym's impact—a Certificate of

Recognition from the City of Los Angeles and photos of champions who have trained at Barrio Boxing.

As Barrio Boxing opened its location in El Sereno, two critical neighborhood boxing gyms–turned–community spaces shut down. Pico-Union Boxing's six-year tenure of providing youth with free boxing lessons and a safe place to go after school ended when the Pico-Union Housing Corporation, which manages the low-income housing units in the area, shut down.[13] Cleland House's ninety-four-year history ended after the Los Angeles County Sheriff Department's Youth Activity League walked away, private benefactors stepped in, and its board of directors decided to open a new location that did not include boxing.[14] The loss of these community institutions highlights the promise and indignities that places like Barrio Boxing face—the possibility of changing lives while struggling to make do in the face of disinvestment from the city.

Barrio Boxing's founder, Sergio Ramirez, embodies the transformative power of boxing and the belief that it can transform the lives of Black and Brown youth even as his own experiences demonstrate the need for systemic social change. He founded this gym with the hope that it will create a different path for youth than the one he followed. Ramirez was born in Juárez, Mexico, and immigrated to the United States at the age of five with his parents and six siblings. His family settled near El Sereno in Boyle Heights, an immigrant community and critical center of Latino life and culture in Los Angeles. For Ramirez, growing up poor and not speaking English resulted in his being bullied in school because of his clothes. Unable to fight back in English, he began to use his fists to navigate the social isolation he felt.

He joined a gang as a young teenager in the 1990s, not an uncommon occurrence in Boyle Heights, which at the time was a hub of gang violence. The gang welcomed him with open arms, something Ramirez had not experienced before. One day he began fighting in a parking lot. A Catholic priest by the name of Father Greg Boyle took notice and encouraged him to trade in street fighting for formal boxing training. Father Boyle had begun ministering in Boyle Heights in the late 1980s at a time when intense gang violence claimed the lives of young men with unnerving frequency. His focus on ministering to gang members gained him respect from youth of color, which allowed him to have an impact on generations of people. For Ramirez, Father Boyle changed his life when he encouraged boxing. When Ramirez describes how he first discovered boxing, he says he fell in love with the sport "before I fell in love with anything else. Even before I fell in love with myself."[15] In retrospect, Ramirez expresses a desire to make the type of impact on youth that Father Boyle does by offering boxing as a lifeline to youth that resemble himself many years ago.

As Ramirez explored his newfound love, he soon learned of his inability to pursue amateur and professional boxing because he lacked proof of US citizenship. By the time he secured a green card, his participation in a gang had already taken him down a much different path—toward incarceration. When telling his story, his face is conflicted and mirrors the stories of criminalized youth who pursue boxing. Prison is not a place he would want to return to or want youth to experience, but it was where he learned to read and write in English. That he did not learn to read and write in school reflects the forms of disinvestment in Black and Brown youth that young boxers face today in Los Angeles and across the country. For example, Lucia Trimbur's (2013) study of amateur boxers at the famed Gleason's Gym in New York explains three experiences the majority of them share—incarceration and juvenile delinquency programs, short educational backgrounds in which prisons were among their largest educators, and difficulty finding and keeping employment. After his second release, at the age of thirty-three, Ramirez combined his love of boxing with a desire for structure to forge a new path and set out to start a boxing gym with educational opportunities for youth from similar backgrounds.

Ramirez builds on his own life experience to put forth the power of boxing to prepare young boys and girls who face poverty and unequal access to education for life outside the ring. In doing so, it fills a gap created by the disappearance of publicly funded boxing programs in the sprawling, postindustrial city. He defines the mission of Barrio Boxing as one that is committed to "youth at risk of violence, drugs, bullying, obesity and those at risk of falling victims to the streets." While his mission seems to echo language about boxing as an antidote to "at-risk youth," it deemphasizes delinquency and considers them potential victims of social problems. His mission statement honors the vulnerability of youth to the consequences of, rather than the perpetrators of, social problems. In aspiring to create a collective space of empowerment, he builds on a larger history of communities of color that transformed boxing gyms into sanctuaries for youth.

Ramirez established Barrio Boxing in the barrio and immediately encountered policing and regulation. When not working to support his family through construction work, he began training his children and other youth in the park until he was threatened with a fine for not having the $60-per-hour permit. In a moment when public spaces are compromised through large-scale public-private partnerships with developers that run the gamut from upscale housing to retail complexes, Ramirez's use of the park was quickly shut down. Then he moved his sessions to an alley behind his home. This solution was short-lived, though, as his neighbors started complaining, so Ramirez set his eyes on opening a gym. He went to the boxing equipment store and put $5 down on three hanging punching bags that retail for about $150 apiece. A week later, he needed his money and had to go back and retrieve it. Despite the setback, he continued to save until he was eventually able to lease a space on Huntington Boulevard and fill it with equipment.

Ramirez began making waves in the local boxing scene for producing champions in a relatively short amount of time while working to secure the gym's future beyond 2019. He continued to work in construction to support his family while doing everything he could to keep the brick-and-mortar Barrio Boxing open, including using his construction paycheck to cover business expenses. In the context of a rapidly changing neighborhood, Barrio Boxing faced an uncertain future in El Sereno. Researchers identified sections of El Sereno as gentrifying, with the latest gentrification mapping conducted four years earlier marking the area only two blocks away from Barrio Boxing. In response to the influx of first-time home buyers and trendy retail development, residents founded the group El Sereno against Gentrification in 2014. Barrio Boxing is located within a mile of two organizations that champion social justice, Barrio Action Family and Youth Center, a nonprofit and collaborator, and Eastside Café, a Zapatista-inspired community space that successfully fund-raised to buy their building in the face of closure. Although Ramirez shares many of the goals of these collectives—to empower young people to create healthy and successful futures—he has not yet been able to secure nonprofit status as a number of other gyms and major boxing councils have. Boxing gyms that do establish nonprofit organizations benefit from public and private funding for their youth boxing programs. However, for Ramirez, the application fees and legal advice needed to set up a nonprofit are considerable. He has approached the city, local police, firefighters, and foundations in hopes of garnering support to set up a program but has come to feel that they do not want to work with him. He remarks, "I wish the city could look at me with fresh eyes. They don't take me seriously just because I have tattoos and have been incarcerated. But that's why I do this." While his tattoos and personal history are what make him effective with youth and have instilled in him an unwavering drive, others read him differently.

The potential loss of the brick-and-mortar Barrio Boxing gym would also mean the loss of a place where stability and family reign supreme in an unpredictable city. Though boxing is a sport, boxers will be the first to say that it is not something you simply play. When you approach the sport with the type of discipline it requires, your gym becomes a collective and second family. Ramirez ingrains this idea in his youth when they first arrive. One kid, he recalls, was being bullied at school and came to him for advice. Ramirez handed him a Barrio Boxing T-shirt, promised him the shirt would be his shield, and encouraged him to remember, "You are Barrio Boxing." The next day, the boy showed up at the gym excited to report that no one had harassed him that day. Although for Ramirez a gang offered this kind of belonging and family, he now offers Barrio Boxing as a family to neighborhood youth. Every new boxer who arrives is introduced to the new community by standing in the center of the ring with everyone surrounding them in a circle. The new boxer introduces themselves and states why they want to box before everyone excitedly welcomes their new peer. They are expected to help one another and belie the idea that boxing is an individual sport; at Barrio Boxing it's a team thing. This collectivity is central to the success of fighters and provides an example of dissent in a sport that markets individual prowess and achievement. Ramirez acknowledges the support of parents who understand this philosophy and are grateful to the changes in their kids. They have worked at the gym installing the carpet and knocking down a wall to give the young boxers more space. Through potluck holiday celebrations, the gym becomes a larger site for community and sharing, where families come together in the very space where their youth are learning the skills that will serve them inside and outside the ring.

Barrio Boxing youth literally run the streets and get a firsthand view of the ongoing changes in their neighborhood. In preparation for their training runs, Ramirez walks their route, which includes alleys and sidewalks, in order to remove trash and harmful objects like syringes to protect his boxers' feet. Beyond that, he does not shelter them from the realities of their neighborhood. They run past people whose homes are literally the streets and who are engaged in a daily battle for survival. Training sessions have been interrupted by police chases, and Ramirez recounts one particular day when youth huddled inside the gym as a person across the street waved a rifle. On these days, Ramirez and his boxers have conversations about the challenges they face and what they can achieve by creating structure in their own lives. Thus, he reframes capitalist narratives of individual success through discipline and resilience into a collective recognition and resistance of the inequality that structures their lives. In these conversations, Barrio Boxing is about creating different futures by learning how to fight inside and outside the ring.

While the future of a brick-and-mortar location is uncertain, Barrio Boxing serves as an example of how boxing gym owners are resisting neoliberal capitalist disinvestment by creating spaces for community. Ramirez thinks constantly about the path that led him to this point and the significant obstacles he has encountered along the way. It's a reflection of the ways that immigration status, unequal education, and poverty have shaped his experiences and now continue to shape the lives of youth of color with whom he identifies. Ramirez does not hold out hope that the government will solve these issues and so dreams of creating a boxing gym that doubles as an educational site. He keeps an eye out for desks and chairs wherever he goes. He has already collected a few and hopes to acquire enough to set them up between the three punching bags. He has a plan to trade private boxing lessons to local college students in exchange for homework help for the youth. His face brightens as he describes the ideal routine, one in which neighborhood youth come straight to the gym from school, do their homework, and train—everything under one roof. Ramirez's refusal to stop planning for the future of a space that remains uncertain demonstrates the overlapping responses to struggle that boxing and the city invite—you do not only fight for the victory; you fight to survive.

City of Angels Boxing: A Global Intersection in Los Angeles

As Barrio Boxing fights to create a space of neighborhood collectivity, City of Angels demonstrates the efforts to create a regional identity in Los Angeles. City of Angels Boxing gym in South Los Angeles draws adults from across Los Angeles and every social stratum of the city. Owner Alex Brenes has certainly faced the pressures of economic restructuring but today confidently claims his gym is the "best boxing gym in LA." If Ramirez's Barrio Boxing reflects the immigrant and working-class neighborhood of El Sereno, Brenes's status as a more recent immigrant and the gym's location in South LA reflects the ways in which lifelong residents and recent arrivals intersect in the changing city. Taking its name from the lyrics of the Red Hot Chili Peppers' classic song "Under the Bridge," the gym offers a civic identity for residents, new and old, from across the city.[16]

Brenes's path to professional boxing provided him with not only skills he needed but also an appreciation for what would be considered an "authentic" and "gritty" boxing gym that respects the history of the sport. Brenes grew up in what he describes as a tough neighborhood in Costa Rica. When asked about how he got into boxing, he regards his story as a common one. He was hanging out with the wrong crowd until the owner of a tae kwon do studio saw him get into a fight and convinced him to train. Brenes went on to join the Costa Rican national boxing team. He immigrated to Miami, Florida, after marrying his wife, a US citizen. In the

United States he won amateur tournaments, becoming a Golden Gloves boxer and enjoying a seventeen-fight professional career. As a professional fighter, he also began teaching classes. He arrived in Los Angeles in 2010 to partner with a friend to run a pop-up gym in West Hollywood. The pop-up gym, which was located inside a clothing store, lasted a year and a half before he opened his own place.

South Los Angeles is the gym's second location. The first location was miles away in an industrial part of Chinatown, on Spring Street. The warehouse space was used by houseless people, one of whom was an artist who would paint on the walls. Although the owner had offered to whitewash all the walls, Brenes refused because the original walls added a sense of authenticity to the space. The large blank spaces also inspired him to reflect on the many people whose paths he's crossed to arrive at the location. He decided to map out these circuits on the walls and began asking everyone who used the gym to sign the wall. Shortly after he had built a consistent consumer base, his landlord decided to capitalize on the development projects that were spilling into Chinatown from neighboring downtown and creating a demand for space. He unreasonably raised Brenes's rent, forcing him to leave and search for a new location.

Brenes new location on Hill and Thirtieth Street demonstrates an appreciation for the city's history and the migratory circuits of people in the face of a highly segregated Los Angeles. Flags from all around the world hang all around the gym. When Brenes moved to the new gym, he brought the autographed drywall from the Chinatown warehouse and attached it to his new walls, bringing the past with him. Gymgoer testimonials emphasize that City of Angels Boxing offers entry into a close-knit community that is rooted not in claiming a particular neighborhood but in occupying the same space. City of Angels' ninety-nine-dollar monthly membership fee still allows the gym to draw from a wider social stratum than boutique boxing studios. The gym's aesthetic and Brenes's own relationship with Hollywood has attracted models, actors, and the film industry. Whereas the original *Rocky* took place at Main Street Gym, today's Creed (Michael B. Jordan) visits City of Angels during Oscar weekend. However, celebrities do not receive special treatment. Brenes does not close his gym for them, and it is precisely that sense that everyone is equal that gives City of Angels its character.

The gym's personality is one rooted in the history of boxing and of Los Angeles while combining the aesthetics of Instagram-worthy places with the feeling of the "authentic" boxing gym. This combination draws both boxing gym and boxing studio audiences while still offering a sense of community. Brenes makes use of Instagram as free advertising and has cultivated a personality that is legitimate to the world of boxing while also welcoming to novice fighters, with a range of goals from fitness to competitive fighting. Novice fighters are relegated to the bags and classes, while those fighters who want to enter the ring for sparring must have a valid amateur boxing license.[17] The gym's exterior has a vivid mural featuring boxing greats Muhammad Ali, Julio César Chávez, and Mike Tyson by MADSTEEZ, a multifaceted artist who has been described as "a human color wheel spinning on overdrive."[18] Next to it is a smaller mural by well-known Los Angeles artist Never. This mural depicts a cadre of greats from Los Angeles sports history—Fernando Valenzuela, Magic Johnson, Wayne Gretzky, and Landon Donovan. Inside the warehouse, Brenes achieved an atmosphere akin to places like Broadway Boxing. He uses his experiences in gyms from Costa Rica to Miami to Los Angeles to give gymgoers a sense of participation in a broader history by inviting artists to paint murals of boxing greats, including hometown heroes like Oscar De La Hoya. Forty hanging punching bags between the two boxing rings ensure that trainers never turn anyone away. Three black steps leading to the gold boxing ring feature three key words: dream, believe, and achieve. Ultimately, the gym aesthetically centers a history of boxing in the feel of neighborhood gyms in Black and Brown communities while incorporating a broader Angeleno audience.

The success of City of Angels Boxing could be attributed to Brenes's emphasis on being what he calls "a real boxing gym" that combines the feeling of grit and struggles with people and collectivity. His training in other boxing gyms in the United States and Costa Rica has made him keenly aware of their depth, one that studio gyms do not have when they attempt to capture the feeling of a neighborhood gym in a commercial storefront near craft breweries, coffee shops, and independent stores. Studio boxing gyms tend to share a minimalist aesthetic characteristic of gentrifying businesses that tends to include refinished concrete floors, exposed brick, or reclaimed wood. Ceilings are open, often giving an industrial feel as pipes are visible. They are also sometimes accompanied by commissioned exterior art that changes the streetscape and provides photo opportunities. City of Angels does not resemble an industrial space; it is actually a warehouse that, in the words of one gymgoer, has graffiti and a "gritty bad-ass aesthetic to it which everyone can appreciate when working out."[19] Brenes's own authenticity—as a boxer and somewhat recent arrival to the city, who has navigated the tough and gritty world—also helps to draw people to the gym.

While Brenes does not put forth boxing as a solution to social ills, his gym has created a space of inclusion and congregation in an unjust city.

For Brenes, social justice and a belief that we are all a part of the human race fuels his responses to inclusion. In addition to Instagram posts that define the gym as a "safe space," where all genders, races, ethnicities, and sexualities are welcome, the gym itself articulates these same values. A flag hangs that articulates a vision for "our America," which includes racial, sexual, gender, and environmental justice. On another wall are the words "No human is illegal. I'm Alex Brenes. I'm an immigrant." Elsewhere are hashtags that lead gymgoers to find images and articles about Martin Luther King Jr.'s and Rosa Parks's mug shots, Bob Marley's "One Love" song, and Nelson Mandela's prison identification number. The proclamation of the gym as a safe space also supports the practice of creating an inclusive atmosphere. While mainstream boxing continues to privilege male boxing, Alex Brenes argues that boxing is one sport and "there is no 'female boxing.'" This perspective is evident in the hanging of USC sorority banners alongside fraternities, the inclusion of female trainers, and the regular features of women on the gym's Instagram page. Unlike many boxing gyms in Los Angeles, women regularly frequent City of Angels.

While City of Angels seeks to create connections among people from all walks of life within the city of Los Angeles, Brenes supports a variety of social justice causes beyond the gym. The gym sponsors boxing teams in Kenya and Costa Rica. The space also hosts Athletes in the Making, an organization that fills the gaps created by the decline of funding for physical education and sports programs in the United States. In addition, the gym holds charity art and music events in collaboration with local organizations that work to alleviate social problems, ranging from the lack of funding for music programs to homelessness. While Brenes's own migratory story propels a regional and global conception of community, the space itself creates a rare opportunity in the contemporary segregated city, one where people converge.

Counterpunches

The determination that boxing requires also doubles as a lesson of how to survive in the city. It takes a special type of courage to be willing to take a punch to the face—often many—and keep going. In many ways, places like Barrio Boxing and City of Angels Boxing demonstrate the power of the counterpunch. It is more than a landing a punch in exchange for the one received. According to the website Law of the Fist, self-identified "youngsters" who are passionate about boxing and martial arts say the purpose of counterpunching is to create an opening for yourself so that you can swing momentum in your favor.[20] As part of a broader constellation of boxing gyms that harness the transformative power of boxing and commitment to community at various levels, Brenes and Ramirez create spaces that fuel the struggle to survive—and even thrive—in the city. They also provide a ray of hope in the hostile city that reminds us to fight, not because we are certain of the victory but because not fighting is certainly defeat.

Yet, nothing about boxing is a clean loss or victory. Not long after this chapter was originally drafted, Barrio Boxing moved from its location in El Sereno to a home garage. This was not the end of Barrio Boxing since it served as much an identity as it is a physical space. Barrio Boxing lives on as Ramirez strives to create a boxing community among youth and partner with other gyms. Shortly after the closing of Barrio Boxing's physical space, the novel coronavirus shut down all gyms across Los Angeles.

As coronavirus continued to ravage Los Angeles, Alex Brenes made the difficult decision to shut down City of Angels Boxing. Brenes reasoned that even though his patrons were very healthy, his collective mind-set swayed him from putting any families at risk. The decision to close became even more certain when reopening at reduced capacity with increased cleaning costs made the business economically unviable. Adapting to the needs of the moment, he transitioned to virtual boxing. The flexibility of virtual boxing allowed him to move his family to his homeland of Costa Rica for the remainder of the quarantine while maintaining the City of Angels community. In effect, he modeled the ethos of the physical gym: Wherever you are and wherever you're from, you are part of the community. In December 2022, Alex Brenes returned with his family to the United States and reopened City of Angels two blocks away from its original location and continues to build community across neighborhoods.

The past couple of years have also rocked the foundations of the landmark Broadway Boxing Gym. When the heart and soul of the gym, owner Sauchsee Larkins, passed away, the gym shut down. There were no major news publications mourning its loss, yet those who benefited from being there and participating in its community were still heard. Two such people were rappers G Perico and D Smoke. G Perico's So Way Out streetwear clothing store is connected to Broadway Boxing Gym, while D Smoke had joined the gym more than ten years ago after a friend had died and he "needed an outlet."[21] Upon hearing of the gym's closure, D Smoke reached out to businessman David Gross and pitched him the importance of the gym and the possibility of a community center within the space that could further invest in neighborhood youth. David Gross agreed and they purchased the gym through Gross's Own Our Own initiative, which works with high-profile entertainers and athletes to invest in Black communities while helping local residents to become shareholders. Thus, G Perico and

D Smoke are the most visible owners of Broadway Boxing Gym, but they have created a fund in which anyone from the neighborhood can invest alongside them.[22] In this move, Broadway Boxing Gym has become part of a larger constellation of efforts to create a sense of agency among Black and Brown people over their own communities and their future.

The changes experienced by Broadway Boxing Gym, Barrio Boxing, and City of Angeles Boxing demonstrate the precarity of a dramatically changing Los Angeles landscape that mirrors widening inequality. However, it also demonstrates the precarity that dissent requires. All three gyms were born out of movement and a goal to make their city better. Efforts to envision a different future for oneself, for one's community, and for the city are not guaranteed unequivocal success. Rather, like the sport of boxing, dissent requires struggle. Boxing gyms remind us that the punches are not defeat. As boxers and as communities of color, it is one thing to lose a fight; it is quite another to give up.

Notes

1. "Broadway Boxing Gym LA," accessed March 27, 2019, https://broadwayboxingla.com/.

2. Rudy Mondragón notes that private gyms operating in the 1980s and 1990s often had to lower their prices to compete with city-funded boxing gyms. He notes that places like Azteca Boxing Gym in South East Los Angeles widened their purpose to include serving youth, girls, and women after the recession in the early 2000s. "Where Julio Cesar Chavez and Macho Camacho Became Stars: How Azteca Boxing Club in Bell Became a Training Ground for Champions," L.A. TACO, accessed March 27, 2019, https://www.lataco.com/history-of-azteca-boxing-gym-bell/.

3. See George Lipsitz, *How Racism Takes Place* (Temple University Press, 2011).

4. Justin Frimmer, dir. *Born and Bred* (Purebred Films, 2011).

5. "L.A.'s Homelessness Surged 75% in Six Years. Here's Why the Crisis Has Been Decades in the Making." *Los Angeles Times*, accessed March 28, 2019, https://www.latimes.com/local/lanow/la-me-homeless-how-we-got-here-20180201-story.html.

6. This notion has been supported by scholarly studies. In a quantitative study combining Yelp data with US Census, Federal Housing Agency, and Streetscore information, researchers found that gentrifying neighborhoods tend to have a growing number of specific types of businesses such as cafés, restaurants, bars, and local grocery stores.

7. See Jan Lin, Taking Back the Boulevard: Art, Activism and Gentrification in Los Angeles (New York University Press, 2019).

8. The term "gentrification" emerged in academic and popular discourse in

the 1960s. Sociologist Ruth Glass described how working-class neighborhoods in London were "invaded by the middle classes—upper and lower." Since the 1960s, gentrification has become integrated into wider urban processes that make the experience pervasive across urban centers. Neil Smith, *The New Urban Frontier: Gentrification and the Revanchist City* (Routledge, 1996), 33.

9. Allie Flynn, "Every It Girl Is Trying This Fitness Trend: Here's Why You Should Too," TZR, November 9, 2017, accessed March 28, 2019, https://www.thezoereport.com/living/wellness/boxing-workout-trend; "Why Boxing Is Becoming the Most—The Active Times," accessed March 28, 2019, https://www.theactivetimes.com/why-boxing-becoming-most-popular-new-way-work-out; "Why Boxing Is LA's Hottest New Fitness Trend," accessed March 28, 2019, https://www.alderapartments.com/blog/boxing-las-new-fitness-trend.

10. These areas include downtown LA and surrounding neighborhoods such as the Arts District, Echo Park, South Central, and Lincoln Heights.

11. For more on the relationship between boxing and US imperial projects in the Philippines, see Linda España-Maram, *Creating Masculinity in Los Angeles's Little Manila: Working-Class Filipinos and Popular Culture, 1920s–1950s* (Columbia University Press, 2006).

12. For more on juvenile antidelinquency programs, see Elizabeth Hinton, *From the War on Poverty to the War on Crime: The Making of Mass Incarceration in America* (Harvard University Press, 2016), 27–62.

13. "Why the Pico-Union Boxing Club, a Godsend to Youth, Is at a Crossroads," *Los Angeles Times*," March 20, 2016.

14. Thomas Curwen, "After He Spent Time on the Street and in Prison, This East L.A. Gym Saved Him. Now, He's Fighting to Save It," latimes.com, accessed September 13, 2018, http://www.latimes.com/local/lanow/la-me-boxinggym-20160823-snap-story.html.

15. Sergio Ramirez, interview with author, January 19, 2019.

16. Alex Brenes, interview with author, January 14, 2019.

17. Brenes's own experience as a professional boxer and recognition of its dangers guide his commitment to protecting fighters by not allowing them to spar until they are officially licensed to do so.

18. "Mad Steez," Long Beach Walls, http://www.powwowlongbeach.com/madsteez, accessed April 2, 2019.

19. "Testimonials Archive," City of Angels Boxing, accessed April 2, 2019, https://www.cityofangelsboxing.com/testimonials.

20. "Complete Guide to Counterpunching in Boxing," Law of the Fist, October 4, 2019, https://lawofthefist.com/complete-guide-to-counterpunching-in-boxing/, accessed December 29, 2019.

21. Ural Garrett, "Interview: D Smoke Describes Meteoric Rise between 'Rhythm + Flow' Win and Debut Album 'Black Habits,'" *Hip Hop Dx*, accessed July 16, 2022, https://hiphopdx.com/news/id.54569/title.interview-d-smoke-describes-meteoric-rise-between-rhythm-flow-win-debut-album-black-habits#.

22. Andre Gee, "How David Gross Is Helping Black People Invest in Their Own Communities," Complex, accessed July 15, 2022, https://www.complex.com/music/david-gross-own-our-own-initiative/.

References

Aguilera, Gene. 2018. *Latino Boxing in Southern California*. Arcadia Publishing.

De La Cruz-Viesca, Melany, Zhenxiang Chen, Paul M. Ong, Darrick Hamilton, and William Darity. 2016. "The Color of Wealth in Los Angeles." Federal Reserve Bank of San Francisco, 1–60. https://www.frbsf.org/wp-content/uploads/sites/3/color-of-wealth-in-los-angeles.pdf.

España-Maram, Linda. 2006. *Creating Masculinity in Los Angeles's Little Manila: Working-Class Filipinos and Popular Culture, 1920s–1950s*. Columbia University Press.

Gems, Gerald R. 2004. "The Politics of Boxing: Resistance, Religion, and Working-Class Assimilation." *International Sports Journal* 8, no. 1: 89–103.

Hinton, Elizabeth. 2016. *From the War on Poverty to the War on Crime: The Making of Mass Incarceration in America*. Harvard University Press.

Huante, Alfredo, and Kimberly Miranda. 2019. "What's at Stake in Contemporary Anti-Gentrification Movements?" *Society + Space*. https://www.societyandspace.org/articles/whats-at-stake-in-contemporary-anti-gentrification-movements.

Johnson, Gaye Theresa. 2013. *Spaces of Conflict, Sounds of Solidarity: Music, Race, and Spatial Entitlement in Los Angeles*. University of California Press.

Lin, Jan. 2019. *Taking Back the Boulevard: Art, Activism and Gentrification in Los Angeles* New York University Press, 2019.

Lipsitz, George. *How Racism Takes Place*. Temple University Press, 2011.

"Los Angeles—Gentrification and Displacement." Urban Displacement Project. https://www.urbandisplacement.org/maps/los-angeles-gentrification-and-displacement.

Massey, Doreen. 1994. *Space, Place and Gender*. University of Minnesota Press.

Mondragón, Rudy. 2018. "Where Julio Cesar Chavez and Macho Camacho Became Stars: How Azteca Boxing Club in Bell Became a Training Ground for Champions." L.A. Taco. https://www.lataco.com/history-of-azteca-boxing-gym-bell/.

Ong, Paul M., Silvia R. González, Chandara Pech, C. Aujean Lee, and Rosalie Ray. 2018. "The Widening Divide Revisited: Economic Inequality in Los Angeles." UCLA Center for Neighborhood Knowledge, 1–55. https://knowledge.luskin.ucla.edu/wp-content/uploads/2018/01/Haynes-Report_WideningDivide_Ong_UCLA_1.3.2017.pdf.

O'Rourke, Bryan K. 2015. "The Rise of Boutique Fitness Studio Concepts." Stephens: Capitalize on Independence, 1–3. https://www.slideshare.net/slideshow/the-rise-of-boutique-studio-fitness-concepts/66643673.

Smith, Neil. 1996. *The New Urban Frontier: Gentrification and the Revanchist City*. Routledge, 1996.

Trimbur, Lucia. 2013. *Come out Swinging: The Changing World of Boxing in Gleason's Gym*. Princeton University Press.

Waters, Sean. 1994. "School of Hard Knocks." *Los Angeles Times*.

Zuk, Miriam, Ariel H. Bierbaum, Karen Chapple, Karolina Gorska, and Anastasia Loukaitou-Sideris. 2018. "Gentrification, Displacement, and the Role of Public Investment." *Journal of Planning Literature* 33, no. 1: 31–44.

10

Boxing as an Art for Community Engagement

A Conversation with Khnum Muata Ibomu

GAYE THERESA JOHNSON
and RUDY MONDRAGÓN

Khnum Muata Ibomu, also known by his stage name stic (previously "stic. man"), is an award-winning hip-hop artist, activist, platinum producer, and published author who makes up half of the legendary hip-hop duo dead prez. Ibomu created the RBG Fit Club, "a holistic lifestyle movement" and brand that centers wellness and healthy living in its mission. On the musical side, stic created Fit Hop, a subgenre of hip-hop that, according to stic himself, aims to inspire well-being through "heartfelt hip-hop that is devoted to holistic healthy living, strong enough for the streets yet uplifting for the whole family to enjoy." In April 2011, stic released his solo project and RBG Fit Records–produced album, *The Workout*, which featured "Joe Louis," a track inspired by the great Black heavyweight boxing champion of the 1930s. Listening to this track for the first time further solidified Rudy Mondragón's belief that hip-hop and boxing form a powerful reciprocal cultural relationship beyond the use of hip-hop tracks for a fighter's workout or ring entrance song.

• • •

RUDY MONDRAGÓN: My honest belief is that everybody has a boxing story or is connected to the sport in some way. These stories often remind us of the past—who we were as children and how we've become who we are right now. What is your story when it comes to the sport of boxing?

KHNUM MUATA IBOMU: Man, you know what? Boxing is the only sport that I wasn't bored to death of. Coming up, everyone was hyped about football. Then it was basketball season, and then there was baseball, which is super boring to me. I wasn't a kid that was into watching sports. But when boxing would come on, it would grab me. I got to feel the excitement, I guess, like what other people were getting from football or whatever.

I identified with the individual performance of it. I draw; so you're sitting by yourself drawing. I write; that's you and the paper. Even as a runner, you know. And if I'm engineering in the studio, I'm just sitting there. So it's like something that you can control your space, your talent, your development. And I know these are team efforts; you don't do any of this stuff truly alone. But as opposed to the basketball team or the football team, I think I identify with that. That guy must show what he's got in the ring. And the courage and just the realness of like, "You gotta show what you've got in front of everybody."

And it's fighting. I've been in fights in school and different things, so I could just relate to what it takes. I appreciate that "Warrior walk alone" in a way, that kind of spirit of it.

And then from there, just the parties or the gatherings around boxing was something that I appreciated. I would see my dad happy. It was a good time. They're excited. So it's a good thing in the house, as opposed to when it's drama and other shit going on. And then, in my family, this is the sport we watch now. And we make food, and . . . It's like when we have gatherings, it's usually around somebody's fight. I see it as . . . It's definitely a cultural thing that I appreciate, we appreciate as a family.

My son got into boxing. We have a two-year minimum of self-defense as one of our family values, right? Some kids wanted to do box; others wanted to do martial arts. He got introduced to different martial arts. Boxing is the one he wanted to keep doing. It allows us father-son time. It allows us the rich metaphors of boxing. We're always talking about using boxing as an analogy to explain something else. If we're here talking about hip-hop, if we're talking about life, if we're talking about marriage, relationship, it's an analogy pulled from a shared experience. I know he knows what that means to "keep your hands up." Boxing is a universal thing, and the principles translate to all kinds of conflict resolution. It's a lot for us. Boxing weaves its way in our family.

GAYE THERESA JOHNSON: I was hoping I could go back to something you said earlier. You said when boxing would come on, it grabbed you. And it made me think about the sound of boxing, because it's very different from football or basketball. And I just wondered, What did you hear that grabbed you?

KMI: The bell, the excitement of the crowd. Having been in loads of playground fights, I know what that feels like. I know when I'm afraid. I know what that feels like when it's like, "Yo, you got beat up?" And tomorrow when it's like, "You handled your business." The currency of that. I responded to that.

We're doing this in this organized ring, and you can watch it. And I'm picking up game. I'm watching the techniques. I'm seeing the feints, and I'm trying to do that. And then I'm doing it with my cousins. Like we used to have sock tournaments. So you take one sock and you wrap it around your knuckles. And then you take another sock and you roll it, and you hold it, and then you put a sock over that, and then you box. We had no special training, but that was a part of like, "Yo, you coming over Saturday? Then we'll sock box." You get to feel like the champ. You get to feel like [Muhammad] Ali or whatever. And these are like rite of passage things. This is something in us that wants to test our courage, test our skills, physical, mind, spirit. We cut off from a lot of our ancient, cultural traditions. And so we look to things to do that in gang culture. Certain things that we would do, like we're gonna run up in the spot where we . . . Some of it is out of economic necessity. But some of it was hard and we need to know who I'm running with. And we would make these terrible penitentiary risk choices. But to define our own character.

Martial arts and boxing are ways to do so without the negative consequences. That's another reason why I really value it, because young men and women need that. You must express your warrior side, in a supportive environment. You got protective equipment, you got counsel, and expertise. I love to be at the gym when all the OGs are saying like, "Bring it. What are you doing?"[1] You know what I mean? And encouraging that in an art, sportsman context, I feel like that is the proper balance of that energy, and it needs to be expressed.

GTJ: I feel like that's the best I've heard it expressed. People who don't know about boxing talk about "Oh, the violence that it elevates" and whatever. And then we do talk, of course, about the toxic masculinist stuff. But the idea that the same feeling state could happen where you're in absolute peril. Like where you could be on the playground, or you could be somewhere you ain't supposed to be, and then you could come back to fight another day, or you could die, or you could go to prison for the rest of your life. But to have that actually happen as you explained it in a safe space where there are people around you, saying like, "You could try it this way." You're not alone in this situation. It sounds like for some people it could be the only place you get to win. And get it witnessed, like children need to see themselves. They need to be seen.

KMI: Right. Absolutely.

GTJ: That's why it touches me so much, because I feel like that is the answer to that accusation that it's only about violence and a way to channel violence.

KMI: And even that is when we describe certain things, like, as violence. There's a lot of loaded cultural baggage saying it's violent. Why? Because we're touching? If it's consensual. When we coming up, you wrestle. You do all kind of stuff. Put someone in a choke hold and it's fun. It's a little uncomfortable, but we're agreeing to do this 'cause I'm gonna get you and it's just part of our being.

At the end of the day, you must have certain amount of survival skills. In a society that wants to oppress people, they're trying to domesticate that out of you. There's no place for your warrior instinct in an oppressed society, right?

An animal will bite your ass if you're trying to do something they don't want you to do, but is he violent? And that's what we say as humans. We say tigers are violent and all this stuff, but animals are very peaceful. They don't ever kill for malice. They don't ever kill for greed. They kill to eat and they kill for protection. And otherwise, this wild animal is the most peaceful creature ever. But human beings kill for pride.

Warrior culture is its own religion, is its own understanding, is its own philosophy. And is what's behind sport, is what's behind football and all these different competitions, because that energy has to be directed in some way. It's just a part of who we are that needs to be in balance.

RM: I remember an article I read where you said something like, it's not a war until the oppressed engage back; otherwise it's just a slaughter.

KMI: There you go.

RM: This makes me think about what Muhammed Ali once said about Jack Johnson: "I know I'm bad but he was crazy."[2] Jack Johnson was talking smack to white people, driving sports cars, and dressing in the dandy fashion, which was not common for Black men during that time.

GTJ: Talking back to cops.

KMI: Yeah, dating white women, whatever he wanted to do.

GTJ: Yeah, whatever he wanted to do.

RM: I thought about that because white journalists would write about the threat that Johnson's victories posed to a white society. They feared that Johnson's wins would inspire Black workers to revolt against them, so they would lie and refuse to share the information with them. It also made me think about your song "Joe Louis." Joe Louis was a very different kind of fighter than Johnson, because his handlers around him didn't want him to be unapologetic like Johnson. They advised him to be different, because if he was like Johnson, they felt that would cost Louis his career. What inspired that song and why did you select Joe Louis for that track?

KMI: The song "Joe Louis" is actually not about Joe Louis. Joe Louis is a symbol that represents an era of boxers including Jack Johnson, Jack

Dempsey, and others. It is a symbol for the old-school work ethic, the old-school training ethic. The hook on that song is, *I train to live, I live to train / It's go hard or go home / No pain, no gain / Hard work just another daily routine / Healthy and strong like Joe Louis in the ring.*

It's more about the work ethic of training. When I look at that era, that's what it inspires me the most. I like watching their training footage more than the old fights because I'm interested in what makes someone a champion, not just your champion moment. And I love how they would be running in work boots and shit like that and the aesthetic of that, in the old leather jump ropes. And this shit is heavy. This was working-class.

Joe Louis represented that vintage, old-school. To this day, our whole brand and when I make beats, I literally score to old footage. I'll put it on just to put that vibe in the room and channel that. Somebody might do this and I'll be like, the snares is gonna follow that. I'm just trying to put that in audible form, in my own artistic way. But every track that I have has been played to some kind of footage. And if the emotion and the scales that I'm using don't fit, then I'm like, "No, I don't feel right. It can go with that." So it was not so much his politic, but it was, he's like a symbol of that era to me.

RM: Dave Zirin says that Martin Luther King Jr. talked about a Black man who was on death row and was about to be executed in the gas chamber and the last thing that person said was "Save me, Joe Louis."[3] The symbolic power that Joe Louis represents is something that goes beyond the moment. We're so far removed from Jack Johnson's and Joe Louis's fights, we have some footage on YouTube from their fights, but our generation right now is inspired by a lot of the things that happened to them in addition to their victories. That's what I think about when it comes to that track. So powerful.

GTJ: I love that it's visual for you, because for so many people who do sonic work, it's a sound that's inspiring, not a visual that's translated into a sound or vice versa.

I was also thinking about Joe Louis and Jack Johnson and their supporters were also different in their era because you couldn't really cheer. They didn't want people to know that they won, but people still found out. There were these networks of information that were like the underground railroad because it's like, "What time is he fighting? What's happening? Where are people gonna see this? Listen on the radio? When is this gonna happen?" And the collectives that come together to celebrate is powerful. You can't have no celebration even in your house. In the 1930s and '40s in the South, you could not be heard celebrating unless you're in church. It's interesting to think about that era.

You also mentioned the heavy ropes. Boxing must have sounded differently and surely the ropes created a different pace.

KMI: Yeah, it's like the aesthetic of boxing is its own chamber. In football, what do they call it, the pigskin? There's this era of the old uniforms versus now, and there's value in that. Those are metaphors or symbols of certain time periods, which really means certain values, certain seasons of values. That era speaks to me different than the way I'm inspired by Sugar Ray Leonard and Marvin Hagler and Ali's era, which is different than Roy Jones Jr. and Mike Tyson and Lennox Lewis and Shannon Briggs. That era, it's not the same. But they all are inspiring, but I guess the real one, the one that gives me that Rocky feeling—you know what I mean?—is that old-school. That's why with my album *The Workout*, that's why it's black-and-white instead of color. That's why we wanna show you the bag with the tape on it instead of the new state-of-the-art gym. You know what I mean? It's about the . . . the *rasquachismo*?

RM: *Rasquache.*

KMI: *Rasquache.*[4] You know what I mean? Like that part of it is the fighter part. That's the fight in you to work through your injury, to work through your doubt, to work through your circumstance, your situation and be a champion regardless. That spirit. That's it. That is the hero's journey. That is [what] Joseph Campbell talks about.[5] The unlikely outcome, the underdog meets a figure or a team; it is part of the journey they go on. They become something that's in them. Yet, in order to get to the victory, they put the work in. And I think that's why boxing is so universal because it's that universal hero's journey coming out of nowhere.

GTJ: We're curious about the RBG Fit Club, how it started, but also what's the role of boxing in the fit club?

KMI: Well, RBG Fit Club is a holistic lifestyle movement, born out of me having gout in my leg in my early twenties from getting high and drinking and smoking and all that stuff. A plant-based diet and lifestyle helped me heal naturally, opening my mind to that world, that space of health.

With that, I got back into martial arts. When I was a little kid, I did martial arts, but I was like, "Oh yeah, there's more to this." It was a calling. For ten years I did various martial arts.

When my son got into boxing, I got into long-distance running because a boxer at our gym named Bones had, like, a twelve-pack. I was like, "Yo, Bones, what are you doing? For your ab game, man?" And he was like, "How much you run?" I told him that I di[d]n't really run. I've done all kind of training, but not really running. He told [me], "Man, you gotta run." He challenged me to start with ten minutes. When I had started, I couldn't do ten minutes, but he challenged me to work up to is, like, thirty, then forty-five, then maybe an hour. I was so inspired by that whole grittiness of everything. It was something new that I hadn't done in all the other training.

I started my five-minute walk and jog, all the way to twenty-six miles nonstop. It came from the boxing work ethic. And seeing footage of Tyson at four in the morning, you know, hating the run and Ali saying, "I hate these runs but it'll make you a champion." It was shit like that that got me through the five miles to ten miles, thirteen, eighteen, twenty, twenty-six. It was that whole passion and the spiritual profit from these physical things.

I thought we had to have a platform that shared this shit. I felt a calling to create a space in my music and in any other platform I would have to get that out, to echo that with people. That was the impetus behind it. I wanted to create a space that people can explore the wealth of healthy living from a deeper dimension. So that's what we are experimenting with, with our brand.

We have five principles that we use and inspire everything we create that came out of our process: knowledge, nutrition, exercise, rest, and consistency. It's really the process of getting to know yourself deeper. That's the fundamental principle. That's why you're running. That's why you're going to dojo. Self-awareness, nutrition, how do we feed our focus? How do we nourish our bodies? What's right for us, and what's the science around that? What do we have access to? What's our habits and our psychology around nutrition?

Exercise is moving the body, but we break it down into four pillars: strength, flexibility, endurance, and vitality. Exercise is addressing the different components. You're building your strength but you're also building flexibility and endurance. Trying to have a balance.

We've heard of strength training, we've heard of flexibility training, we know about endurance, but vitality training is like breath work. It's like the Qigong.[6] It's like resting and valuing the spa, the sweat, so your vitals are also being strengthened. Then restoration, rest, that's the fourth principle and that's meditation. Again, we emphasize the break, the rest. Not just to go hard but to rest hard. And then consistency, that's the thumb on the fist. That holds it all together.

RM: Roadwork and consistency, that's what stuck out to me, and it goes back to boxing. I think about fighters like Juan Manuel Márquez, who used cupping therapy when he was training for his fight against Manny Pacquiao. He was also doing yoga. And then you have Deontay Wilder of this era, who did a lot of visualization. Whatever he puts out there, he puts it out there because he wants it to manifest.

KMI: Speak it into existence, right?

RM: Right, and then you have Keith Thurman, who meditates all the time. You've seen these non-Western practices that are being applied by some fighters and the roadwork and consistency, which is one of the pillars of RBG Fit Club. What metaphor do you think roadwork serves for RBG Fit Club?

KMI: I'm gonna come back to that, but something just came to me in terms of that in Mike Tyson's book *Iron Ambition*, about how Cus D'Amato taught him about meditation and visualization. So that's a whole chamber of Tyson learning how to go into his subconscious mind and deal with his doubt and his feelings of unworthiness and just the shit he's been through. He had dealt with a lot. Cus D'Amato used these holistic alternative techniques to supplement his training. He wasn't just his trainer. Helping him understand that your mindset is a huge part of you believing in your ability to be a champion. If you don't work on that, that's gonna be in the way. And Tyson would tell you he still doesn't feel like he's capable of the things he's done. But somehow it happened and it's because he had these techniques.

Back to the roadwork and the consistency: I remember being inspired by roadwork. Running is my go-to practice; that's my main form of exercise. There's a whole lot of parallels in our brand, about one step at a time, about continuing. There is something I learned when I was training for the twenty-six miles is that if you've never ran longer than ten minutes, you have a perception of running. Once you run, let's say, two miles, right? Okay, you're like, "I know what that takes. I know what that feels like." But there are thresholds at different points in your journey of running that is different. For example, after the second mile physiologically in your body, your body says, "Okay, you're gonna keep going? Okay, so we're gonna have to change the formula of when we send lactic acid. We're gonna move some shit around because you're gonna keep going." So your third and fourth mile you're like, "Hold on, what is this? A second wind?" You would have never known that because you would assume that if I keep going, it's gonna be harder, and harder, and harder. But the body, like a car has these gears and it shifts with your consistency, and I learned that firsthand. Right now, if we go run two miles, I'm gonna be feeling like, "Do I wanna run two miles?" But I've been through that zillion[s] of times, so I know that's just the mind. It has nothing to do with "Am I in shape?" The athletic capability of the body or nothing. It's purely mental. But you have to get to know that. And in running I've learned that we personify phenomenons [*sic*]; we personify energy and forces.

So I was like, "Oh, that's Mr. Doubt." He got on a trench coat and a hat. And he sits on the bench, and he show up every time I train, he comes out to check on me. And Mr. Doubt is gonna sit there and see what you got today. And once I started projecting that outside, I was like, "Oh, he's keeping me company."

It's a whole chamber of what consistency unlocks for your wellbeing, for your personal growth, for your understanding of yourself. That's the value of consistency. Consistency means that the deeper benefits can have time to show up. No boxer has started out the champion of the world. Consistency is that investment that unlocks your wealth in major ways.

GTJ: In many ways it makes a bridge. Some of the things you started off talking about, even just about animals and the spiritual payoff for the physical challenge. So much of this is so much simpler than we allow it to be because of the way that we let our minds get in the way of what our bodies want to do. And the body is an animal. It doesn't lie. It lets you know what it needs. It also strikes me as something that is very anticapitalist in terms of practice and rest. Because rest is totally not in the model of capitalism that was ever made for Black people. Period. But just for all of us. And any time you try to monetize something, rest is not in that equation either, whether you're trying to make it into an industry rather than a way of life or a philosophy of action. And I feel like when you really are focused on healing people, like whole people over generations, that strikes me as very intentionally anticapitalist.

KMI: And they align too. The principles are cumulative. Everything starts with awareness. For something to grow it needs to be nourished. And then exercise it. Let it get strength in its legs; let it do what it do. Let it manifest; let it try. Let the cub try to hunt a little bit. It's exercising what is to come, right? But then rest. Don't go so hard. You're not a full-blooded cheetah yet. Rest, grow, 'cause that's when we grow is when we rest. That's when muscles grow, when we rest. And that's what, the rest is what allows you to continue and to be consistent. So those principles are a wheel that feed each other in that way.

RM: RBG stands for so many things. Listening to the music and checking out the website, RBG stands for Reaching Bigger Goals; Revolutionary but Gangsta; Red, Black, Green. What are some of the goals and the vision that you're currently working towards for RBG Fit Club?

KMI: We wanna just continue to be a bridge of hip-hop culture and holistic living. Our big game is to fuse the elements of hip-hop culture with a holistic practice through multimedia, through events, experiences, books, and music.

Ultimately, we want to invest in what we call wellness real estate. To create locations that we can engage in practice in our own curated space. It might be a cousin of a gym, but it's not like a gym. It might be a cousin of a spa, but it's not just for rest and relaxation. It's the coming together of that, and in the mind-set aspect, the affirmations and just being in a space that you can practice a holistic way.

GTJ: I feel like what we're hearing is a whole other thing here, how boxing and martial arts functions for our communities. What it has meant and what it can mean as a transformative whole thing.

KMI: The key is the art of boxing. A lot of people don't recognize boxing as an art form. They see it as a violent sport. When you go in a gym and you decide to box, you see other people who are putting in that work, you start to recognize talent as opposed to this "It's violent, it's this and that." You start to recognize speed like, "Yo, son is nice!" Or you start to see bad habits. You start [to] see attitudes or you start to see self-control. You start to notice the art just like you would in music. The nuances like the breath control of Big Daddy Kane versus the charisma Eazy-E had. He had no rhythm, but he was effective. And there's some boxers that are incredibly skillful in the basics. And then there's some boxers that's like brute, knock 'em out. So those are expressions of an art. And there's a reason why these things work in context with everything going on, you know? And I don't think the average person don't get the benefit of appreciating boxing as an art. So I feel like that's one thing, just gratitude of that. We have a music side, RBG Fit Records. And our whole premise of Fit Hop music is based on boxing like 100 percent. The same way a fighter goes to a gym to learn techniques to become a champion is the same way our artists, we go to the studio to learn certain techniques to become a champion of healthy living. To learn how to make music about healthy living that's gonna connect with audiences. There's an art to doing that. Where it's not corny, where it's not preachy, but it's still giving inspiration and value.

When I'm coaching our artists, I'm speaking like a boxing coach. I'm giving homework, like roadwork. And just so many analogies that we're using it in that way. It's an easy metaphor that our guys [use] to identify with and to see themselves as: "I'm like a fighter, but for this rap shit." It's something that's easy to connect and then we run that metaphor all the way. Like Coach Nym is our recent release, he went through that process.[7] He didn't know how to produce. He had never completed an album. He had been doing gangsta music here and there. He's a Blood. Whoop-dee-whoop. And when he told me he wanted to work with me, I was like, "You gotta be ready to become a champion. You gotta be ready to let go just like a boxer." This is our conversation: "Just like a boxer gotta give up burgers and fries and all this type of shit to be the champ, you gotta do that too. Are you ready?" We worked for like a year and a half. He had to learn the software. He had to make wack beats all the way to understanding musical theory and how to not be corny.

Just like a boxer has to learn all the form and then you gotta put it together your way. And then you must adapt to the person in front of you, who's totally different than the dude from last week. And you gotta continue to do your thing so every song, every beat, you gotta adapt that; you can't do the same shit. So that's just like our running metaphor in creating Fit Hop. That's, like I said, that's why our tag line is the Champion Sound of Healthy Living.

Notes

1. "OGs" refers to coaches, trainers, and former boxers with a great deal of expertise and years of experience in the sport of boxing.

2. "Muhammad Ali 1978 Says 'Jack Johnson' the GREATEST," uploaded by Robert Sevier, June 4, 2016, https://www.youtube.com/watch?v=MSj3hsabWmc.

3. Dave Zirin, What's My Name, Fool? Sports and Resistance *in the United States* (Haymarket Books, 2005), 57.

4. *Rasquachismo* is a Chicano phenomenon or view of the downtrodden that Tomás Ybarra-Frausto has defined as an underdog perspective (*los de abajo*) that presupposes a worldview of the "have-not." It is also an oppositional worldview that has both cultural and practical dimensions. In other words, making do with what you have is both a way to resist as well as affirm. stic uses *rasquache* here to emphasize how within a boxing context, using duct tape on a punching bag is both a way to extend the life of a used-up punching bag as well as affirming a working-class experience.

5. Joseph Campbell, *The Hero's Journey: Joseph Campbell on his Life and Work* (Harper & Row, 1990).

6. Qigong is a centuries-old system of coordinate body postures and movements, breathing, and meditation that is used for the purpose of health, spirituality, and martial arts training.

7. Coach Nym is an Afro–Puerto Rican artist originally from the Bronx, New York, who is part of the RBG Fit Club and has collaborated on music with stic.

11

Solidarity or Sanction

The Moral Economy of the Urban Gym

LUCIA TRIMBUR

Around noontime on an otherwise uneventful day in Gleason's Gym, Harry, a boxing trainer, approaches me and, with flattened affect, asks if I "wanna take a ride." Harry knows that traveling anywhere with him and listening to his stories is one of my favorite pastimes, and he laughs when a smile stretches across my face and I nod enthusiastically. He tilts his head sideways toward the door and says, "Let's go." Before he has told his fighters when he will return, I have grabbed my jacket and am waiting at the gym's exit.

We climb into Harry's minivan, the vehicle he uses for trips from Brooklyn to gyms in the other outer boroughs where he trains prospects and contenders. Today, however, we head into the heart of Manhattan, where Harry will work with a "white-collar client."[1] As we battle traffic for close to an hour, Harry explains that we are visiting a well-known comedian who likes a quick boxing workout before he tapes his daily TV show. The performer's energy is low by nature, but hitting pads with Harry helps him energize for his twenty-one-minute program. The arrangement also helps Harry. Though he trains the client for under an hour four days a week, the job adds over one thousand dollars to his monthly income. Because most of the amateur boxers that Harry coaches cannot pay for their training, and because the professional fighters he works with pay only when they have a sanctioned fight, consistent clients are crucial to Harry's income. Some months, payment from this comedian alone comprises nearly half of his earnings. On the way back to the gym after his workout, we chat about the client, of whom Harry is quite fond, and the possibilities this job has given him. Harry stresses that not only does the position provide needed income, but it also offers him a break from the pitch, intensity, and insularity of the gym, where he spends upward of fifteen hours a day, six days a week.[2]

Several weeks later, I notice Harry is not leaving the gym at midday as usual. When I ask if he still works with the comedian, he explains that he has given the position to Leon, a talented amateur fighter whom Harry has been training for almost a decade and who Harry believes needs the income more than he. When my eyes widen with worry, Harry reassures me: "It's a good job for him."

And it *is* a good job for Leon. It would be a good job for most of the gym's young men of color, an overwhelming number of whom have been distanced from the wage, have histories of incarceration, and struggle to locate adequate housing. This job allows Leon—who lives at home but receives no financial help from his parents—to train, earn a modest income, and pay his bills. But gifting this lucrative post places Harry back into a precarious financial position, out of which he has spent nearly two decades trying to move. Why did Harry do this?

Harry's gift to Leon is remarkable and one of the more generous offerings in circulation during my fieldwork, but it was not an aberration. During over a decade of ethnographic fieldwork in this Brooklyn boxing gym, I watched trainer after trainer, boxer after boxer, and even client after client share in what, at first glance, looks like a surrender of personal well-being. After studying these practices of generosity over time, I saw that gym members were not relinquishing but rather redefining the very concept of well-being.

This chapter looks at how and why members rearticulate well-being in the gym when living in an economy of scarcity outside of it. I take Harry's gift of the job to Leon as a starting point to consider how people in this sporting space act counter to market-based self-interest in order to share and create a sense of the common good.[3] I look at why, in an otherwise brutal market economy, gym regulars reconsider personal accumulation, choosing other economic priorities instead. I argue that the collection of these individual acts constitutes what E. P. Thompson (1991) calls a "moral economy," in which members of the gym are able to claim and actualize a set of rights that are unavailable outside (188). Through this moral economy, gym regulars enforce social norms, obligations, and behaviors that often run counter to free market exchange. The moral economy of the gym is a collective, though not uncontested, sense of what the community considers fair and just. It is both an answer to the racial hierarchies of postindustrial capitalism and unique in its own right: not merely a response to inequality but an anticapitalist indictment and a system of morality.

My hope is that an analysis of the moral economy of the gym might expand understandings of sporting practices, of the social relations surrounding them, and of the spaces where many sports are played and significant labor for lucrative sporting enterprises is supplied. My motivation comes from two reigning strands of thought in sport studies. The first is marked by a focus on labor, or the economic dimensions of sporting industries and the forms of exploitation that workers, especially Black and Brown men from under-resourced urban centers, experience in their line of work. Of course labor is crucial to our analyses of what Norbert Elias and Eric Dunning (2009) call "sportization," and configurations of labor power and labor discipline remain central to any examination of sport in society.[4] However, reductive debates about profit and pay can obscure closely related social and cultural phenomena, threatening to conceal meaningful opposition to those very economic arrangements. The second strand emerges from work attempting to articulate the emancipatory possibilities of solidarities formed through play as an anti-market or even a market event. For scholars dedicated to this strand, a joy—fleeting but significant—can be found in the solidarity and excitement of physical striving, training, and competition.[5] My goal in analyzing the appeals and critiques embedded in the moral economy of the urban gym is to expand on the insights of the first strand while drawing on the generative features of the second.

Custom and the Moral Economy

The term "moral economy" has become polysemous and is often deployed in contradictory ways. My use comes directly from E. P. Thompson, who, in 1971 published "The Moral Economy of the English Crowd in the 18th Century," though he had written the essay almost a decade earlier while waiting on the page proofs for *The Making of the English Working Class*. The idea stirred significant controversy and prompted Thompson to pen "The Moral Economy Reviewed," which was published with the original essay in *Customs in Common* in 1991.

In his original essay, Thompson is eager to understand how the poor fought for access to basic resources as markets transformed from paternalist to free. By analyzing the skyrocketing price of cereals and the uprisings the poor activated in response, Thompson argues that the motivation for food riots was rooted in long-standing belief systems rather than merely a spontaneous and hysterical outburst propelled by participants' base hunger. Unrest, which occurred all over Britain in the 1700s, was social protest: disciplined, invested with objectives, and considered legitimate by the community. In asserting what they perceived as unfair prices for food, protesters offered "alternative economic imperatives" to an emergent capitalist market system, such as fair prices rather than set prices. These alternatives functioned as protection against unbridled market forces as other checks were phased out.

Customs undergirded the traditional belief system that structured daily life. Developed to regulate patrician power, Thompson (1991) sees customs as "survivals," where the old agrarian order and the law intersected (2, 126). Though not always articulated as such, customs were considered privileges or even rights by their users. They changed over time rather than remaining firm or static and could be contradictory or even in conflict. And they transformed with each progeny as they were handed down from generation to generation both orally and locally. But they were guarded with the threat of social protest or outright unrest; when imperiled, they were defended vigorously (3–8, 57). Thompson, for example, suggests that many of the protests undertaken at the beginning of the Industrial Revolution were about customs as much as wages and working conditions.

As markets changed, customs were increasingly used to fight new economic practices that were detrimental to survival: "enclosures, time-discipline, unregulated 'free' markets in grain" (9). Thompson explains, "When people search for legitimations for protests, they often turn back to the paternalist regulations of a more authoritarian society and select from among those parts most calculated to defend present interests" (10). When fighting the encroachment of the free market, customs gave primacy to the non-economic over the economic (11). Combined, these customary practices formed an economy that gave priority to mutuality and reciprocity. This moral economy eschewed personal accumulation and self-interest and was intentionally created by its practitioners to protect the collective. Participants were not just randomly responding to individual circumstance but were acting together according to an established code of traditional rights (181–88).

To Thompson, an analysis of a moral economy is not to evacuate politics or abandon political economy. In "The Moral Economy Reviewed," (1991) his follow-up essay to "The Moral Economy of the English Crowd in the 18th Century," he is at pains to emphasize that there is no separation between moral and market economies. The "moral" is derived from the content of the crowd's claims as well as the fact that protesters were not opposing the "whole system of prosperity and power." Rather, Thompson links morals-as-values, or values as they are lived in their social contexts, to economic roles and practices. Morals are both norm and cognitive structure.

More recently, Paul Gilroy (2010) has used the concept of a moral economy to structure his work *Darker Than Blue*, in which he analyzes the moral features of the Black Atlantic's freedom struggles, utopian imaginations, and critiques of consumer capitalism. Gilroy's moral economy draws upon a number of interpretive resources to enlarge the concept beyond food to "elements of life." Like Thompson, Gilroy does not jettison political economy but rather sets it alongside and overlapping with alternative systems of judgment and value. He writes, "I do this not to downplay the fundamental significance or scope of political economy, but to contest the limited place provided in that paradigm for questions of morality and political culture" (Gilroy 2010, 7).

Harry's gift to Leon is a small part of a moral economy that gym members have created in which their alternate systems of judging value run counter to those of a free market system. They, too, give primacy to alternative economic imperatives and, through their actions, enforce protective market controls. And like its counterpart in the eighteenth century, the moral economy of the urban gym does not challenge the entire system of profit and pain. Rather, it is a stop-gap measure that uses available resources—material and interpretive—to respond at the local level.

From the Manor to Gym: The Elements of Life

In the gym, fighters and trainers use existing resources and options to create a moral economy. Though members are under stress and under-resourced, men of color make it a priority to improvise arrangements for one another's well-being as well as to admire and enact sharing and mutuality.[6] There are several features of this moral economy. For the purposes of this chapter, I look at the two most significant: time and value.

Time

One of the more radical reassessments of market-based capitalism in the gym is made through the use of time. And here, understanding changes to the gym's overlapping political economy is helpful. Historically, the urban gym has been frequented almost exclusively by competitive male boxers—Irish, Italian, and Jewish fighters and, later, African American pugilists—as well as trainers and other types of professional men invested in the sport, such as managers, promoters, matchmakers, and sportswriters. Professional boxers worked to advance their paid careers while amateurs trained to "turn pro" at some point in the foreseeable future. Trainers coached their fighters early in the morning before their full-time jobs, often in the city's manufacturing sector or public agencies, or late in evening after leaving work for the day. Only well-known trainers who worked with famous boxers could afford to relinquish outside employment.

This demographic arrangement continued through the golden age of boxing into the early eighties. But in the mid-1980s, as the fitness craze hit New York City just as the city's wealthiest residents were amassing even more capital due to new financial practices, new groups of athletes expressed their interest in the sport.[7] The most important of these—businessmen and TV network executives—offered to pay substantial sums of money to be trained.

Boxing trainers quickly offered their expertise to this new group, called "white-collar clients" for their professional backgrounds outside the sport. Trainers realized early on that if they worked with white-collar clients in large enough numbers, they could support themselves from income earned in the gym. Being released from outside employment meant that trainers, most of whom were Black, modestly educated, and increasingly locked out of a postindustrial labor market, could devote time to the work they considered most meaningful. Uses of time began to change as trainers actively asserted how they wanted to apportion it. They devoted a larger portion of their days to amateur boxers, who, overwhelmingly, could not pay for their training but with whom many trainers most enjoyed collaborating. Instead of training clients full-time to extract the most possible profit, trainers developed portfolios that balanced the exact number of clients needed to make a living wage with the number of amateur fighters they most preferred to coach. Trainers, in effect, used time with white-collar clients to subsidize time with amateur fighters.

The ability to structure their time, in turn, opened up another possibility: engaging in the work their consciences dictated. Harry, who grew up in Bedford-Stuyvesant during the height of the crack cocaine boom and lived in deteriorating social housing, considers it is his responsibility to help young men of color avoid the mistakes he believes he made. His desire to make a difference is propelled not only by his past mistakes but also by a vision of society in which the government and everyday people help each other more. When I inquire if he thinks all trainers should give their amateurs the athletic, social, and psychological attention he devotes, he responds, "Sure, because if everybody thought in those terms, you'd have better people."[8]

Mike, another trainer with whom I worked closely, did not face the same struggles as Harry but argues that as a Black youth in Crown Heights, his opportunities to escape racial segregation and class oppression were limited. He seeks to provide his amateur boxers with the opportunities to which he did not have access:

> Nobody navigated me. If somebody had navigated me, I'd probably be in Harvard somewhere. Street navigator. Yeah, that's what kids need . . . They want to do right, but they haven't been navigated. They don't know what to do . . . You counsel them on more things than this boxing shit. They don't know what to do. Baby stuff, how you do the baby stuff. Things like—even how to get the baby circumcised when he little. You gotta counsel them on everything—where to get a job, what to do. (Interview, March, 9, 2004)

Mike uses the time he has created as a full-time trainer to provide his amateur fighters with the knowledge he never had. Mike argues that society's biggest failure is not mentoring Black men and providing them with the resources to leave poorly resourced areas of New York City. His social and athletic work is motivated by a critique of racial exclusion and an existing need in the next generation.

Finally, trainers were able to reapportion time for their own well-being, shifting time-discipline to task-based labor, giving them more control over their days. Full-time trainers spend a significant number of hours in the gym and go to great pains to make themselves available to their clients. Harry, for example, arrives around 6:00 a.m. and leaves around 7:00 p.m. Mike arrives around 5:30 a.m. and leaves around 10:00 p.m. But despite these grueling hours, trainers insist on setting their own schedules, choosing to leave the gym between sessions, running errands when needed, taking lunch breaks or walks to the waterfront, and even scheduling days off. This is extremely important to men who feel they had little autonomy in their previous jobs. Trainers would rather work longer hours in the gym than labor fewer hours in their former places of employment, where they had no influence over how their working days were spent. When I was doing my fieldwork at Gleason's Gym, there were roughly seventy-eight trainers, about forty of whom make their livings entirely from income earned there.

Value

Like time, value in the gym is produced in ways different from the market economy; not all exchanges are motivated by the desire to make money and not all forms of value are defined by the demand for profit. In the gym, amateur boxers use bodywork to engender their bodies with value after being locked out of other forms of formal work and to earn recognition based on that value.

The young men who train at Gleason's Gym trek from similar neighborhoods, where they often live in social housing units. They tend to have experienced periods of forced confinement, and because they were condemned to state prisons before completing high school, they earn their highest educational credential—the General Education Development certificate (GED)—while behind bars. They have a difficult time securing dignified—or even adequate—employment, and without jobs they cannot create the identities traditionally associated with wage labor or experience the benefits generated from those identities (Willis 2000). Some amateur athletes go to Gleason's Gym to create identities and enjoy their by-products through bodywork, such as the sharpening of their minds and the disciplining of their bodies.

Bodywork requires between three and five hours of arduous training a day. But despite not being compensated for this time, amateur boxers consider this pugilistic labor to be their job. This is true for fighters who have professional aspirations and for those who do not have any plans to turn pro. It is true for boxers who can secure jobs, and it is true for those who participate in extralegal economies outside the gym. Amateur boxers consider themselves, by occupation, to be boxers, and they approach their boxing activities with the insistence and purpose of a job rather than as a pastime or hobby. When they work, they borrow features of traditional wage labor—such as regimentation and disciplining—and recast these features to create a new kind of labor, which allows them to forge new identities. Pugilists can find meaning in their daily routines and fashion the conditions by which they can learn, be challenged, and succeed. They create the rules and systems of meaning and invest worth in the practices and social relations of boxing.

Bodywork does not fit a standard notion of work. Amateurs are not employed in the formal sense, their labor is not paid, and their toil is not recognized by most sectors of society. But through bodywork, amateurs understand their time, their bodies, their labor, and their lives in new ways. Most importantly, they engender their bodies with value and recognize that value after enduring forms of social and economic injury. In doing so, boxers disentangle traditional moral and emotional features of work from economic compensation. The social status and cultural recognition achieved from training one's own mind and body is neither the product nor the source of financial gain. Yet value *is* produced when pugilists invest in the intellectual disciplining of their minds and the strength and skill of their bodies. Whereas value has primarily been understood as the by-product of formalized work, amateur fighters illuminate that status can be generated in alternative institutions in a postindustrial landscape—but without wages.

Conclusion: Citizenship Reviewed

Like Thompson's eighteenth-century bread crowd, gym members assert alternative social and economic practices, values, and beliefs. They advocate the importance of social obligation, and their moral economy improvises arrangements for members' well-being, enacting gifts, favors, and redistribution. The gym exists as a place where those who are frustrated, excluded from full citizenship by criminal records, and unable to meet the expectations of dominant society can create work, perform the work, and be recognized for that work.

Gym trainers have created positions in which they control their time, and they use this time in ways that are different from those in the formal labor market. Here notions of labor and identity are troubled; even the work relationships that most closely adhere to a traditional economic transaction—namely, those between trainers and white-collar clients, where there are overt monetary exchanges—are made possible by the other nontraditional work relationships. The phenomenon of white-collar boxing at Gleason's is driven by the cultural cachet—attended by no small amount of racial stereotyping—of training in the same institution as amateurs working without wages and in a gym with a revered and hard-core boxing reputation, a reputation bolstered by the presence of those so committed to the sport that they work at it full-time without getting paid.

The value boxers create through bodywork demonstrates the inventive ways young men develop dignity and earn respect as well as how they intervene in their own lives and attempt to control the conditions of their experiences when maneuvering room is constrained. They recreate within the gym the right to work, which they have been denied outside the gym. In other words, when there is no lawful or paid work, they fashion work. And this self-fashioning is both political and symbolic. As Robin D. G. Kelley (1996) points out in *Race Rebels*, "Daily acts of resistance and survival have had consequences for existing power relations, and the powerful have deployed immense resources in order to avoid these consequences or to punish transgressors" (9). In the case of the urban gym, young men's improvisations reveal that they recognize the ability to work as fundamental. Amateur boxers have found a way to meet their own unspoken demands for work and value, and in a worksite that is fair and instructive and that supports them.

For amateur boxers—Black and Brown men who have been all but shut out of a restrictive labor market and disproportionately forcibly confined in the US's prison industrial complex—the gym offers a place to fashion work that provides opportunities for building individual and collective forms of identity and for forming intimate social relations with other men. This work departs from conventional social scientific understandings of the concept; in many sociological schemas, the social and psychological features of work and the economic sustenance it provides are co-constituting. While some of these social and psychological effects and benefits may accrue along with material recompense in some forms of labor, the connection does not hold in the context of Gleason's Gym. Rather, for amateur boxers, the sort of work that pays the bills, when available, rarely delivers the potential for the recognition, status, dignity, and sociality that amateurs cherish and seek in the urban gym. And, conversely, whatever social and cultural capital or moral and emotional fulfillment participants achieve from training their bodies is not a product of any sort of economic gain.

Gleason's moral economy represents both a plea for and a critique of citizenship. Through the uses of time and revaluations of bodywork, gym members expand and redefine the idea of citizenship to include a broad right to dignified work. The social protest embedded in their labor reacts to postindustrial structural circumstance but is also generative and forward-looking. Their claims do not emerge from birthright or naturalization but instead something social; members of the gym expand the notion of citizenship and link civil rights to the common good rather than individual profit. The gym's moral economy, then, shows that actions can occur both within and in response to the market, revealing at once solidarity and sanction. My car ride from Gleason's Gym to Manhattan reveals more than just how a group of men in postindustrial New York create work when there is none. It also illuminates the ways people come together to resist and accommodate contemporary forms of belonging and accumulation while generating their own meaningful elements of life.

Notes

1. White-collar clients are practitioners of white-collar boxing, a form of the sport in which white middle- and upper-class professional people who are not registered as amateurs or professionals are coached by boxing trainers. Clients possess varying degrees of investment in their activities and use a range of training regimens: Some train but do not spar; some spar but do not compete; some fight in special white-collar shows. This pugilistic practice began in the mid-1980s in New York City when businessmen expressed their

willingness to pay substantial sums of money to be coached. For more on white-collar boxing, see Lucia Trimbur, *Come Out Swinging: The Changing World of Boxing in Gleason's Gym.*

2. When I was conducting fieldwork, Gleason's Gym was open six days a week. Now it is open seven days a week.

3. Here I use the idea of the gift in a loosely Maussian sense to highlight a commitment to reciprocity and the collective. But unlike the systems of exchange Mauss analyzed, gifts in the gym encourage but do not demand a particular form of reciprocity and, unlike, say, the potlatch, certainly do not lead to stratification. See Marcel Mauss, *The Gift: Forms and Functions of Exchange in Archaic Societies* (Norton, 1967).

4. See Norbert Elias and Eric Dunning, *Quest for Excitement: Sport and Leisure in the Civilising Process* (University College Dublin, 2009). For a Marxist approach, see Tony Collins, *Sport in a Capitalist Society: A Short History* (Routledge, 2013).

5. I am grateful to Ben Carrington and Santiago Colas for a lively discussion on the political possibilities of play in the discussion following paper presentations on "The Fun and the Fury: New Dialectics of Pleasure and Pain in the Post-American Century" panel at the 2014 American Studies Association Conference in Los Angeles. Drawing on the work of Baruch Spinoza, Johan Huizinga, Roger Caillois, and even the surrealists, we debated ways to move beyond the protest/pleasure, work/play binaries to consider more nuanced ways of thinking about liberation and emancipation in sport. As Carrington warned in his paper, "A normative slippage occurs wherein resistance is not just privileged over pleasure but that the latter is seen to be somehow problematic. Stated reductively, resistance and protest is good, pleasure is suspect if not outright bad. Such an approach to thinking about politics risks suggesting that pleasure is apolitical and, by implicit contrast, that protest cannot be fun." Instead, Carrington suggested pushing "back against the notion that we have to frame the discussion as sports moving *from* places of play and entertainment *towards* locations of political transformation by arguing, instead, for the politics of play and for playful forms of politics, be they conducted in the sports arena or elsewhere" (Carrington 2014).

6. When I was conducting fieldwork, the gym's moral economy was created and used almost exclusively by men; though there were an increasing number of women joining the gym, they did not participate in the moral economy. First, women boxers came from very different social and economic circumstances, ones that rendered redistribution and gifts less necessary to survival. Second, as women were still slowly creating a place for themselves in the gym's social world, they had not yet developed the intense relationships as those found between male amateur boxers and gym trainers.

7. For an excellent analysis of the emergent fitness industry, see Shari Dworkin and Faye Linda Wachs, *Body Panic: Gender, Health, and the Selling*

of Fitness (New York University Press, 2009). For an explanation of the financial restructurings of the 1980s, see Saskia Sassen, *The Global City: New York, London, Tokyo* (Princeton University Press, 1991).

8. All quotes in this essay were generated from four years of formal ethnographic fieldwork and seven additional years of informal follow-up research. The quotes are from both semi-structured interviews and participation observation.

References

Carrington, Ben. 2014. "To Protest or Not to Protest: Athletic Resistance and/or the Pleasure of Fans." Unpublished paper presented at "The Fun and the Fury: New Dialectics of Pleasure and Pain in the Post-American Century" panel. American Studies Association Annual Conference. Los Angeles, November 6–9.

Collins, Tony. 2013. *Sport in a Capitalist Society: A Short History*. Routledge.

Dworkin, Shari, and Faye Linda Wachs. 2009. *Body Panic: Gender, Health, and the Selling of Fitness*. New York University Press.

Elias, Norbert, and Eric Dunning. 2009. *Quest for Excitement: Sport and Leisure in the Civilising Process*. University College Dublin.

Gilroy, Paul. 2010. *Darker Than Blue: On the Moral Economies of Black Atlantic Culture*. Harvard University Press.

Kelley, Robin D. G. 1996. *Race Rebels: Culture: Politics, and the Black Working Class*. Free Press.

Mauss, Marcel. 1967. *The Gift: Forms and Functions of Exchange in Archaic Societies*. Norton.

Sassen, Saskia. 1991. *The Global City: New York, London, Tokyo*. Princeton University Press.

Thompson, E. P. 1971. "The Moral Economy of the English Crowd in the 18th Century." In Thompson, *Customs in Common*.

Thompson, E. P. 1991. *Customs in Common: Studies in Traditional Popular Culture*. New Press.

Thompson, E. P. 1991. "The Moral Economy Reviewed." In Thompson, *Customs in Common*.

"The Fun and the Fury: New Dialectics of Pleasure and Pain in the Post-American Century" panel discussion. American Studies Association Annual Conference. Los Angeles, November 6–9.

Trimbur, Lucia. 2013. *Come Out Swinging: The Changing World of Boxing in Gleason's Gym*. Princeton University Press.

Willis, Paul. 2000. *The Ethnographic Imagination*. Wiley Publishing.

12

"Boxing Is Essentially Exploitation"

Labor, Value, and Narrative Structures in Boxing

A Conversation with Max Kellerman

RUDY MONDRAGÓN

Max Kellerman is a preeminent authority in the world of boxing. Kellerman emerged as a widely recognized ringside commentator for the HBO series *Boxing after Dark* in 2006. He joined the *World Championship Boxing* broadcast team in 2007, appearing on *The Fight Game with Jim Lampley* and then with his own show, *Face Off with Max Kellerman. Face Off* featured Kellerman and fighters sitting face-to-face. This popular show allowed boxing enthusiasts to learn more about the boxers. Kellerman has had a long tenure at ESPN, hosting the series *Around the Horn* and then co-hosting *First Take* and *Sports Nation.* Over the two decades with the network, he has also served as broadcaster during boxing matches and was the host of *Max on Boxing.* As a leading voice and authority in the world of boxing, Kellerman is part of a long tradition and lineage of sports journalists and commentators who have covered boxing and sport as a form of dissent.

• • •

RUDY MONDRAGÓN: As a broadcaster of boxing, you have moved me in many ways. I've seen how impactful you've been, with a lot of my friends who watch boxing on a regular basis. When you get into your concluding monologue at the end of HBO broadcasts, it always has people on the edge of their seats. You're on the ground level and we're at home in the living room saying, "Shut the fuck up, everybody shut up, shut up. Max is about to talk."

MAX KELLERMAN: That's awesome. That's what you're hoping, that you can contextualize what's happening in what they say now is real time. And the thing that Larry Merchant did that no one else really did until him, at least in boxing broadcasts, is he wasn't really analyzing left hooks and right hands.[1] He was telling a story. And that's how I view my job too. We understand the world through narrative structure; that's the way even scientific models are, essentially stories we tell that best map onto reality. And stories are only as interesting as the characters are interesting, as invested as you would be emotionally in the character. And so you need to know who the characters are, what's at stake, what are the obstacles, how daunting are they? And you tell that story.

RM: Our book explores boxing and how fighters have performed or become symbols of dissent and resistance to dominant structures. The biggest figures that we could think of in the political realm of boxing are Jack Johnson, Joe Louis, Sugar Ray Robinson, and Muhammad Ali. This book adds to that rich list.

MK: I'm from a left-wing secular Yiddish background from the labor movements in the 1930s, '40s, and '50s. That's where my family is. My grandparents were immigrants. My father was first generation, and Yiddish was spoken in the house because his grandmother lived in the house with them; that's how they spoke. But to learn the written language, he went a couple of days a week to a Yiddish school that was secular not religious. He was just learning the culture and the formal language and stuff. And he had a teacher named Haika Klabonski, who also taught me Yiddish when I was a little kid. When the kids were acting up and they wouldn't listen, she would say, "*Kinder, ich bin nicht kein* Joe Louis." Like children, I'm not Joe Louis. I don't have the strength to do this, you gotta cooperate with me. So Joe Louis, he was a cultural reference, especially in the years leading up to the Second World War.

RM: Martin Luther King Jr. once shared a story about the last words uttered by a Black man who was going to be executed in a gas chamber. King said this man's last words were "Save me, Joe Louis" before being killed.[2]

MK: Joe Louis was a symbol. Some say Muhammad Ali and Joe Fraser's first fight was the fight of the century. The most important fight ever was the rematch between Joe Louis and Max Schmeling in the late 1930s. A Black fighter from America was going up against the symbol of Aryan supremacy even though Schmeling had a Jewish manager and was great friends with Louis after his career. He was also a paratrooper for the Germans but was really forced into that. After he lost that fight to Louis, he was sent as a paratrooper behind enemy lines and given the most dangerous stuff to do. Joe Louis knocked him out in one round, in front of Hitler's High Command. Louis hit Schmeling with the right hand to the body and Schmeling cried out in pain and knocked him out. For oppressed people all over the world, Joe Louis meant things to people.

Ali is the greatest heavyweight champion of all time, and Ali took a stand, but Joe Louis was a symbol that I don't know if people today can truly appreciate the power of Joe. Jack Johnson so alienated white America because he was so far ahead of his time that no Black fighter got a title shot at heavyweight until Joe Louis got his title shot. Louis was this phenom, the way Mike Tyson was, just knocking everybody out, and when he won the title, the kind of symbol he became for African Americans in the United States, but also for Jews because of the Second World War. Joe Louis became this very emotionally powerful symbol for the free world, and there's irony, of course, that he's fighting in a country—and then eventually for a country—in a time where he couldn't drink at the same water fountain. And yet he was; when you don't look at the way he could be used as manipulative propaganda in a bad way, right? When you look at the kind of symbol of hope and strength he was, I think you could even contextualize the way you might say, "Well, it's not all great because he can be used as that symbol for a country that still oppressed people who looked like him." But the idea was, "We have high hopes for you." So he represented—not just at the time, he wasn't just a symbol of strength at the time, but even in retrospect, he represented in the best light—the kind of hope that you could have for America.

RM: How did you find boxing, or did boxing find you?

MK: I was a scrappy kid that liked fighting. My dad took me to the PAL [Police Athletic League] around the time Duk Koo Kim was killed by Ray Mancini.[3] So my mother and my grandmother said no to boxing. So, of course, that made me more interested in it. But I don't know: I like a fair fight.

RM: I know you are a Columbia University graduate and have a history degree. Do you feel like your history training plays a role in your life as a boxing broadcaster?

MK: I never planned on really being a broadcaster, nor did I plan on being a history major. I looked up and it was time to declare a major and I had the most credits in history. But in both cases, you don't choose your profession; your profession chooses you. So that's what happened. In terms of how it helps? I don't know that it so much helps as it reflects the kind of things that interest me. Boxing has a very rich history and is inextricably tied to social phenomena throughout, especially, the twentieth century.

RM: In our current moment, Colin Kaepernick has become an icon of athletic protest. I don't know if boxing has a Colin Kaepernick, in that his political demonstration became very overt and very clear, as he was able to articulate that he was fighting against police brutality, racism, and black lives not mattering.

MK: Well, I don't think Kaepernick is quite Kaepernick, to tell you the truth. I've obviously publicly supported Kaepernick on television. In Kaepernick's case the reason I don't agree with you that it is clear, as you say. At first, I said, Look, maybe he didn't feel as though teams didn't feel he was a starter, and he's a kind of a bubble starter. And then after a while it became clear what was happening. But one of the issues with Kaepernick is [that] teams can credibly say, "We don't think he's worth it. He's a back-up quarterback." Kind of, or maybe, if he's a starter, he's not one of the better starters. And he didn't start the protest as a protest per se; he started it as a conscientious objection. And he didn't start it with a spotlight on him; he did it quietly. The media caught wind of it, then he articulated his position more clearly, but the fact [is] that he wasn't a star.

In order to be Muhammad Ali, Kaepernick would now have to come back and lead a team to a Super Bowl. Part of how we view these things is the significance of the athlete is based upon his success in his field. The reason Ali resonates today still as the greatest athlete who ever lived is because, ultimately, he beat Sonny Liston, Joe Frazier, and then beat George Foreman and had multiple title defenses. That's why his stances are still remembered to the extent that they are. Kaepernick was not that kind of football player. And that, I believe, does have an impact. Jack Johnson could say whatever he wanted. If he lost the title shot to Tommy Burns, we would not be talking about Jack Johnson today.

Boxing does not have a Kaepernick today, but boxing has had Muhammad Ali, and Kaepernick is not Muhammad Ali. And the reason that's significant is Kaepernick did not risk the same things. In other words, at the time Kaepernick took the stance, his career wasn't taking off, he wasn't walking into some enormous contract, he had already turned down a contract, [and] it turned out to be a mistake. So what risk did he really take? Well, he risked his career; actually, he's in a better position to earn money now than he was then. I'm not impugning his motives. Whereas Muhammad Ali clearly was risking a lot in order to stand up for what he believed in and Kaepernick less so. So the waters are muddied.

RM: For me, the question is also due to this current moment. In the classroom, when I talk with students, the consensus is that Kaepernick is the athlete that is center stage right now when it comes to this idea of athletic activism.

MK: Well, the irony of Kaepernick is that, forget about the specificity of police interactions with communities of color, right? Basically, the protest is [that] there is social racial injustice in this country. And I don't feel good about standing up for this flag ceremony, which, by the way, is based on a racist song. When our country is not doing its best to live up to its ideals, I don't feel good about it. The irony is, because the league does not have one single African American owner, he has been drummed out of the league because of that stance, just saying, "Hey, this is not fair." The irony is, in fact, that unless you believe Black people are intrinsically inferior at making money, then you also must acknowledge that, in fact, systemic racism—including the slave trade, the institution of slavery, and Jim Crow—is what has created the imbalance in the first place. That's the very injustice that Kaepernick is protesting. And yet that power imbalance, based on that injustice, is the reason that he doesn't have a job. He doesn't have a job because he's protesting forces that led to him not having a job in the first place.

RM: From watching you on *First Take*, it was very powerful for me because you're not just talking about racism only happening on an individual level.[4] No, you were saying structurally, systematically, there's a design here of how things work, and this is how it manifests. In addition to Kaepernick and talking about boxing in the present moment, do you feel like there's a boxer or boxers who are using their platform or are articulating their politics and performing dissent?

MK: I haven't even thought of that. None come to mind, but just activism is not the confluence of events, circumstance, and a man's character. That's why we all know Kaepernick, that's why we all know Ali, and so there may be fighters today who, were they put in a situation, would behave in such a way that would draw attention to social or racial injustice in such a way that would make them some kind of iconic social justice figure, but the circumstances haven't led to that.

RM: Dave Zirin talked about Allen Iverson as the bridge between Michael Jordan and today's political athlete. He said, "Being a political athlete isn't always about grabbing a microphone and doing a discourse about racism and oppression. Being a political athlete can also be about how you represent yourself."[5] Iverson's representation of hip-hop culture is political.

MK: In that sense, Floyd Mayweather and Al Haymon flipped the paradigm, which was that boxing is essentially exploitation. You could argue all labor in some ways, with the Marxist view of exploitation. But boxing is essentially exploitation. Fans, TV networks, and promoters exploit—usually people of color in this country from the very bottom of the socioeconomic ladder in desperate circumstances—for their own enjoyment. When fans say they need to see a fighter's toughness or their need to overcome adversity to be a great fighter, what they're saying is, we need to make sure that this guy will be brain damaged by the time he's done—and usually wind up broke, too.

Al Haymon and Floyd Mayweather flipped that around and said no. We are not going to be exploited by fans and networks, we are going to exploit networks and fans. So Floyd took minimal risk. He fought everyone at the right time, he talked a great game and fought beautifully, but not in an especially exciting manner, and got out. We don't know what the effects of his boxing career will be on his brain and his body, but so far so good. And he got out with a lot of money, and he may spend it all, but that's on him. In that way, you may say, fighter as entrepreneur, or as in Floyd's case, it's just because he's self-interested. I don't think he's making a larger statement, but in the way that Iverson didn't need to consciously make a statement and could be used by people as a symbol, Floyd Mayweather may be used in a similar way. You don't have to be a pawn in the game; you can exploit the game.

RM: I agree with you. Boxers are pawns in an underregulated sporting industry and most of them exist in a constant state of vulnerability, subject to the shifting market as well as the effects of dominant ideologies and structures. Given their instability, boxers use fashion, music, and their entourages as powerful tools that they deploy during their ring entrances to communicate their politics and sometimes even perform dissent. I think about Sugar Ray Robinson and how when he would negotiate his fight contracts and demand money he felt entitled to. As a result, people labeled Robinson as a difficult person to work with. The question for me is why was he labeled as such? Was it because he was trying to negotiate a fair compensation for his labor?

MK: Vernon Forrest was a very good welterweight contender. His biggest purse was about fifty thousand dollars and he was getting up there in age. And he seemed to be in the same class of fighter, give or take, as "Sugar" Shane Mosley and Oscar De La Hoya and others who were making a good living in boxing and were considered stars. Yet he just wasn't given the opportunity. Then he got a fight with Shane Mosley. And it's funny, because fighters like that, it becomes an exercise in righteousness for members of the press and fans, that he deserves a shot. But once he actually got his shot, everyone picked the other guy. They think, "There's a reason he hasn't gotten the shot; he's not quite as good as the other guy." So, at any rate, I was looking at it through that kind of template and being influenced by that kind of thinking in ways I wasn't aware of. Vernon got offered a million dollars to fight Shane, and he turned it down, thought he was worth more, and I was critical on TV. I looked into the camera on HBO *Friday Night Fights* and said, "Vernon, you're almost thirty years old. You have guys like me on TV saying, 'He deserves a shot,' you get offered a million dollars for the shot, and you turn it down? You gotta take the opportunity."

Vernon sees me at a fight in Atlanta a couple months later. He comes up to me, sits down, and we start talking. "Max, do you take the first offer the company makes you? I'm negotiating. I know my worth; I'm negotiating." And I had to acknowledge that I wasn't extending the same kind of courtesy to Vernon Forrest that I extend to myself. There's this sense with fighters—"Why, it's a child's game, and you're getting paid to play. You should be happy to take whatever the team gives you." Well, that's a labor issue. And in boxing there is a corollary to that, which is not why you should be happy with it, but like, "Damn, you come from nothing. You have a chance here; you gotta take that chance." And Vernon was like, "No, no, no. I can take a smart chance; I don't have to take the first chance offered."

And Floyd, when HBO offered him a twelve-million-dollar contract, two million a fight for six fights, he called it a "slave contract" and was roundly criticized. And I talked to him about it: "Floyd, you didn't win a gold medal; you're an African American junior lightweight who's not a big puncher. Those guys don't make a lot of money. They're offering you two million a fight." But he was right. I was wrong. People like me didn't have the *imagination* to see how big he could become, because the easiest story we tell ourselves is "the next guy should look like the last guy," and the last guy was Oscar De La Hoya. If you're Mexican American or you have a gold medal, or you're a big puncher, or you're a heavyweight, then maybe. But if you're African American, and you're not a puncher, and you don't have a gold medal, you should be lucky to take what you get. But Floyd made a billion dollars doing it his way. And whatever you think of him as a person—because he's done a lot of reprehensible things—whatever you think about him as a person, he flipped the script, as we used to say.

RM: I love that breakdown. With Floyd, there are the reprehensible things that we need to address and talk about. He has challenged the paradigm. Especially when you think about how he has maintained his faculties and health in a sport that loves to watch boxers fight in a kill-or-be-killed style.

MK: Why should someone have to behave perfectly—ethically in other respects, or morally in other respects—for them to make a point or to even be a symbol through which a point is made? He doesn't need to be a perfect angel. I don't think it's disqualifying as an example of someone around whom you could build a sound kind of argument. There's a lot of talk that Jack Johnson was a pimp. Does that make him less important? Maybe it does to some. And he also won the heavyweight championship of the world beating up white fighters who would have otherwise denied him the opportunity.

RM: It's complex and nuanced. At the core, perfection is unrealistic to attain. When I speak to people, I emphasize the need to talk about Floyd's history with domestic violence and violence against women as well as how he did things his way in boxing and came out of the sport with his faculties.

MK: Yeah, perfect is the enemy to good. When Floyd says, "I'm TBE, the best ever," what he's really saying is "I played the fight game better than anyone ever did." And he's right; he did play the fight game better. If you think of it as a game, he got in and took kind of the least amount of punishment that could have been taken among the world class. For a long career and being a world-class fighter, he made almost a billion dollars, got out with an undefeated record and a legion of fans who swear he's the best fighter ever, even if it's not true, and he avoided risk. That's playing the fight game better than anyone ever. It's true.

RM: Absolutely. And you talked about the things that he did, the reprehensible things, the domestic violence and violence against women. As a broadcaster, how do you reconcile that?

MK: There is no reconciling; it's not an issue of reconciling. It's an issue of observing. He's done bad things; he's also kind of been a jerk to a lot of people just generally, right? My interactions with him, for the most part, have been good, going back to when he was a 130-pound prospect. Listen. The New Journalism, right? Once upon a time, Babe Ruth got gonorrhea and it was like, "Why, he has a belly ache from eating too many hot dogs." And then the New Journalists came and said, "Look, the fiction that we try to tell ourselves or sell is not as interesting as the truth." Forget about any kind of moral imperative as a journalist, even. It's not as good a story. I think, like Kevin Durant, the easy story to tell was that he's a good small-town kid. And what did it turn out to be? Not that simple. He's a three-dimensional human being who is very sensitive to what's said about him, who's angry at negative coverage in the press or just being bombarded by criticism on social media. He is also a very competitive, complicated person who's more interesting than a stereotype. So, like Floyd, if you pay attention to the details and you conclude wherever those details lead you—and they're going to be of any human being—it's gonna be complex; it's not going to be a simple story.

RM: As I mentioned when we were walking in the hallway, the ring entrance is what I pay a lot of attention to in my research. How important do you see the ring entrance being to the production of boxing?

MK: I think boxing could do a better job with showmanship. It's a lesson that the Ultimate Fighting Championship seemed to have learned from the World Wrestling Entertainment. When a fighter has shown the willingness to present some showmanship, it has generally paid off for the fighter. Prince Naseem Hamed was not only knocking guys cold but was giving people a show even before the fight started. Boxing has always traded on ethnic rivalries, like, the "Brown Bomber" [Joe Louis]. In the old Lower East Side, it was Italian versus Irish versus Jewish. Mexico versus Puerto Rico, or even Mexican American versus Puerto Rican. Boxing has always traded on ethnic identity or racial identity. When I see elaborate ring walks, I just think someone's trying to bring some production value to the proceedings.

RM: To what extent do boxers have total control and agency on deciding and curating how they bring themselves into the ring? And has there been a ring entrance that you found to be very spectacular and impressed you?

MK: It's usually in conjunction with their promoters more than the TV networks. It depends on the personality of the players. It may be a fighter who feels they have a vision for this stuff. It may be a promoter who says, "It would be good to play this up." I have not noticed that it's generally the TV network. Everyone will tell you the same thing: When Mike Tyson would come in, it was the juxtaposition of the kind of showmanship of others, where he's just marching to the ring, no robe, no socks, like a gladiator. That increased, it amplified his aura and scared opponents. His ring walk, because it was stripped down, the aesthetic sensibility said, "I'm all business." That's the one that jumps to mind, if you ask. Because the smoke and pyrotechnics, you can think of the Klitschko brothers over in Germany, but, like, in the end, you still got to fight. So Tyson was like, "I'm coming to fight." Jorge Arce used to ride a horse into the ring.

RM: I was going to mention Arce's because I have watched and analyzed that video, and I remember you saying something like, "The horse is dancing in. It's not just walking in, it's dancing in!" What do you think is the significance of Arce coming in on a black horse, sucking on a lollipop, and wearing a Tejana hat to the ring?

MK: Right. He's dancing; the horse danced to the ring. It's pretty good. I would say that getting back to character, right? Melodrama is when the story is driven forward by what happens next—as opposed to real drama is driven by character.

When someone like Arce comes into the ring like that, he's defining his character as an individual. As a fan, you can live vicariously through him: "Oh, I too am an individual. My life has some meaning. Right? I have some value. I'm not simply a member of this group."

At some level the viewer can live vicariously through the showman, because the showmanship is really saying, "I'm specific. I'm not just general." And as someone who is not a famous fighter, you can feel kind of general. You can feel that your life, you're toiling away in anonymity, but when you see a personality, you can connect to it.

"Yeah, I too am an individual. I'm a person, and this person's from where I'm from, and he's expressing that. And I'm not allowed to do that really, but I feel some of that stuff inside and I can relate to that."

RM: Do you think that is a unique power that boxing has versus other sports?

MK: I think showmanship in any sport can make someone feel that way, or it could even be, conversely, it can be, "I'm amused by that because, boy, that's out of my experience," right? But I hadn't thought of it, until you just asked, but I suppose that I would say the former is actually probably, if I had to guess, more right. It connects to you because there's some side of you, even if you're a stoic, work fifteen hours a day, can't get too high or too low because this is your lot in life, and you got kids to feed. There's a part of you, like in every human being, that if you see Arce, flamboyant, insisting on his own individuality, that there's a kind of—even if it's not exactly an identification—there's some piece of you that identifies with it or at least gives you some hope.

RM: I'm remembering Anthony Joshua's ring entrance for his fight against Wladimir Klitschko, which lasted over five minutes.

MK: But they're very much in the Klitschko domain. They're not specific to who Joshua is. They are just, "I am a big important heavyweight champion." I remember when Raekwon led Floyd Mayweather in on a "Boxing After Dark," or a "KO Nation" fight card. I wasn't on that broadcast, or I'd have said it at the time, but I remember thinking the significance of that was Raekwon was rapping a song where he said, "The man like Floyd Mayweather."[6] That was a line in the song. As soon as I heard the beat, I recognized it. What Floyd was saying by having Rae walk him in was "Yo, Rae didn't write this song for me. It's not like I called him up and said, 'Walk me into the ring,' so he put me in a song. He put me in a song. I'm showing you that I'm important." Floyd came in with that dude from a song where he'd already put him in, and Floyd's saying, the streets are recognizing. I thought that was significant.[7] Yeah, but you wouldn't get it unless you knew that. Floyd's really sending that message; he's the antihero to mainstream America but also a hero to counterculture and the streets.

RM: I always think about the moment he went from "Pretty Boy Floyd" to "Money Mayweather," that transition that took place during the buildup of his fight against Oscar De La Hoya in 2007. To me, that was a very pivotal moment in his career.

MK: Top Rank is a brilliant promoter. Top Rank is the most successful promoter of all time. And they tried to package Floyd like Sugar Ray Leonard. That was very much the idea. "An African American star, he's the best in the world, but he's the good guy." The thought was, it was difficult to market African American fighters, if they weren't punchers or didn't have gold medals by just telling their stories. You had to fit them into a category like "The Golden Boy" or "The American Dream Guy." And Floyd was chafing under their control of that image. You understand why Top Rank had to do it. It makes sense. It had always been done that way. But the next guy doesn't look like the last guy. As I said, the biggest fight in terms of money and actual dollar generation was Floyd Mayweather versus Manny Pacquiao. It was between a Filipino flyweight champion versus an African American junior lightweight, non–gold medalist, and who's not a puncher. That's gonna break all the records? So you understand why people didn't necessarily see that coming ten years before it happened. So Top Rank understandably said, "This is the easiest way to promote this." And Floyd was like, "That's not me! I'm not Pretty Boy Floyd, like your Golden Boy . . . I'm Money Mayweather. And if that seems like it's not gonna work for you, because it's gonna turn people off, then I'm gonna do me." And he also had a sense of it being marketable, because that's who he is.

Floyd talks a lot of shit, is from the streets, and that's an expression of him. And the authentic expression of someone's personality is going to resonate more than the attempt to be what you think the audience wants. When he was Pretty Boy Floyd, it was two million dollars a fight offered in a deal. And when he was Money Mayweather, eventually he made two hundred million in a fight.

RM: What do you think his fight with De La Hoya represented for his career?

MK: The De La Hoya fight branded him as the number one moneymaker. So it was a lot like branding. In Hollywood, for example, this A-list actor is, they can open a movie, because they've selected scripts carefully, and as a result, the audience knows "When I see this person in a movie, it's really good." And after they do that a couple of times, the presence of that actor indicates to the audience that it's a good script. It's directed by a good director. If the actor has a couple flops, suddenly that brand starts to be tarnished. So is it really the actor that's driving it? Well, in a way, but the actor's driving it because of the selection process, because they are only associated with big event films.

And likewise, Floyd's branding in the De La Hoya fight was what was important. Floyd had De La Hoya as his dance partner. He took the mantle as number one cash cow in boxing from De La Hoya in that fight. He had just had a big event with Arturo Gatti and now he had a big event with De La Hoya, and because he was the winner of that event, and because he could generate interest with his talking outside the ring and his excellence inside the ring, he was better than everyone else. He branded himself as the money fighter.

Notes

1. Larry Merchant served as a boxing commentator for HBO Sports from 1978 until his retirement in December 2012.

2. Dave Zirin, *What's My Name, Fool? Sports and Resistance in the United States* (Haymarket Books, 2005), 57.

3. Duk Koo Kim was a fighter from South Korea who collapsed into a coma minutes after the conclusion of his fight against Ray Mancini. Doctors found a subdural hematoma consisting of 100 cubic centimeters of blood in Kim's skull. Kim died four days later, on November 18, 1982. On December 9, 1982, the World Boxing Council announced that they would reduce the number of rounds in championship fights from fifteen to twelve and would allow referees to issue standing eight counts. The standing eight count, also known as the protection count, is a judgment call made by the referee inside the ring. When using the standing eight count, the referee stops the action in the ring and starts to count to eight after a fighter is knocked down. During that count, the referee determines whether or not the fallen boxer can continue.

4. In this video, Kellerman discusses systemic racism and oppression as being the reason why Colin Kaepernick was denied a job with the National Football League. This video was uploaded by "The Rational National" and is not the official ESPN *First Take* video, which omits Kellerman's participation on the show. "Max Kellerman Obliterates Racist NFL Owners. ESPN Hides the Clip," YouTube, September 19, 2017, uploaded by "The Rational National," https://www.youtube.com/watch?v=AD6ne4zfz1k&t=41s. This is the video uploaded onto ESPN's YouTube channel, which omits Kellerman's participation in the discussion: "Stephen A. Smith, Snoop Dogg and Magic Johnson Discuss Colin Kaepernick | First Take | ESPN," YouTube, September 12, 2017, uploaded by "ESPN," https://www.youtube.com/watch?v=LLGENw4C1jk.

5. *Shut Up and Dribble*, season 1, episode 2, "102," directed by Gotham Chopra, written by Adam Feinstein, Alexa Stapleton, Rob Ford, Victor Buhler, narrated by Jemele Hill, aired November 10, 2018, Showtime, 2018.

6. Funkmaster Flex and Big Kap Featuring Raekwon, "Dem Want War," released December 7, 1999, track 11 on *The Tunnel*, Def Jam, compact disc.

7. The fight Max Kellerman referred to is the March 18, 2000, match between Floyd Mayweather Jr. and Gregorio Vargas. See video at "23rd FIGHT Floyd Mayweather vs Gregorio Vargas FULL FIGHT," YouTube, September 11, 2022, Uploaded by "TaleOfTheTapeBoxing," https://www.youtube.com/watch?v=1D6uVW2EL5w.

13

"Sincerely, These Hands"

Mayweather, Money, and Masculinity

JAVON JOHNSON

Round One

Boxing
[**bok**-sing]
1. the act, technique, or profession of fighting with the fists, with or without boxing gloves.
Origin of Boxing
First recorded in 1705–15; box +-ing
—Dictionary.com

Round Two

In his final fight, Floyd "Money" Mayweather returned from his second retirement to soundly defeat mixed martial arts superstar Conor McGregor in a technical knockout after referee Robert Byrd stopped the fight one minute and five seconds in the tenth round. After having returned to beat Oscar De La Hoya, Ricky Hatton, Juan Manuel Márquez, Shane Mosley, Victor Ortiz, Miguel Cotto, Robert Guerrero, Saúl "Canelo" Álvarez, Marcos Maidana, Manny Pacquiao, and Andre Berto, Mayweather, ever the ringmaster, made a circus out of the entire sport of boxing when he made easy work of McGregor to earn a ridiculous $275 million payday and an undefeated record of 50-0 to surpass Rocky Marciano's 49-0. At the end of the historic night, Mayweather said, "I think we gave the fans what they wanted to see."[1]

I'll be honest. I loved watching Mayweather's career, the way he tactically outsmarted and outlasted all of his opponents. There is something amazing in knowing that this 5′8″ (173cm) Black man, with his fragile knuckles, ingeniously figured out how to leave the sport well paid, with his wits intact, and with an undefeated record. After constantly witnessing how Black men have been and are disenfranchised, there was a poetry watching him master the sweet science and consistently display a brilliance that shattered not only men's faces but also the idea that Black men are disempowered, even though he simultaneously reinscribed troubling myths of Black males having innate violent predispositions.

I am fully aware of the problems with championing violence. Among others, the glorification of Mayweather's physical prowess in the boxing ring substantiates claims of Black males as naturally violent, which can, in turn, be used to justify the state-sanctioned violence enacted upon Black males on an everyday basis. Floyd Mayweather, however, like Jack Johnson, Joe Louis, and Muhammad Ali before him, held promises for Black masculinity squarely in his fist. Though not a first like Johnson, not nearly as political as Louis (who fought Italian boxer Primo Carnera while the world was learning that Mussolini's Italy was to invade Haile Selassie's Ethiopia) and Ali (who put his career on the line to protest the Vietnam War and gave us the oft-cited line "No Vietcong ever called me nigger"), Mayweather, with his display of cunningness and power, which might be read as excessive or hyper, often acted as an empowering symbol of Black male possibility (opening some doors while simultaneously closing off others). Riffing on Roland Barthes's (2013) discussion of the French poet Minou Drouet's tree, boxing "as expressed" in the ways it now "is no longer quite [boxing], it is a [boxing] which is decorated, adapted to a certain type of consumption, laden with literary self-indulgence, revolt, images, in short with a type of social *usage* which is added" (109; original emphasis). While I am sure he inspired his fair share of violent moments, Mayweather's unmatched skill had "social usage" in that it was galvanizing for me in a nonviolent way, teaching me, as I am sure it did many other young Black males, about Black male brilliance, strength, and agency in a white supremacist world that want us to have little of either.

The broader politics surrounding Johnson, Louis, and Ali, plus the times in which they fought, make it easy for us to mark them as heroes by allowing us the ability to focus less on their fighting and more on their politics. In this so-called post-racial world, Mayweather, who does not offer us any of those larger "political moments" to hang our hats on, forces those of us who like him as a fighter to admit that what we love most about "Money May" is solely his boxing prowess and that physical Black power, even when displayed in a fight, can be a symbol of empowerment and hope for many Black people. This is not to excuse Floyd Mayweather for his multiple accounts of domestic violence, the battery, his use of homophobic slurs, gross capitalism, or any of his other problematic behaviors and actions. Instead, this reading is an argument for a human face for the infamous boxer and, more importantly, for those Black folks who use figures like Mayweather to engage in "a politics of disrespectability," or a tactical countering of a strict, unfair, and near impossible Victorian ethos imposed on Black performativity.

Providing yet another way to think through what Evelyn Higginbotham (1994) called "the politics of respectability," or the demand "that every individual in the black community assume responsibility for behavioral, self-regulation and self-improvement along moral, educational, and economic lines," disrespectability openly attacks and challenges the troubling racial, gendered, classed, and sexualized practices that establish those very lines (198). In what follows, I want to reread the ways in which we understand Floyd Mayweather's supporters, hypermasculinity, and Blackness and search for something critically salvable.

Round Three

How do we write about a troubling figure like Floyd Mayweather in ways similar to how we write about other Black boxers, some—if not all—of which were problematic in their own rights, without glossing over his atrocities or reducing him to monster?

Round Four

Recently, many outlets, including sellers on Amazon.com, began offering T-shirts that read "Dear Racism, I am not my grandparents. Sincerely, these hands." While I cannot say for certain when the phrase or shirt was born, I can say that the phrase "these hands" originated from Black youth as a way to invite or demand someone to a fist-fight, as in "Catch these hands," "You don't wanna see these hands," or "Dear racism, come get these hands." Grammatically awkward indeed, one can and should, however, make the argument that "these," the adjective that precedes the action verb "catch," is used in lieu of an indefinite article for added emphasis. And because racism is so pervasive and pernicious, it is easy to see how "these hands," vague and nonspecific so as to remain ever available for anyone who might cross a particular boundary, might be a correct construction.

Reminding us that the history of Black resistance is ingeniously complex, rife with violent and nonviolent responses to white supremacy, and ought not be reduced to simple passivity as meekness, Ivory A. Toldson (2016) writes, "Following the controversial election of Donald Trump, and during a time when racist acts have reached unprecedented levels, the T-shirt resonates with many who are motivated to resist racism 'by any means necessary.'" Indeed, the phrase resonates so much, despite its lack of nuance (which I am not sure is ever the goal of such a shirt), that people continually use it in conversation and on social media sites. Used jokingly, politically, problematically, and wrongly, the hashtag #thesehands has well over twenty thousand posts on Instagram, is used multiple times every day on Twitter (now "X"), and has a ridiculous number of memes attached. In other words, social media would have you believe that it is as easy to catch these hands as it is to catch this cold.

In *The World Made Meme*, Ryan Milner (2016) asserts that memes are employed "to emphasize the social processes essential to the creation, circulation, and transformation of collective texts, regardless of the individual text itself," and, in so doing, the memetic is shaping our public discourse (2). Calling memes "cultural building blocks that are articulated and diffused by active human agents" within certain social and cultural constraints, Limor Shifman informs us that given most people "choose to work within the borders of existing meme genres," despite having the freedom to generate any kinds of content, points to the necessity "for creating a sense of communality in a fragmented world" (qtd. in Jenkins 2014). As for Shifman, memes and "memetic media are significant" for Milner (2016) "as individual strands in vast tapestries" in that they offer people participation in a larger conversation through embellished images circulated across social media platforms, providing new commentary and criticism through mediated dissemination of old ideas (3). In this way, "these hands" are an attempt, however forgetful or short-sighted, to offer different lenses, discourses, and paths on and to Black liberation, and I want to think about Mayweather, money, and masculinity sincerely through and with "these hands," these Black hands that require, crave even, different lenses.

Round Five

Mayweather, incredibly dominant, has put together arguably the greatest boxing career in the history of the sport. Of his 50-0 record, which surpassed boxing legend Rocky Marciano's historic 49-0 record, twenty-four wins were against current or former champs, twenty-six were world title fights, and he held world titles in five weight divisions, one of only five boxers to achieve such a feat. Equally important, in a sports era rife with performance enhancement drugs (PEDs), he has never truly been accused or suspected of using PEDs. Although Mike Tyson had far more punching power, and though Muhammad Ali's brilliance in and out of the ring might very well mean he is still the greatest, Mayweather's unblemished record and numerous titles across a staggering five different weight classes, which spans two decades, is an impressive feat that speaks as much, if not more, about his brilliance in the ring as it does his physical abilities. In other words, Mayweather not only dominated his opponents, but he also dominated boxing, a sport intimately associated with causing brain damage, so much so that chronic traumatic encephalopathy, a brain injury not entirely dissimilar to shaken baby syndrome, is also called boxer's encephalopathy and dementia pugilistica. And, somehow, despite toying with it for decades on the highest, most dangerous level, he seemingly beat that too to leave the sport as perhaps, as my uncle once quipped, "the baddest man alive."

Nearly a century before, Jack Johnson was the baddest man alive, with documentarian Ken Burns calling him "the most famous and the most notorious African-American on earth." As the first Black heavyweight champion, Johnson's narrative "exemplifies one of many ways Progressive Era men used ideas about white supremacy to produce a racially based ideology of male power" (Bederman 1995, 5). Examining white men's inability to reconcile Johnson's success with their understanding of manliness, historian Gail Bederman argues, "As white middle-class men actively worked to reinforce male power, their race became a factor . . . [and] whiteness was both a palpable fact and a manly ideal" (4–5). The excessive furor of those white men who successfully whitened masculinity through their violence and vitriol set up a continual need for Black people to support any and all fighting back, which often meant supporting the fight and the fighter even when conflicted about the particular fighter or violence as a means of justice. Poet William Waring Cuney's "My Lord, What a Morning" evidences that claim:

> Oh, my Lord
> What a morning,
> Oh, my Lord,
> What a feeling,
> When Jack Johnson
> Turned Jim Jeffries'
> Snow-white face
> Up to the ceiling.
> Yes, my Lord,
> Fighting is wrong,
> But what an uppercut.
> Oh, my Lord,
> What a morning,
> Oh, my Lord

What a feeling,
When Jack Johnson
Turned Jim Jeffries'
Lily-white face
Up to the ceiling.
Oh, my Lord
What a morning,
Oh, my Lord
Take care of Jack.
Keep him, Lord
As you made him,
Big, and strong, and black.

For Cuney, "Fighting is wrong," but given the extreme violence early twentieth-century Blacks faced, there was a joy—a certain poetry, even—in watching Johnson demolish the white James J. Jeffries with a heavenly "uppercut" in what was dubbed "The Fight of the Century." In this way, boxing has never been just boxing but instead a social-cultural fight for power, legitimacy, visibility, and bragging rights, all caught up in patriarchal notions of male power, and I argue that many Black folks' love for the too often grotesque and indefensible Mayweather is grounded in many of the same race, class, and gender politics.

Round Six

What makes Mayweather such a useful figure in this argument is quite precisely his troubling legacy. Since 2001, Floyd Mayweather has been accused of multiple acts of violence against women, one of which he was convicted, and in two others he pleaded guilty. In one incident, in which his then eleven-year old son wrote a harrowing letter to the police, Mayweather, who was not with Josie Harris, the mother of their children, at the time, was apparently so upset that she was dating Chicago Bull's player C. J. Watson that he beat her in front of their children while his friend James McNair aided Mayweather by not allowing them to get help for their mother. Shanteal Jackson, Mayweather's girlfriend at the time, alleged that the infamous boxer pointed a gun at her feet and asked her which one would she like to keep. However, he has only received slaps on the wrist by the justice system, the boxing commission, and his fans alike. In *Iron Mike: A Mike Tyson Reader*, Michael Eric Dyson (2002) forces us to ask how such a despicable person like "Tyson still commands loyalty in the black neighborhoods" (xix). Whether it was Rev. Dr. Theodore J. Jemison, the then seventy-three-year-old president of the National Baptist Convention, who threw his support behind Tyson during his rape trial; members of various Black congregations; or folks in the streets, "Iron Mike," in Dyson's words, "became [Don] King's field general in the ghetto rebellion," or a symbol of rebellion, for many Black people (Dyson 2002, 163).

The love for Tyson was so profound that shortly after the rape conviction, after the hoards of excuses, Michael D. Shanabrook (1992) was compelled to pen a brief "Letter to the Editor" in the *Washington Post* in which he lamented "the 'seemingly' large number of members of the black community who 'appear' to condone [Tyson's] actions or at least feel he is not guilty of anything." Charles A. Williams (1992) followed that up with his own letter, ending with "To my African-American sisters and brothers, let us stop crying racism, blaming the victim; and let us start demanding that Mike Tyson and others like him take responsibility for their actions."

In this way, unlike the aforementioned Johnson, Louis, and Ali, Floyd Mayweather, like Tyson, is not clean-cut, "respectable," or politically motivated. This is not to suggest that those figures are not without their problems but rather that Mayweather's particular checkered past and performance of Black masculinity does not allow us the space to hide. Instead, it forces us, those who love him, to admit that in addition to his fighting, we love—or least put up with—his filth, his grotesqueness, and his monstrousness.

Like Adilifu Nama (2009) suggests of Black comic books, I want to read Mayweather, those who love him, and to some extent hypermasculinity, with a "critically celebratory perspective" (5; original emphasis). This is not to "uncritically embrace" Mayweather and hypermasculinity, accepting them wholesale; rather it is an attempt to "steer the discussion away from theoretical dead ends or conversations that lead only in one direction to one conclusion" (5). Using Nama's "critically celebratory perspective" is undeniably Black in the ways it allows us to move beyond "the tired tropes about blackness" that service white supremacy, and it provides us the opportunity to use "these hands" to salvage what has been discarded and tossed away.

Round Seven

On May 2, 2015, two multidivisional world champions collided in the ring when Floyd Mayweather fought Manny Pacquiao in what Jason Gay (2015) of the *Wall Street Journal* and many others dubbed "the fight of the century." Seemingly a decade in the making and one that happened at least five years too late, Mayweather–Pacquiao was still highly anticipated and had an audience that was a circus of celebrities. In the text *Money: The Life and Fast Times of Floyd Mayweather*, Tris Dixon (2017) writes:

> Beyoncé was there with Jay-Z, so were Ben Affleck, Mark Wahlberg, Don Cheadle, Sugar Ray Leonard, Mike Tyson, Michael Jordan and Yvette Prieto, Tom Brady, Donald Trump, Sean Combs, Jon Voight, Nicole Scherzinger, Drew Barrymore, Nicki Mina, Andre Agassi, Steffi Graf, Christina Milian and dozens of others from the A and B lists.
>
> There were so many celebrities and high-rollers in town for the event that McCarran International [Airport] closed its clogged runways to private planes later in the day. (353)

Moreover, it was an incredibly expensive event that sold out in minutes with tickets that "were priced at $7,500, $5,000, $3,500, $2,500 and $1,500. There were also some $10,000 tickets, though they were not made public. On the secondary market, some agencies started by offering floor seats (not ringside) for $45,000" (346). However, I argue that it was billed as a mega-fight not merely because both Mayweather and Pacquiao were at the top of their game, as they were not. Nor was it that the highly anticipated mega-fight was expected to be, at that point, the highest-grossing fight of all time; instead, it was the way Pacquiao's respectability, as well as his proximity to whiteness, worked in stark contrast to Mayweather.

By the time the match had come to fruition, it was more about the model minority showing the bombastic and problematic Black guy how to do it "the right way." Dixon (2017) argues, "Of course, the good guy–bad guy dynamic for Mayweather–Pacquiao was in play" (353). In what was continually reported on going into the boxing match, "Pacquiao had worked his way up from poverty to become a national icon, an international star and a congressman in the Philippines who always gave back to his people. One athlete inspired a nation, the other—at times—had been loathed by one" (353). My colleague Constancio Arnaldo is a Filipino American who examines the larger-than-life Manny "Pacman" Pacquiao's performances of nationality and masculinity. Arnaldo makes necessary arguments about the ways race and gender are both packaged and travel from the Philippines to those Filipinos not in the country; he has has illustrated how the love for Pacman, especially when he fought Mayweather, was grounded in the "myth of the model minority" that conveniently glossed over Manny's well-documented sexism and homophobia in service of anti-Blackness and white supremacy. The "myth of the model minority" is when a minority group (typically Asian Americans in the United States) is propped up for having the "right" values and culture for the sole purpose of being pitted against other minoritized groups in order to blame their culture and values for failures and to dismiss and undermine any claim of structural-based inequality. Indeed, how else are we to understand the US love of Pacquiao, who has his own well-documented problems with homophobia, womanizing, and cockfighting, in relation to the disdain for Mayweather, who also made true the American bootstraps metaphor by literally fighting his way out of poverty, and who also gives back, and, as I have argued, inspires?

Beyond Pacquiao, the media covering the Floyd Mayweather versus Conor McGregor match conveniently glossed over the racist actions of McGregor until they became too much to ignore, such as when he told Mayweather to "dance for me, boy" or when he called Black boxers "dancing monkeys," hoping that he himself could be the "Great White Hope" that would put this Black man in his place. None of this is to suggest that Pacquiao or McGregor is worse than Mayweather, as Mayweather has also said racially problematic, homophobic, and sexist, things; rather, I point out how media attention is especially problematic. And, I argue, they do so partly because he is problematic but also because he is Black, unapologetic, and has managed to control his own career in a capitalist market that was never designed for him to do so. I struggle here because I want to read Mayweather with a certain grace not often extended to Black men and still hold him accountable for his atrocities, as the discourse surrounding him informs us that the subject-object of "proper" critique is constructed along anti-Black (as well as sexist, classist, homophobic, transphobic, xenophobic, etc.) lines.

Round Eight

While many boxers struggle to gain and keep their earnings, Floyd "Money" Mayweather, with his signature defensive skills, has managed to become one of the most financially successful sports figures in history. After parting ways with International Boxing Hall of Fame promoter Bob Arum a decade ago, Mayweather controlled his financial future and has accrued earnings of nearly one billion dollars. In an industry known for ruining boxers financially, Mayweather was almost perfect with money, promoting himself and negotiating his own contracts. Also, his particular "hit and not get hit" boxing style will likely allow him to live in a healthier manner during his later years, when other boxers might feel the effects of such a brutal career choice. And it is how this unapologetic Black man managed himself, controlled his purse, his health, his image, and his career that is especially telling of how Mayweather is both read and understood.

Race and sports scholar David J. Leonard (2010) writes extensively about how Black athletes are treated and imagined very differently from their white counterparts. What he says of Black NBA players can be extended to all major sports in the United States. He writes that the NBA's desire to control the rights of Black players "demonstrate[s] the powerful ways in which black bodies, even those living the 'American Dream,' [function] as million-dollar commodities [who must be] contained and imagined as dangerous, menacing, abject, and criminal" (259). In this way, I argue, while there are legitimate reasons to figure Mayweather as "dangerous" and "menacing," it is mainly the domestic abuse, homophobia, misogyny, and his ability to gain financial freedom that mean he functions as a dangerous "liberatory" model who must be reeled in, and racist hatred serves that very function.

As Cedric Robinson (2000) informs us in the monumental text *Black Marxism*, "Somewhat paradoxically, the more that Africans and their descendants assimilated cultural materials from colonial society, the less human they became in the minds of the colonists" (119). Mayweather's performances of hypermasculinity and gross capitalism take place in a sociohistorical context that always imagined him as an object to be used in service of white supremacy, and in some ways he uses those performances and the context against themselves. By privileging a style that focuses on the maintenance of his health, managing his career and earnings, and his use of the villain role to promote his fights, Mayweather illustrates one way "objects can and do resist," to cite Fred Moten (2003), and every victory was, to some degree, a blow to an industry that relies on the punishment and disciplining of Black fighters (1).

Round Nine

In elementary school, I spent a good amount of time at my great-aunt and-uncle's home. Partially to save my single mother money in after-school care costs, and to have us around people she trusted, my younger brother and I would walk to my aunt and uncle's house immediately after school, where a hot meal and a demand to immediately finish homework always awaited us. One day my brother, my cousins, our friends, and I were all outside playing when the ice cream truck approached. While everyone ordered more-elaborate frozen treats, I, having only a quarter left, ordered a Popsicle. Upon seeing me unwrap it, my uncle knocked it from my hand and said, "Real men don't suck things." My eyes welled in anger because I really wanted that Popsicle, in embarrassment because everyone saw this, and in hurt because I could not understand how my beloved uncle could do such a thing. As I started to cry, he said, "Don't cry or I'll give you something to cry about. This world doesn't need another soft Black boy. You won't be able to survive. It'll eat you up and spit you out."

I have never been able to reconcile that brutal moment, and perhaps on some level this essay is an attempt to think through and make sense of it. That moment and others like it color my "odd, irregular, and slightly off-kilter" understanding and reading of Mayweather and, more generally, my performances of masculinity (Johnson 2005, 2).

Interestingly enough, my uncle was incredibly nurturing in that he cooked for and cleaned up after us, was never afraid to hug or say, "I love you," and stressed the importance of respecting women. He openly criticized my father, his biological nephew, for not being an active parent, saying, "Money cannot raise those boys. They need you there. They need you to hold and care for them." In this way, my uncle's troublingly homophobic lesson, complicated by his at other times careful and brilliant love, illustrates that Black masculinity is an "always already 'queered'" complex set of strategic and contradictory performances that cannot be readily reduced to an either-or but instead an also-and (51).

Mark Anthony Neal (2005) discusses in full detail the problems with fixed masculinity in his oft-cited text *New Black Man*. While I largely agree with Neal that my uncle's problematic teaching moment, however well intentioned, "unfortunately helps reinforce a rigid model of black masculinity that allows for little if any flexibility," I wonder if there is a space for a Black masculinity to exist somewhere betwixt and between "Strong Black Man" and Neal's more progressive "NewBlackMan" (2005, 27). While my uncle reinforced a particular brand of homophobic masculinity, he did so not because he questioned my Blackness—quite the opposite: He did so because he felt that my Blackness requires, at times, a strong and straightforward defense (problematic pun intended).

While, for him, some queer possibilities (e.g., the Popsicle, the crying) troublingly threatened my masculinity and my ability to protect myself in this harsh anti-Black world, other queer possibilities (e.g., affection, emotion, caretaking) further established my manliness. My uncle knew that even my adolescent Black male self was understood as threatening, as it is/was always, by virtue of being loud, excessive, unruly, illegible, pathological, and outside the confines of white neoliberal, liberal, and conservative structures alike. He understood that I was a threat to safety because I am Black and that in this unforgiving world I would need to call on a number of performative options to survive. Though I cannot disagree with my uncle any more on what constitutes a "real man" as it pertains to his homophobic and sexist derision of fellatio oddly placed in a Popsicle, I understand his desire to keep me "safe," which rests, at times, on my being tough, strong, or, dare I say, hyper, which beckons me to at least think about the feasibility, practicality, or possibility of a usable, even if only situationally, hypermasculinity.

A quick survey of the literature would reveal that discussions of hypermasculinity are almost always centered on Black people. Jack Halberstam (1998) agrees, writing, "Arguments about excessive masculinity tend to focus on black bodies (male and female)," and even more, hypermasculinity is almost always discussed in terms of the pathological (2). In this way, without ever asking "excessive as compared to what?" all of the problems associated with the hypermasculine (violent, sexually aggressive, overly aggressive in general, etc.) are automatically extended to Black folks. This kind of thinking further adds to the ways we pathologize Black people at birth.

Traditional critiques of masculine performativity vituperate the hypermasculine, figuring it as little more than a villain gender that must be rooted out. Rather than eliminating the hypermasculine and finding more usable or controllable masculinities, I propose a move toward new racialized gender understandings that might, at times, view the hypermasculine as a viable option. I am not disputing the broader criticisms of hypermasculinity; rather, I want to trouble those too easy readings that label the hypermasculine as simply problematic. I want to point to those moments when hypermasculinity cannot be readily reduced to an antihero but might be better understood as a symbolic jolt, a protective measure, or a counter-performance.

Exploring "how the criminal justice system shapes the development of specific forms of masculinity," sociologist Victor Rios (2011) asserts that for many Black and Brown males hypermasculinity becomes an "ideal of survival" (152, 159). Indeed, Rios fully understands how "hypermasculinity serves both as resistance and a resource for self-affirmation" but ultimately concludes that "it impedes desistance and social mobility and further entitles the system to punish" Black and Brown bodies (161). I wonder if there are performances of hypermasculinity that are grounded in resistance to a near-totalizing racist system without contributing to sexism and homophobia. Is there a way to think about the hypermasculine as a series of raced performances that are simply working to keep white supremacy, the criminal justice system, the unfair labor market, and harmful people at bay?

On some levels, the exaltation of Mayweather by many Black people, despite all of his woes, is a rejection of white "normalcy" standards and an attempt to avoid them. In his now oft-cited text *Constructing the Black Masculine*, Maurice O. Wallace (2002) reminds us that "Black men come to embody the inverse picture necessary for the positive self-portrait of white identity" (32). Examining Albert Watson's now-famous photos of various Black people, Wallace so poignantly highlights how it is not the image "per se that tricks the (mind's) eye, but the . . . frame that fools" (29). This is why so many Black people refuse to sit still and smile for the camera, why so many of us strategically reject the direction of the white gaze. Championing Mayweather is a way we might understand the often push back against the "trick."

Hyper-toughness, symbolized and performed in a walk, constantly clenched fists, and scowls, is not only a defense mechanism but a hypermasculine currency that purposefully pushes back against dominant structures and discourses that seek to discipline Black bodies at every turn. Even if we are going to continually read hypermasculinity as nothing more than a problematic text, we must not continue to do so without the proper context (a play on Tricia Rose's "Black Texts/Black Contexts").[2] We cannot talk about violent and excessive Black males without simultaneously talking about the excessive violence enacted *upon* Black males on an everyday basis. In other words, we cannot talk about hypermasculinity without critically discussing all the moments that create the spaces for young Black males to act in these so-called illogical and self-destructive manners as well as talking about what these performances do to and for many Black people. In a white supremacist, anti-Black America, Black folks are troublingly surveilled by the state, constantly under attack by unfair police practices, subjected to a harsh justice system that repeatedly fixes us as the problem, and unjustly scrutinized by scholars and politicians who discuss us as always already pathological and the hypermasculine. Floyd "Money" Mayweather, with all of his issues, offers a symbol of strength and power that not only fights back but wins. To be clear, I am not articulating a world where we would be unable or unwilling to critique (problematic) performances of hypermasculinity; rather, I am gesturing toward one where hypermasculinity is, on some levels, depathologized.

Round Ten

I got into boxing as an adult. I regularly attended a local gym in Oakland, California, just up the street from where I once resided. It is a small but expanding boxing gym, now complete with a ring, various boxing bags, a cardio room, humble locker rooms, and a dizzying number of posters lining the walls. Founded and owned by Miguel Lopez, Oakland's Boxing for Health gym is more than a space for exercise and training; it is a community for those interested in learning more about the "sweet science" of boxing. After intense classes, we usually sit around for a bit to talk about boxing, sports, music, family, personal histories, politics, and many other topics.

One day, after the class I usually attended did a series of four-round sparring sessions, a young woman, also a regular, asked Miguel why he proudly displays posters of Floyd Mayweather on the wall given all of the "stuff he's done." He responded, "Because there are few like him. Ever. He wasn't just a boxer; he is more like a superhero. The money, the way he gamed the business showed me how to use my hands . . . not for destruction, but to build this gym and hopefully a community." She later said, "I get that. He totally grosses me out, but I can see how he can be that for you."

To continue along the boxing metaphor, she dealt a blow that left me thinking about my defense of Mayweather for quite some time. Mayweather, his promises and problems, and how he is championed and criminalized do not exist in a vacuum but in a robust history of race and gender expectations. Like Mayweather's 2006 photo shoot, where he posed in the Top Rank Gym in Las Vegas, Nevada, which produced a series of darkened images of a sweaty boxer with an almost electric glow in front of a brick wall, Mayweather's public image—that is, his performance of black masculinity—is "a messy assembly-line construction" (Wallace 2002, 25). Indeed, we view Mayweather, his entire career, and his public image—like all Black bodies, hypermasculine or not—clouded in "a vision of what the racial solipsistic among us will not, cannot see: their own self-serving blindness" (31). And while we never came to an agreement, what I love about the conversation I had with him is how it reminded both of us that the first and most important rule of the boxing is to protect yourself at all times.

Notes

1. "Floyd Mayweather vs. Conor McGregor Full Fight," YSU, YouTube, https://www.youtube.com/watch?v=tvbr9-YXDSE.

2. Tricia Rose's "Black Texts/Black Contexts" in *Black Popular Culture* (1998) examines how Black cultural production is often misread or decontextualized within dominant discourses. She critiques the ways Black texts are either co-opted by mainstream culture or dismissed through reductive frameworks that ignore their political and historical specificity. Rose argues for a reading practice that situates Black cultural forms—such as music, literature, and film—within their sociopolitical and historical contexts, emphasizing their resistance, innovation, and counter-hegemonic potential.

References

Barthes, Roland. 2013. *Mythologies*. Hill and Wang.

Bederman, Gail. 1995. *Manliness and Civilization: A Cultural History of Gender and Race in the United States, 1880–1917*. University of Chicago Press.

Cuney, William Waring. 2014. "My Lord, What a Morning." *Beltway Poetry Quarterly*, June 12. https://www.beltwaypoetry.com/cuney/.

Dixon, Tris. 2017. *Money: The Life and Fast Times of Floyd Mayweather*. Hamilcar Publications.

Dyson, Michael Eric. 2002. *Holler If You Hear Me: Searching for Tupac Shakur*. Basic Civitas Books.

Gay, Jason. 2015. "Pacquiao vs. Mayweather: It's Real, Not Talk." *Wall Street Journal*. February 22.

Halberstam, Jack. 1998. *Female Masculinity*. Duke University Press.

Higginbotham, Evelyn Brooks. 1994. *Righteous Discontent: The Women's Movement in the Black Baptist Church, 1880–1920*. Harvard University Press.

Jenkins, Henry. 2014. "A Meme Is a Terrible Thing to Waste: An Interview with Limor Shifman (Part One)." February 17. https://henryjenkins.org/blog/2014/02/a-meme-is-a-terrible-thing-to-waste-an-interview-with-limor-shifman-part-one.html.

Johnson, E. Patrick. 2005. *Appropriating Blackness: Performance and the Politics of Authenticity*. Duke University Press.

Leonard, David J. 2010. Jumping the Gun: Sporting Cultures and the Criminalization of Black Masculinity. *Journal of Sport and Social Issues* 34, no. 2: 252–62.

Milner, Ryan M. 2016. *The World Made Meme: Public Conversations and Participatory Media*. MIT Press.

Moten, Fred. 2003. *In the Break: The Aesthetics of the Black Radical Tradition*. University of Minnesota Press.

Nama, Adilifu. 2009. *Super Black: American Pop Culture and Black Superheroes*. University of Texas Press.

Neal, Mark Anthony. 2005. *New Black Man*. Routledge.

Rios, Victor M. 2011. *Punished: Policing the Lives of Black and Latino Boys*. New York University Press.

Robinson, Cedric. 2000. *Black Marxism: The Making of the Black Radical Tradition*. University of North Carolina Press.

Rose, Tricia. 1998. "Black Texts/Black Contexts. " In *Black Popular Culture: A Project by Michele Wallace*, ed. Gina Dent. New Press.

Shanabrook, Michael D. 1992. "The Mike Tyson Case." *Washington Post*. February 22.

Toldson, Ivory A. 2016. OpEd: "Do These 'I Am Not My Grandparents' Shirts Dishonor Our Forefathers?" November 21. NBC News. https://www.nbcnews.com/news/nbcblk/oped-do-these-i-am-not-my-grandparents-shirts-dishonor-n686761.

Wallace, Maurice O. 2002. *Constructing the Black Masculine: Identity and Ideality in African American Men's Literature and Culture, 1775–1995*. Duke University Press.

Williams, Charles A. 1992. "The Mike Tyson Case." *Washington Post*. February 22.

Coda

Beyond the Dreams of Gold Medals and World Titles

DAVID J. LEONARD, GAYE THERESA JOHNSON, and RUDY MONDRAGÓN

It's the risk that gives the protest its power.
—Dave Zirin

Embodying the endemic nature of the Olympic project, the 2024 Paris Olympics visualizes a range of political expressions and realities. The ways that race, nation, gender, sexuality, geopolitics, war, and the global economy circulated through, shaped, and embedded within the production and consumption of this athletic competition are integral to the Olympics as medals and sports contests. There was great resistance on the streets of Paris as well. As Jules Boykoff and Dave Zirin (2024) reported, "People have been protesting numerous issues—from Israels' attacks on Gaza to the environmental impacts of the Games to the treatment of the homeless." Yet, as these two authors argue, one of the major issues of the Paris Olympics was the invented "controversy" created by a collective of transphobic right-wingers who posited that Algerian boxer Imane Khelif was a male posing as a female boxer.

Prior to the Paris Olympics, Khelif had an amateur record of forty-two wins and nine losses competing in the female division of boxing. Her low knockout rate (seven knockouts total) did not stop her critics, some of those being responsible for her disqualification at the 2023 World Championships. The International Boxing Association, known for its corruption, argued that she possessed competitive advantages over other female boxers, citing the existence of a test that showed Khelif had XY chromosomes. To this day, there is no evidence of those tests. This firestorm carried into the Paris Olympics with hate-fueled messages resting on the idea of "Save Women's Sports," which proclaimed that Khelif was not a female. The implications of these false accusations threatened her safety, as it is illegal to be transgender in Algeria. As Boykoff and Zirin (2024) remind us, "To be absolutely clear, Khelif is not trans—so, making these sorts of unfounded claims could put the boxer's life in danger." Given this unjust fiasco, Khelif's opportunity for dissent was seized on August 9, 2024, when she defeated Liu Yang to capture a gold medal in boxing. Khelif has made the decision to continue her career, now as a professional boxer, which means an opportunity to use the ring to shed further light on how transphobia also hurts cisgender women who don't conform to narrow, Eurocentric visions of womanhood proffered by high-profile harbingers of hate (Boykoff and Zirin 2024).

The nature of boxing, its history, aesthetics, history, and embodiment of the principles of war and combat, results in an Olympic sport that has long been a political avatar and a space for both hegemonic/reactionary political expressions and those concerned with justice and revolution.

As we write this coda, Israel's invasion of Lebanon is well under way; the death toll continues to rise; there is no medical infrastructure left; the international community has come to recognize that what is happening in Gaza and Lebanon is clearly genocide. This is why the presence of Wasim Abusal (also referred to as Waseem Abu Sal in some publications) at Paris as the first Palestinian Olympic boxer is significant. During the opening ceremonies, Abusal wore an embroidered shirt that sought to shine a spotlight on the ongoing war on Palestinians. Alongside olive trees and a sun symbolizing a brighter tomorrow, his shirt depicted planes dropping missiles on innocent children playing. "This shirt represents the current picture in Palestine," noted Abusal. "The children who are martyred and die under the rubble, children whose parents are martyred and are left alone without food or water" (AFP 2024b). Jibril Rajoub, head of the Palestinian Olympic Committee, further highlighted the shirt's antiwar, pro-peace message that sought to bring attention to the devastating loss of life. "It's a message of peace. It's a message to attract attention. This is anti-war, against killing. This abides with the Olympic Charter" (AFP 2024b). Illustrating the power, potential, and possibilities of sport as an instrument of peace, justice, and voice, Abusal was not alone in using the immense platform of the Olympics.

Abusal, along with several other Palestinian athletes displaying "political symbols" on their jackets, used the Opening Ceremonies to perform dissent (Irish 2024). They used the entire games not only to shine a spotlight on the war and the ongoing oppression of their communities in Gaza, the

West Bank, and elsewhere, but also to counter the ubiquitous dehumanization of the Palestinian people. Being at the Olympics and these athletes' respective journeys represent not only an accomplishment but also an act of defiance, resistance, political refusal. They embodied a collective stance against the Israeli occupation, apartheid, the war in Gaza, and the racism that seeks to sanction endless violence.

Valerie Tarazi, an Olympic swimmer who pointed to the Palestinian flag on her arm after the conclusion of her race, highlighted the political importance of their participation. Noting that she and the rest of the delegation were in Paris to "speak up for the people who can't," Tarazi underscored the stakes beyond the pool, beyond the war, and beyond everyday politics. It was about a future: "We're not here to compete for ourselves or represent ourselves. This is more than that" (qtd. in Da Silva and Smith 2024). Omar Ismail noted the larger significance as well, saying, "I'm thinking of kids in Palestine . . . in Gaza, also, and I hope they can see me as a role model" (qtd. in Da Silva and Smith 2024). "France doesn't recognize Palestine as a country, so I am here to raise the flag," notes Yazan Al-Bawwab, who swims for Palestine. "We're not treated like human beings, so when we come play sports, people realize we are equal to them" (qtd. in Janetsky 2024).

For Tarazi and Al-Bawwab, and their Olympic teammates competing under the Palestinian flag, the journey that took them to Paris was made up of acts of defiance, protest, and refusal. Abusal described his participation in the game as an act of protest against the occupation, against war, and against the ongoing assault against the Palestinian people. "I'm going to the Olympics not just for myself, but for all of Palestine. I'm fighting to show the world our dignity and to preserve our identity. It's important to me and to the Palestinian Olympic Committee. My message is one of peace, but also to show the world that we are strong and resilient" (qtd. in Kuehn 2024).

For Abusal, the road to Paris was anything but ordinary, at least for most athletes. Like so many boxers, he started at a young age, learning to box from his father at Elbarrio Gym in Ramallah. His father saw boxing not just as a hobby or an activity but also a means to fulfill his dreams. In this regard, his story is familiar, like many of the boxers discussed in this collection. Yes, Abusal trained for hours; he fought throughout the world; he ran, lifted weights, and sparred with opponents when possible. He developed his craft and endured pain.

More than his training regime, Abusal's journey to the 33rd Olympiad was shaped by war, occupation, and denial of basic human rights. He had to navigate checkpoints, substandard training facilitates, and the realities that shape the lives of all Palestinians. He could not train with his

Cairo-based Gazan coach, Ahmad Harara, who was unable to travel to the West Bank because of the Israeli occupation. Instead, Coach Harara sent him workouts and facilitated his morning training remotely. In the evening, he worked with coach Nader Jayousi at a gym in Ramallah.

And then war hit. As part of its assault on Gaza, following the October 7, 2023, terrorist attacks, Israel targeted every aspect of Palestinian life. It halted all sporting activities. Once athletes were able to resume training, the entrenched obstacles became increasingly more difficult to navigate. In "I'm doing this for all of Palestine," Michelle Kuehn (2024) says, describing this accomplishment as miraculous, an astonishing feat, given the circumstances. "This milestone has not come without tremendous sacrifice, with the everyday struggles of living in the occupied West Bank presenting a far more formidable battle than the endless rounds he [Abusal] faces in the ring." She powerfully describes the conditions Abusal trained under as dire on the best days, making Creed's training in the desert or Rocky's prefight preparation in Siberia seem like a walk in the park:

> Training in Palestine has become increasingly perilous due to a rise in checkpoints, military presence and settler violence, complicating travel even between West Bank cities and thus restricting his access to sparring partners. For international travel, Abu Sal must undertake a journey by road from Ramallah to Amman, Jordan, to catch a flight—if he is fortunate enough not to be denied an entry visa. (Kuehn 2024)

Similar experiences have shaped the journeys of all eight Palestinian Olympians. "Do you know how many approved pools there are in Palestine? Zero," swimmer Al Bawaab noted. "There is no sports in Palestine. We are a country right now that does not have enough food or shelter, and we are trying to figure out how to stay alive. We are not a sports country yet." Al Bawaab, who sees swimming as "a tool for Palestine," knows that it is bigger than swimming. Noting how nobody ever asks him about his race, he sees a more powerful role he can play: "I'm going to be plain and honest: France does not recognize Palestine as a country. But I'm over there, raising my flag. That's my role" (qtd. in Petrequin 2024).

For other athletes who also dreamed of competing on an international stage, the journey didn't end with an Olympic experience. According to reports, over three hundred athletes, coaches, referees, and other officials have died along with almost forty thousand others amid the assault on Gaza. Others endured the anguish from the death and wounding of family and friends.

It is no wonder that Wasim Abusal and others saw their participation as a historic victory even in defeat. Following a loss to a Swedish boxer,

Abusal described his experience as something bigger than the Olympics, as transcending medal counts and the billion-dollar corporate spectacle: "'I am sorry I will not raise the flag for Palestine on the podium. I wanted to have a medal but God willing, I will not be stopped here. The journey will continue for four years. The Olympic Games are already a victory for Palestine'" (AFP 2024a).

Abusal's journey through checkpoints—the training amid occupation and bombs, the perseverance in the face of ample loss, as with the sartorial choices, the visibility of the Palestinian flag and other symbols, and the statements demanding to be seen and heard—all exist as acts of resistance. They are part of a larger history of protest in boxing, where both the G.O.A.T.s and those unknown fighters have used the ring, their entrances, their voices, their training, their identities, and their presence in the sport as a means of resistance. These struggles are directed not just at the larger systems of violence—war; settler colonialism; white supremacy; mass incarceration; hyperpolicing—but at the reactionary politics of sport as well.

As evident throughout this collection of essays, boxing is a space of politics, both dissent and those that offer legitimacy and cover for hegemony. Recent events illustrate the hegemonic politics of boxing. For example, Floyd Mayweather has long used his immense platform in support of Israel. Following October 7, alongside a picture of his 2022 Western Wall photo, he wrote the following caption on Instagram:

> I stand with Israel against the Hamas terrorists . . . Hamas do not represent the people of Palestine but are a terrorist group that are attacking innocent lives! I stand for all humans and wish for the safe return of all Americans and Israelis and any human that were kidnapped as hostages during these horrific war crimes. This is not a time for politics. This is a time for safety first and foremost. God Bless America. God Bless Israel. God Bless Human Kind! (Keene 2024)

He also sent his private jet with five thousand pounds of supplies for both the Israeli Defense Forces and civilian groups (McPhee 2023).

The activism of Kali Reis or Wasim Abusal must be understood alongside the politics exhibited by Mayweather here. Similarly, we cannot understand the many ways boxers have leveraged their training, their talents, and their skills to shine a spotlight on the experiences of oppressed people, to speak truth to power, without looking at the ways that boxers, officials, and others in the fight game have always used their place to speak truth FOR power. The examples throughout history are endless.

In spring 2024, as university students throughout the world built encampments as an expression of solidarity with Palestinian people,

David Kaminsky, an Israeli boxer whose family owns a gym in Los Angeles, decided to give voice to his politics. Known as "the Lion of Zion," Kaminsky clearly saw his boxing career and his participation in "counter protest" as part of a larger mission. While on the UCLA campuses, he used a racial slur and allegedly spit at protesters. According to the *Los Angeles Times*, "Kaminsky admitted using the slur in an interview with The Times, but said he didn't say it with a 'hard R' and that it was 'slang in the boxing community'" (Ormseth 2024).

From the stripping of Ali's heavyweight crown after his refusal to be drafted to Robert Rundo's Rise Above movement, there is a long history of boxing aiding, abetting, and reflecting hegemonic power structure. This is a story that exists alongside dissent.

With the ongoing Russian-Ukrainian conflict, we have witnessed the Ukrainian boxing community use their celebrity platforms to speak out against the violence prompted by Russia. As of October 2024, more than 12,000 civilians, including 551 children, have been killed in Ukraine at the hands of Russia (Gadzo 2024). Former world heavyweight champion boxer, Wladimir Klitschko, has been one of the most vocal Ukrainian fighters. In his 2024 interview with Rudy Mondragón, Klitschko reflected on the Russian aggression and the lesson it has taught him on morality:

> Moral, because that's the core. It really doesn't matter your titles, your money in [your] bank account, your legacy. If you're a piece of shit, you're a piece of shit. And it's your moral. What do you stand for? Because this society, like, generally speaking, globalization, digitalization, we're looking for fancy cars, fancy clothes, fancy life, jet setting. I mean, we're all excited about that. It's [a] very competing society in regards to that. And in the end, what are your morals and what your moral stands for? That's what I understood during the war—what do you stand for? And there are a lot of disappointments of people that [have] been my icons, my idols. And then all of a sudden, they're just supporting the war. They're supporting the killing of the innocent. But who you are as a person, what your moral stands for, and I believe that's what in human kind is important . . . And we have morals or [we] don't. Some animals don't. Speaking of humans. (Mondragón, "From the Fields to the Garden")

Klitschko's reflections on the war reveal a critique of societal values, emphasizing that moral integrity is paramount in a world often obsessed with material success. He suggests that the violent chaos of war strips away surface levels of superficiality, which unveils the true character of individuals and their principles. His expressed disappointment in those he once idolized highlights how their support for violence is a contradiction of the morals, he believes should define humanity. Ultimately, Klitschko's insights challenge us to recognize that justice requires an unwavering commitment to uphold human dignity and morals and to resist state power that seeks to normalize violence and the killing of the innocent.

The ongoing histories presented in this collection illustrate the history of refusal and resistance in boxing; a story of boxers of color refusing to be silent, consistently speaking truth to power; one of fighters leveraging their platform to spotlight their experiences and that of their larger communities, to document and challenge systems of oppression; and a history of resistance to the invisibility and erasure, of fighting hegemonic stereotypes and systemic policing. The story of boxing, as evident by so many fighters and others in the game, is one of courage beyond withstanding the physical pain or the torturous training but also the bravery to speak, resist, refuse, and challenge. As Muhammad Ali noted at a 1984 news conference, "What I suffered physically was worth what I've accomplished in life. A man who is not courageous enough to take risks will never accomplish anything in life" (qtd in Ali and Beydoum 2018) As with the recent Olympics, boxing has long been a place where the fight itself, the walkout, the pre- and post-fight interviews, the training through violence and injustice, and the legacy of the sports itself stands on the shoulders of social movements, reflecting and contributing to our collective freedom dreams of what's possible (Kelley 2002). It has always been bigger than gold medals, wins/losses, championship belts, or career earnings. And this might be the most significant act of refusal, for the ring has always been a place of dissent.

References

Ali, Muhammad, and Khaled A. Beydoun. 2018. "Muhammad Ali Inspirational Quotes on Success and Racism." *Al Jazeera*. January 18. https://www.aljazeera.com/sports/2018/1/18/muhammad-ali-inspirational-quotes-on-success-and-racism.

AFP. 2024a. "First Palestinian Olympic Boxer Defiant Despite Debut Loss." *Barrons*. https://www.barrons.com/news/first-palestinian-olympic-boxer-defiant-despite-debut-loss-9b79b6ea.

AFP. 2024b. "Palestinian Olympian Wore Shirt Showing Bombed Children at Opening Ceremony." July 27. France 24. https://www.france24.com/en/live-news/20240727-palestinian-olympian-wore-shirt-showing-bombed-children-at-opening-ceremony.

Boykoff, Jules, and Dave Zirin. 2024. "We Must Defend Imane Khelif." *The Nation*. August 5. https://www.thenation.com/article/society/imane-khelif-olympics-paris-boxing-transphobia/.

Da Silva, Chantal, and Alexander Smith. 2024. "'We're Here to Speak for the People.'" NBC News. July 17. https://www.nbcnews.com/news/world/paris-2024-olympics-palestinians-gaza-west-bank-israel-hamas-war-rcna160815.

Gadzo, Mersiha. 2024. "Record High Deaths in the Russia–Ukraine War: What You Should Know." *Al Jazeera*. October 16. https://www.aljazeera.com/news/2024/10/16/russia-ukraine-wartime-deaths.

Irish, John. "At Paris 2024, Israeli and Palestinian Athletes Joust over Gaza War." Reuters. July 30. https://www.reuters.com/sports/olympics/paris-2024-israeli-palestinian-athletes-joust-over-gaza-war-2024-07-30/.

Janetsky, Jane. 2024. "Palestinian Olympic Team Greeted with Cheers and Gifts in Paris." Associated Press. July 25. https://apnews.com/article/olympics-2024-palestinians-israel-paris-fc937552b30c921422b2d39bb0999564.

Keene, Louis. 2014. "Floyd Mayweather Has a Long Record of Domestic Violence. Why Are Supporters of Israel Embracing Him?" *Jewish Daily Forward*. March 14. https://forward.com/news/592637/floyd-mayweather-israel-domestic-violence/.

Kelley, Robin D. G. 2002. *Freedom Dreams: The Black Radical Imagination*. Beacon Press.

Kuehn, Michelle. 2024. "'I'm Doing This for All of Palestine' Says Waseem Abu Sal on Making Boxing History." *Arab News*. July 16. https://arab.news/gppx3.

McPhee, Michelle. 2024. "Floyd Mayweather Is Sending Supplies to Israel via Private Jet." *Los Angeles Magazine*. October 10. https://lamag.com/news/floyd-mayweather-sending-israel-supplies-private-jet-exclusive.

Mondragón, R. Forthcoming. "From the Fields to the Garden." Documentary on Jacob "Stitch" Duran.

Ormseth, Matthew, Connor Sheets, Brittny Mejia, Ruben Vives, Jessica Garrison and Summer Lin. 2024. "'Shut It Down!' How Group Chats, Rumors and Fear Sparked a Night of Violence at UCLA." *Los Angeles Times*. May 10. https://www.latimes.com/california/story/2024-05-10/how-social-media-rumors-sparked-a-night-of-mayhem-at-ucla.

Petrequin, Samuel. 2024. "For Palestinian Athletes, the Olympics Is about More Than Sports." Associated Press. July 20. Retrieved October 17. https://apnews.com/article/paris-olympics-palestine-war-gaza-e5d7af095f86ae74f9a99db2aadf629e.

Serhan, Yasmeen. 2024. "The IOC Wants the Olympics to Be Apolitical. That's Impossible." *Time*. July 18. https://time.com/7000067/olympics-2024-paris-gaza-israel-ukraine/.

Afterword

Weary, Resigned, Ready

MARK ANTHONY NEAL

The thing that strikes you, over and over again, is that look of weariness. You see it on Jack Johnson's face in that famous photo of him—well, one of so many—fists balled, shirtless, standing outside what seems to be a woodshed; the photo that likely inspired photographer Annie Leibovitz a century later when she photographed Tiger Woods and somehow made him look like an actual Black American. Or is that resignation we are looking at in Johnson; or Joe Louis, well past his prime; or Sugar Ray Robinson, who after twenty-six years in the ring was certainly weary, if not just tired; or any of those last glimpses of Ali in the ring—with Larry Holmes in 1980 and Trevor Berbick in 1981? Or perhaps it's just exhaustion, which can never be and never has been an excuse for those who still need to be ready for the next fight, whether in the ring or in this Black life.

It's difficult to not look at photographs and footage of Black boxers and not see the experiences of Black folk embodied. For Johnson, it's not the idea that you are drawn into a fight that you can never really win—"the game is rigged" as *The Wire*'s Bodie (J. D. Williams) said so eloquently at the beginning of the twenty-first century—but that you are *always* expected to get up off the canvas (even in victory) with your dignity and perhaps integrity intact, knowing damn well that you can't win. Then there's the reality that you always have to go back in that ring because you are simultaneously the best and the worst of your race—an "unforgivable Blackness" as W.E.B. Du Bois said about Jack Johnson—and it's your duty to uphold that status regardless of how you feel. Indeed, that look on Johnson's face is the look of every Black life that has stoically tried to recover their humanity amid unyielding capitalist exploitation, and, yes, that is even when you are the victor, which far too many of us rarely are.

It is perhaps the resignation of being that credit to your race, especially when there were always bills to still be paid—often behalf of folk you'd never meet but who you knew always had your back, as long as you were willing to go back into the ring, and still look stylish if you were Sugar Ray, even beyond his prime. And that resignation is not just for the old: You could see it on Mike Tyson's face as a twenty-year-old, walking into the ring robeless and unadorned, wise enough to know at that age, on the verge of becoming a champion, that it would never get better than that moment for him, and the price that he would pay for that moment would be unimaginable. That look of resignation has found a home on Tyson's face, and in his demeanor, even now as an old Black man.

And yet we still rise in those rings (like Mama Maya told us to), just as we always still rise in these Black lives, ready for the next and ready for the inevitable. And I find myself thinking of another gladiator who had the misfortune to arrive on the scene when Ali was in his post-Vietnam prime and George Foreman was as hungry as he was ever going to be. So it's often easy to forget Joe Frazier, who managed to lose even as he defeated Ali that first time, and remained undefeated in that ring, to retain his championship. Frazier's reign ended over the course of six minutes in January 1973 in Kingston, Jamaica, to the fearsome forest of a man named Foreman. The fight was punctuated by Howard Cosell's infamous call—made during a televised rebroadcast of the fight on network television—"Down goes Frazier. Down goes Frazier." And what was so miraculous about that call is that it was only the first of the six times that Frazier was knocked down during the course of the two-round fight. Five times Frazier picked himself up off the floor, weary, resigned and ready, as did so many Black folk before him and have continued to since.

Acknowledgments

As the editors of *Rings of Dissent*, we acknowledge that nearly everyone has a personal story that is connected to the sport of boxing. These stories can be about family congregations over boxing matches, attending live matches with their parents, practicing the sport as a child, or the divisions of gender that take place in some boxing gyms and at family parties. As scholars, intellectuals, teachers, and critics of sport and popular culture, we wanted to honor these experiences and ask contributors, both sport and non-sport scholars alike, to use their stories and research expertise as a launching point to ground their chapter interventions on boxing and performances of dissent and resistance. Like the contributors of this anthology, we, the editors, also have our stories that are connected to boxing.

RUDY MONDRAGÓN

The birth of my scholarship on boxing dates back to fall 1992. That was the year my father introduced me to the sport of boxing via the mega-fight between Julio César Chávez and Héctor "Macho" Camacho. As a seven-year-old Mexican American, I saw myself embodied in Chávez because he closely matched everything my friends and family told me I was: a young Mexican American boy who loved sports. Though I related more to Chávez and the romance of Mexican nationalism that surrounded him, it was Camacho's ring entrance performance that caught my attention. He entered the ring first, as the challenger who would try to dethrone the Mexican champion. I remember seeing an unapologetic Camacho wearing a custom-made refashioned Captain America suit that reflected a different kind of superhero: Captain Puerto Rico. The cameras were following his every move in the dressing room. Well aware of the cameras, Camacho kept pacing and at times yelling "Macho Time!" As he made his way into the ring, the sounds of Gene McFadden and John Whitehead's "Ain't No Stopping Us Now" took over the Thomas & Mack Center in Las Vegas as fans were forced to take in Camacho in all of his performative glory. As I look back now, this experience introduced me to the complicated pedagogy and political economy of boxing. It was my introduction to the neoliberal multicultural theatrical script of the intense rivalry between Mexican and Puerto Rican boxers. This script informs the theatrical boxing narrative that is used for promotional purposes and capitalist accumulation. These ethnic, racial, cultural, and national rivalry matches usually take place during Cinco de Mayo and Mexican Independence Day weekend and greatly assists the major beer companies maximize the sale potential of their products. Watching this fight with my father and reflecting on it thirty years later reminds me of how boxing, immigration, country of origin, race and ethnicity, gender, and nationalism are intrinsically connected. For my father and uncles, who all migrated to the United States from Mexico in the 1970s, Chávez was a representation of Mexican homeland as well as a symbolic marker of ethnic and national pride. This was important, especially during the 1990s, in the Southwest, where anti-immigrant sentiment and legislation was on the rise. In the present moment, I am still a fan of boxing and a critical scholar of the sport. In what order? That is yet to be determined. It's a matter that can remain an ongoing question.

GAYE THERESA JOHNSON

The first boxing match I ever saw was between two girls in a small town outside of San Antonio. A friend and I drove an hour south to watch a day of matches. A succession of Tejana teens entered the ring for this regional event, which took place in a venue that was likely also used for livestock shows. The floor was dirt, and the day was hot and dusty. Families swatted away flies and carried food as they crowded into the large tent. During the first fight, a fifteen-year-old girl stepped back after a powerful blow to her face bloodied her nose, and I recall being shocked to see her shake her head and step forward immediately to reengage her opponent. In all the fights, these young women demonstrated such skill and grit; it was fascinating to witness for the first time. But I found myself most interested in what was happening outside the ring. The ring was smaller than I would have imagined, and the families who filled the tent sat on folding chairs. After a few matches, as if by some kind of silent agreement, a few family members began setting up tables and large containers of food and pitchers of water and Gatorade they had brought in the back of trucks and cars. Once the boxing stopped, the music started. Someone had brought a separate sound system and a boom box. Selena, *cumbias*, and rap music blared from speakers with too much feedback, but families sat together, communed over food, and shared memories for forty-five minutes until, again by some silent cue, it was time to rearrange the folding chairs around the ring. The fights were called in a combination of Spanish and English. Siblings, parents, grandparents, teachers, coaches, and fans with no connection to the boxers cheered and encouraged the girls in the ring, who fought, congratulated each other, and demonstrated a resilience I hadn't before witnessed in women's sports. This was my first boxing story.

I don't recall who won the fights, the names of the boxers, or even the name of the town. But I do recall the smell of the air, the encouragement of the spectators, and that families drove long distances—some across the Mexican border—to commune around the pride and promise of young women. When it was all over, everyone helped to clean up, families lingered around large trucks laughing and talking, and the young women were the stars of the day.

DAVID J. LEONARD

I used to love boxing. Maybe "love" is an overstatement, but I have so many fond memories: those Saturday gatherings with family when we would watch Sugar Ray Leonard and countless other fighters on pay-per-view; the endless Tyson matches that saw him destroy his opponent in one second; the shock of hearing about Buster Douglas dropping Tyson in the middle of my high school basketball game; the 1984 Olympics, with Meldrick Taylor, Pernell Whitaker, Mark Breland, Frank Tate, Tyrell Briggs and so many other American fighters winning gold medals.

Yet, this is a story of disgust and disappointment; about rapes and domestic violence, about fallen heroes whose ability to throw an uppercut, land a jab, or otherwise perfect the sweet science seemingly concealed their misogynistic sins, at least for some; about a sport that traffics in racism and xenophobia, that has long imagined the ring as a staging ground for white supremacy and toxic masculinity; about a sport that sells the American Dream, that sells fighting as pathway to financial success, erasing the shattered dreams, the health consequences, and the destruction; about a sport that offers pleasure to the 1 percent, whose champagne and tuxedos don't obscure the fact that boxing is modern-day gladiator event where an overwhelming white wealthy audience finds joy and profit at watching marginalized Others brutalize one another.

My story with boxing is complex, wrapped up in nostalgia and outrage, hope and despair. Yet it is also a story of how boxing taught me so much beyond the ring. It taught me about white privilege. My uncle wanted me to be a boxer. He used to tell me that I wouldn't even have to be good to be successful because white America wants a white champion—half as good for ten times the rewards. A story of white America beyond the ring. Without knowing it, my uncle used boxing to teach me about whiteness, about racism, and about the myth of meritocracy. This was a story I learned from Hollywood as well. This wasn't the only lesson learned. Boxing taught me over and over again that to be a "real man" was to fight, to be aggressive, and to be violent. It is no wonder that as I became more and more conscious about justice, I found watching boxing more and more difficult. While I have learned many lessons from boxing, about greed, misogyny, white supremacy, and violence, I have also learned how the ring has always been a place of resistance and protests. Ali taught the nation about racial justice, global imperialism, and the Vietnam War. Yet it remains hard to think about my relationship with boxing through this history and other examples where men and women have used the ring to stage dissent, not the other lessons.

As editors, we wanted to use this space not only to reflect our complex relationships to boxing but also to acknowledge the people who have influenced us, shaped our journey, and otherwise are part of our teams. We also want to thank the contributors who stuck with this project over many years. It was like the long-awaited fight that kept getting delayed, postponed, and at one point looked like it would never happen. We are grateful for the perseverance of our contributors and the belief from University of Illinois Press. Much appreciation to editor in chief, Daniel Nasset, and everyone else at the press who allowed us to bring this project to the world. Of course, much love and appreciation to our families, colleagues, and communities for always having our backs and otherwise supporting our individual and shared adventures.

Contributors

RUDY MONDRAGÓN is an assistant professor in the Chicana/o and Latina/o Studies Department at Loyola Marymount University. Previously he was a UC Chancellor's Postdoctoral Fellow in the Institute for Research on Labor and Employment at the University of California, Los Angeles. He earned his PhD in Chicana/o and Central American Studies at UCLA. He is the recipient of the UCLA Chancellor's Award for Postdoctoral Research, UCLA Latino Applied Policy Research Award, University of California Cota-Robles Fellowship, UC Berkeley Oral History Center Fellowship, Smithsonian Latino Museum Studies Program Fellowship, UCLA Gold Shield Alumnae Graduate Fellowship, and Arthur Ashe Jr. Sports Scholar Award. Mondragón has published in *Kalfou: A Journal of Comparative and Relational Ethnic Studies, Journal of Sports History, International Review for the Sociology of Sport,* and *Aztlán: A Journal of Chicano Studies.*

GAYE THERESA JOHNSON is the author of *Spaces of Conflict, Sounds of Solidarity: Music, Race, and Spatial Entitlement* (University of California Press, 2015) and co-editor with Alex Lubin of *Futures of Black Radicalism* (Verso, 2017). She is an associate professor of African American Studies and Chicana and Chicano Studies at the University of California, Los Angeles, where she writes and teaches on race, cultural politics, and freedom struggles.

DAVID J. LEONARD is the author of *Playing While White: Privilege and Power On and Off the Field* (University of Washington Press, 2017) and *After Artest: The NBA and the Assault on Blackness* (SUNY Press, 2012) and co-editor of *Visual Economies of/in Motion: Sport and Film* (Peter

Lang, 2006) and *Commodified and Criminalized: New Racism and African Americans in Contemporary Sports* (Rowman & Littlefield, 2011). He is a professor of ethnic studies at Chico State University, where he teaches about racism, sporting cultures, and popular culture.

JOSÉ M. ALAMILLO received his PhD in Comparative Cultures at University of California, Irvine. He taught in the Comparative Ethnic Studies Department at Washington State University from 1999 to 2008. His work is broadly under Chicana/o cultural history with a focus on labor, immigration, gender, leisure, and sports. He is the author of *Making Lemonade out of Lemons: Mexican American Labor and Leisure in a California Town* (University of Illinois Press, 2006) and co-author of *Latinos in U.S. Sport* (Human Kinetics, 2011). His book *Deportes: The Making of a Sporting Mexican Diaspora* was published in 2020 from Rutgers University Press. He is currently working with Latinos in *¡Pleibol! In the Barrios and the Big Leagues*, a multiyear community collecting initiative and exhibition at the Smithsonian Institution's National Museum of American History.

ROBERTO JOSÉ ANDRADE FRANCO is from the El Paso–Juárez borderland, where he attended the University of Texas at El Paso. He is currently a writer for ESPN. He earned a PhD in history from Southern Methodist University, where his dissertation focused on boxing's impact on Mexican and Mexican American culture and identity. Andrade Franco's work has been published, among other places, in ESPN, Yahoo Sports, *Deadspin*, *Bleacher Report*, and *Texas Monthly*.

JAVON JOHNSON is an associate professor and director of African American and African Diaspora Studies at the University of Nevada, Las Vegas. A renowned poet, Johnson is the author of *Killing Poetry: Blackness and the Making of Slam and Spoken Word Poetry Communities* (Rutgers University Press, 2017), the forthcoming poetry collection *Ain't Never Not Been Black (Button Poetry)*, and the co-editor of *The End of Chiraq: A Literary Mixtape* (Northwestern University Press).

PRISCILLA LEIVA is an associate professor of Chicana/o and Latina/o Studies at Loyola Marymount University. Her research sits at the intersections of relational ethnic studies, urban history, and sports history, particularly as it relates to place making and community formation. She is currently at work on a book manuscript that examines the history of stadiums in Los Angeles—namely, how they have produced racialized visions of the city and who belongs. She is co-founder of *Chavez Ravine: An Unfinished Story*, a community–academic partnership that aims to preserve the memories of displaced residents of Chavez Ravine over the course of the long twentieth century. Her public history work has included collaborations with the Smithsonian National Museum of American History, LA Plaza de Cultura y Artes, Boyle Heights Museum, and Los Angeles County Museum of Art.

KYLE T. MAYS (Black/Saginaw Anishinaabe) is an associate professor in the Department of African American Studies and the American Indian Studies Center at the University of California, Los Angeles. He earned his PhD in the Department of History at the University of Illinois, Urbana-Champaign in 2015. He is a transdisciplinary scholar of Afro-Indigenous Studies, Indigenous popular culture, and urban history. He is the author of *Hip Hop Beats, Indigenous Rhymes: Modernity and Hip Hop in Indigenous North America* (SUNY Press, 2018). Mays has a book currently under review titled *Aunt Judy's Detroit: Indigeneity and Belonging in the Motor City* under contract with the University of Washington Press. He is currently writing a book on Afro-Indigenous history in the United States.

LOUIS MOORE is a professor of history at Michigan State University. His classes focus on African American history, civil rights, and US sports history. In his teachings, he uses historical documents, especially news articles, to raise questions and draw parallels. He is the author of *I Fight for a Living: Boxing and the Battle for Black Manhood, 1880–1915* (University of Illinois Press, 2017) and *We Will Win the Day: The Civil Rights Movement, the Black Athlete, and the Quest for Equality* (University Press of Kentucky, 2021). He has also written for a number of online venues, such as *The Shadow League, Black Perspectives, New York Daily News, Vox,* and *Vocativ*. In his role as a public intellectual, Moore has appeared as a commentator on NPR, MSNBC, the BBC, and other outlets.

MARK ANTHONY NEAL is professor in the Department of African and African American Studies and the founding director of the Center for Arts, Digital Culture and Entrepreneurship (CADCE) at Duke University, where he offers courses on black masculinity, popular culture, and digital humanities, including signature courses "Michael Jackson & the Black Performance Tradition" and "The History of Hip-Hop," which he co-teaches with Grammy Award–winning producer 9th Wonder (Patrick Douthit). He also co-directs the Duke Council on Race and Ethnicity (DCORE). Neal is the author of several books, including *What the Music Said: Black Popular Music and Black Public Culture* (Routledge, 1999), *Soul Babies: Black Popular Culture and the Post-Soul Aesthetic* (Routledge, 2001), and *Looking for Leroy: Illegible Black Masculinities* (NYU Press, 2013). The 10th Anniversary edition of Neal's *New Black Man* was published in February 2015 by Routledge. He is co-editor of *That's the Joint: The Hip-Hop Studies*

Reader (Routledge), now in its third edition. Additionally, Neal is host of the video webcast *Left of Black*, which is produced in collaboration with the John Hope Franklin Center at Duke.

LUCIA TRIMBUR is an associate professor of sociology at John Jay College and CUNY's Graduate Center and a Global Fellow at the University of Edinburgh. She completed her doctoral degree in African American studies and sociology at Yale University. Her work focuses on the relationships among embodied practices; perceptions of racial, class, and gender difference; and hierarchies of power. Her first book, *Come Out Swinging: The Changing World of Boxing in Gleason's Gym*, was published by Princeton University Press in 2013. She is currently working on her second book, "Lights Out: An Ethnography of Concussion," which looks at how rule changes in American football transform the play of the game as well as attitudes toward and investments in the sport. Her work has been published in academic journals such as the *American Studies Journal, Antipode, Contexts, Ethnography, Journal of Sociology and Social Welfare, Qualitative Sociology*, and *Quest* as well as popular journals such as *The Allrounder* and *Urban Omnibus*.

DAVE ZIRIN is the sports editor at *The Nation*. He is the author of eleven books on the politics of sports and the host of the *Edge of Sports* podcast. His books include *What's My Name, Fool? Sports and Resistance in the United States* (Haymarket Books, 2005), *The Muhammad Ali Handbook* (Spruce Books, 2007), and *The Kaepernick Effect: Taking a Knee, Changing the World* (New Press, 2021).

Index

The University of Illinois Press
is a founding member of the
Association of University Presses.

Composed in 10.5/13 Mercury Text
with Avenir display
by Jim Proefrock
at the University of Illinois Press
Manufactured by Sheridan Books, Inc.

University of Illinois Press
1325 South Oak Street
Champaign, IL 61820-6903
www.press.uillinois.edu